SUPER SONS

VOL.1 WHEN I GROW UP...

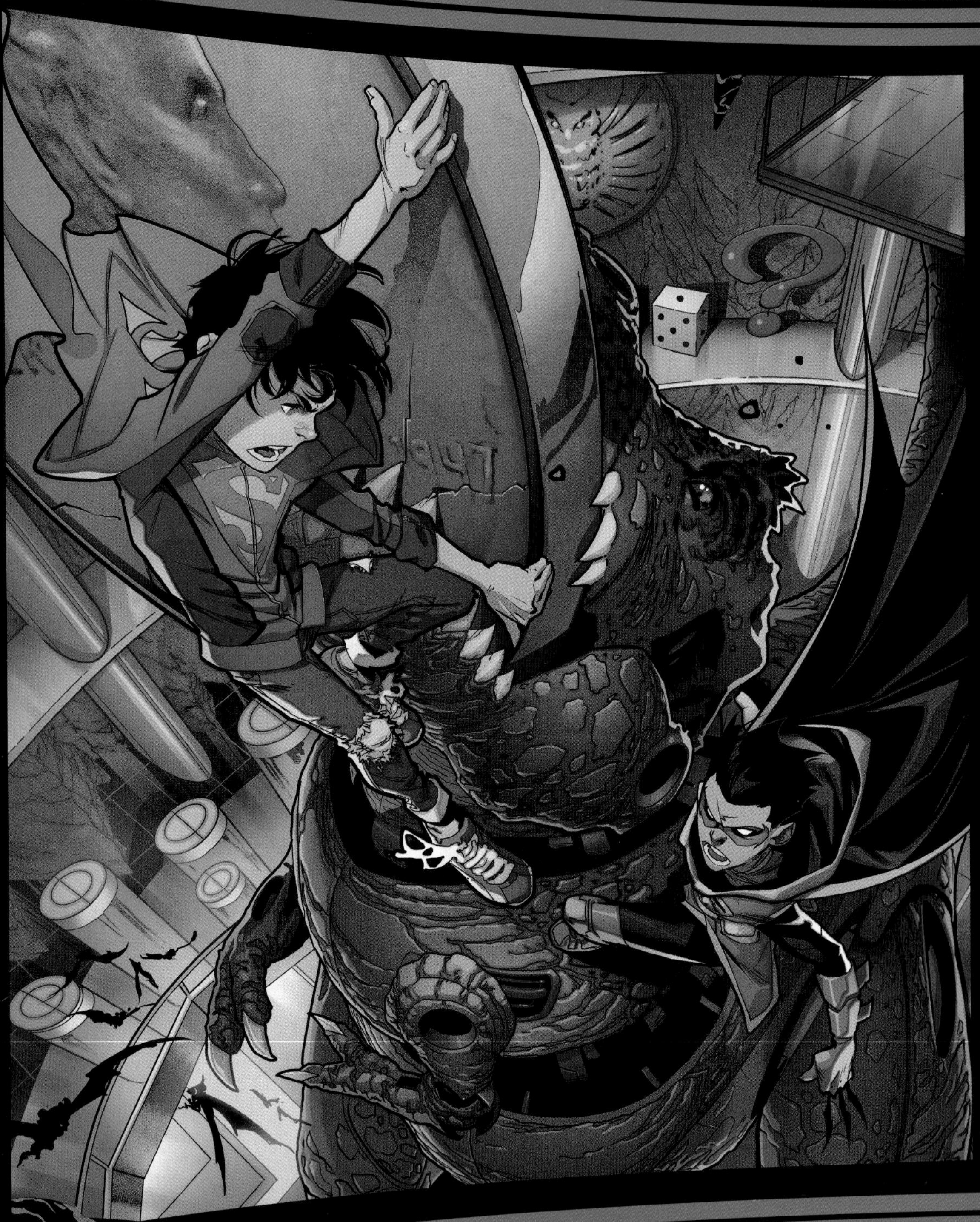

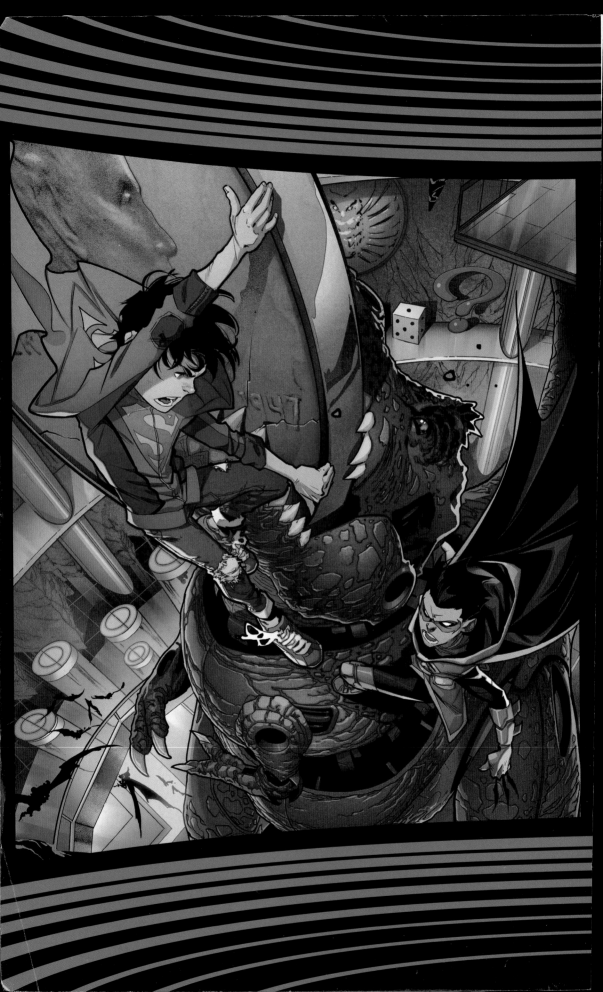

SUPER SONS
VOL.1 WHEN I GROW UP...

PETER J. TOMASI
writer

JORGE JIMENEZ
ALISSON BORGES
artists

ALEJANDRO SANCHEZ
HI-FI
colorists

ROB LEIGH
letterer

JORGE JIMENEZ & ALEJANDRO SANCHEZ
series and collection cover artists

SUPERMAN created by **JERRY SIEGEL** and **JOE SHUSTER**
By special arrangement with the **JERRY SIEGEL** family
SUPERBOY created by **JERRY SIEGEL**
By special arrangement with the **JERRY SIEGEL** family

EDDIE BERGANZA Editor - Original Series ◆ **PAUL KAMINSKI** Associate Editor - Original Series
JEB WOODARD Group Editor - Collected Editions ◆ **PAUL SANTOS** Editor - Collected Edition
STEVE COOK Design Director - Books ◆ **MONIQUE GRUSPE** Publication Design

BOB HARRAS Senior VP - Editor-in-Chief, DC Comics
PAT McCALLUM Executive Editor, DC Comics

DIANE NELSON President ◆ **DAN DiDIO** Publisher ◆ **JIM LEE** Publisher ◆ **GEOFF JOHNS** President & Chief Creative Officer
AMIT DESAI Executive VP - Business & Marketing Strategy, Direct to Consumer & Global Franchise Management
SAM ADES Senior VP & General Manager, Digital Services ◆ **BOBBIE CHASE** VP & Executive Editor, Young Reader & Talent Development
MARK CHIARELLO Senior VP - Art, Design & Collected Editions ◆ **JOHN CUNNINGHAM** Senior VP - Sales & Trade Marketing
ANNE DePIES Senior VP - Business Strategy, Finance & Administration ◆ **DON FALLETTI** VP - Manufacturing Operations
LAWRENCE GANEM VP - Editorial Administration & Talent Relations ◆ **ALISON GILL** Senior VP - Manufacturing & Operations
HANK KANALZ Senior VP - Editorial Strategy & Administration ◆ **JAY KOGAN** VP - Legal Affairs ◆ **JACK MAHAN** VP - Business Affairs
NICK J. NAPOLITANO VP - Manufacturing Administration ◆ **EDDIE SCANNELL** VP - Consumer Marketing
COURTNEY SIMMONS Senior VP - Publicity & Communications ◆ **JIM (SKI) SOKOLOWSKI** VP - Comic Book Specialty Sales & Trade Marketing
NANCY SPEARS VP - Mass, Book, Digital Sales & Trade Marketing ◆ **MICHELE R. WELLS** VP - Content Strategy

SUPER SONS VOL. 1 WHEN I GROW UP...

Published by DC Comics. Compilation and all new material Copyright © 2017 DC Comics. All Rights Reserved.
Originally published in single magazine form in SUPER SONS 1-5 Copyright © 2017 DC Comics.
All Rights Reserved. All characters, their distinctive likenesses and related elements featured in this publication are trademarks of DC Comics.
The stories, characters and incidents featured in this publication are entirely fictional.
DC Comics does not read or accept unsolicited submissions of ideas, stories or artwork.

DC Comics, 2900 West Alameda Ave., Burbank, CA 91505
Printed by LSC Communications, Menasha, WI, USA. 9/19/17. First Printing.
ISBN: 978-1-4012-7401-6

Library of Congress Cataloging-in-Publication Data is available.

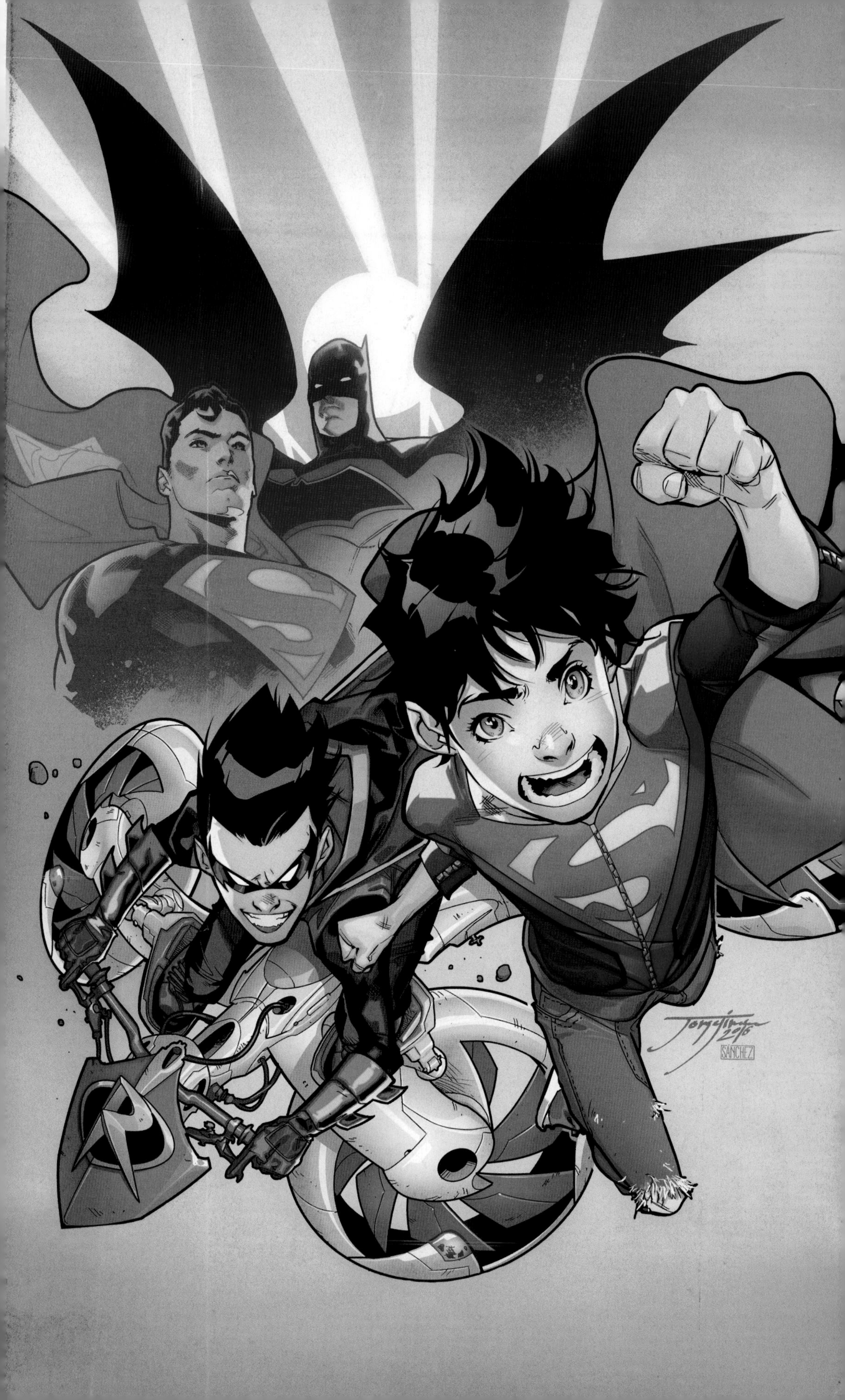
SÁNCHEZ

WHEN I GROW U PART ONE

JORGE JIMENEZ artist * ALEJANDRO SANCHEZ colorist

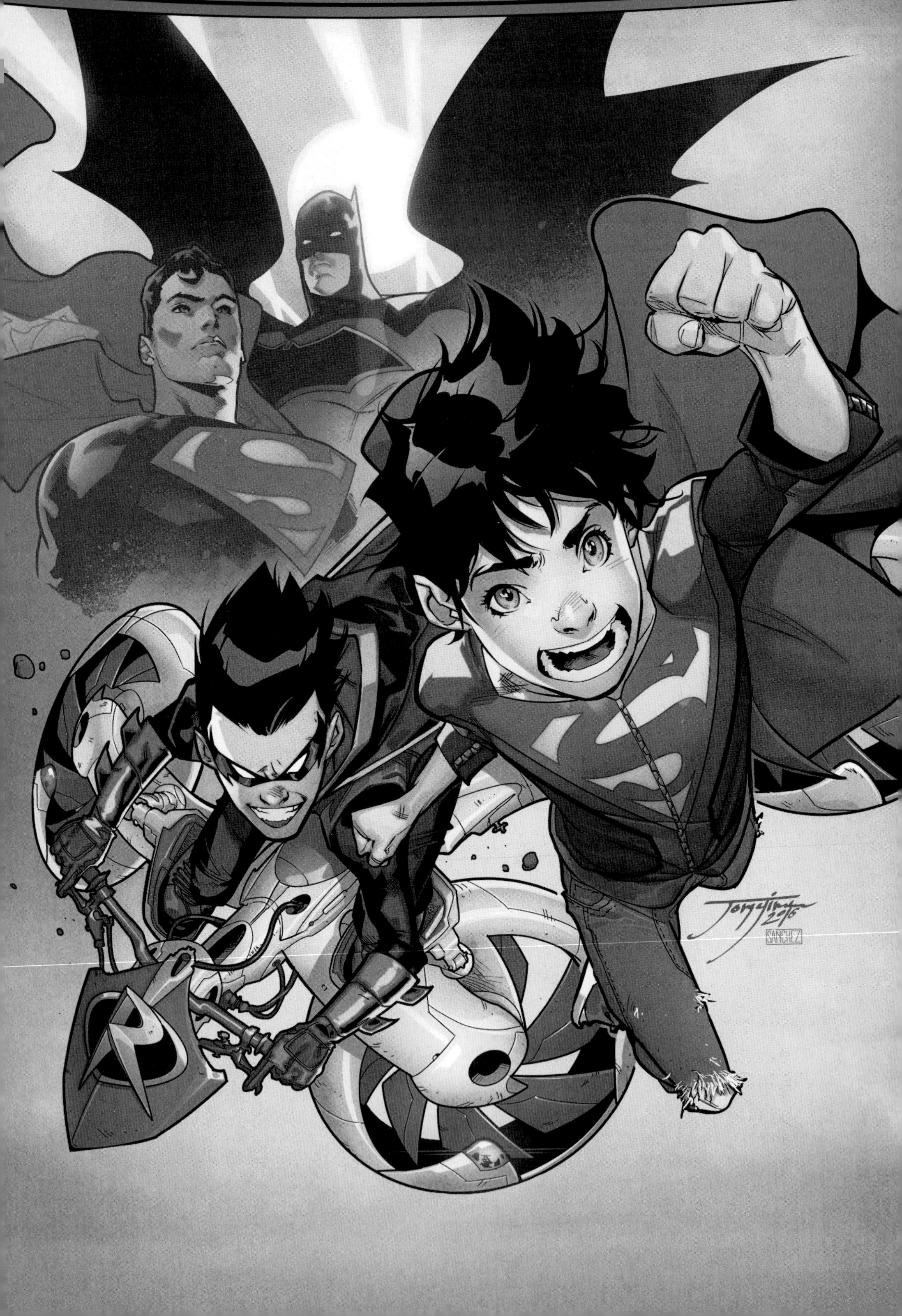
SANCHEZ

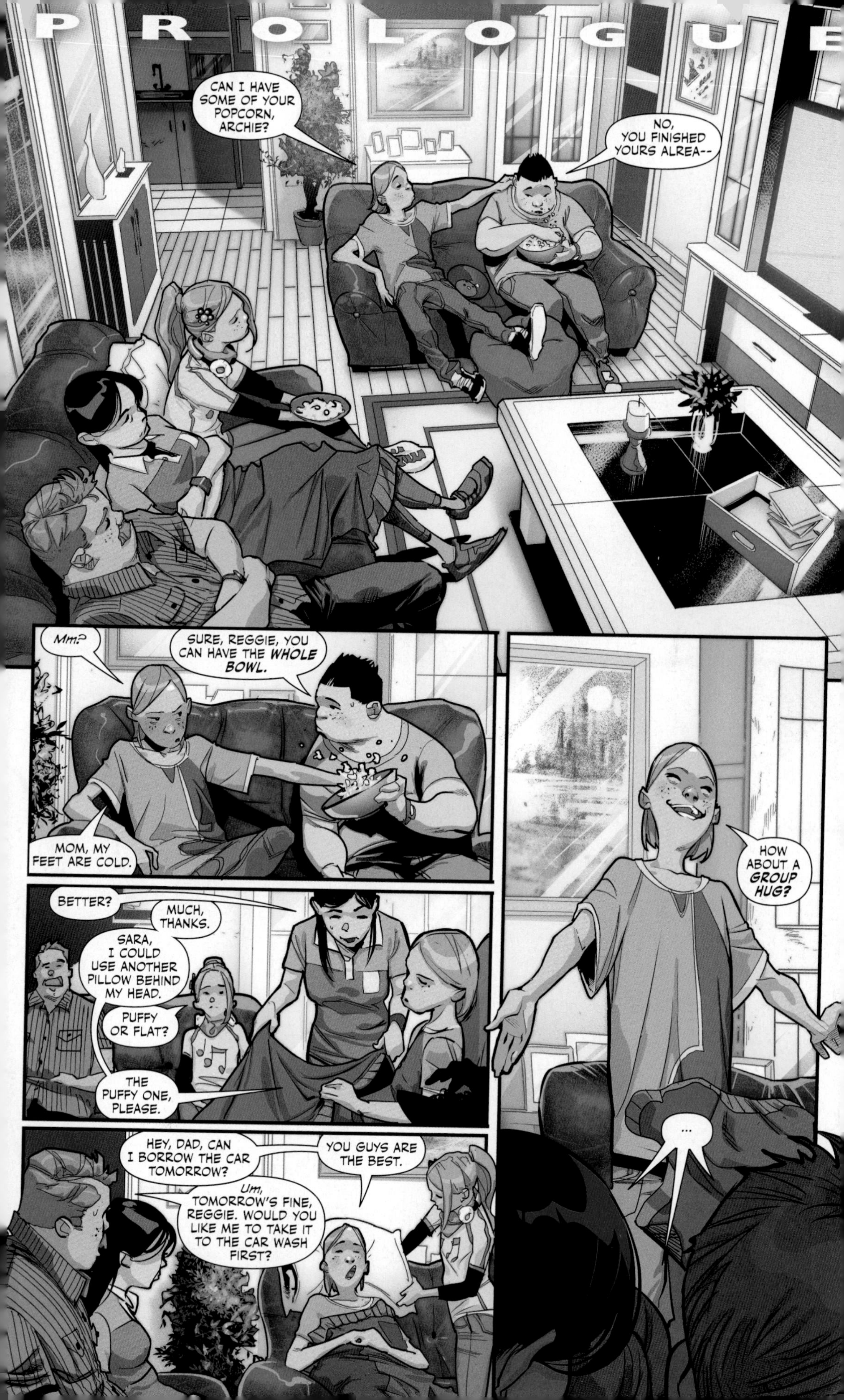
PROLOGUE
CAN I HAVE SOME OF YOUR POPCORN, ARCHIE?
NO, YOU FINISHED YOURS ALREA--
Mm?
SURE, REGGIE, YOU CAN HAVE THE *WHOLE BOWL.*
MOM, MY FEET ARE COLD.
BETTER?
MUCH, THANKS.
SARA, I COULD USE ANOTHER PILLOW BEHIND MY HEAD.
PUFFY OR FLAT?
THE PUFFY ONE, PLEASE.
HEY, DAD, CAN I BORROW THE CAR TOMORROW?
Um, TOMORROW'S FINE, REGGIE. WOULD YOU LIKE ME TO TAKE IT TO THE CAR WASH FIRST?
YOU GUYS ARE THE BEST.
HOW ABOUT A *GROUP HUG?*
...

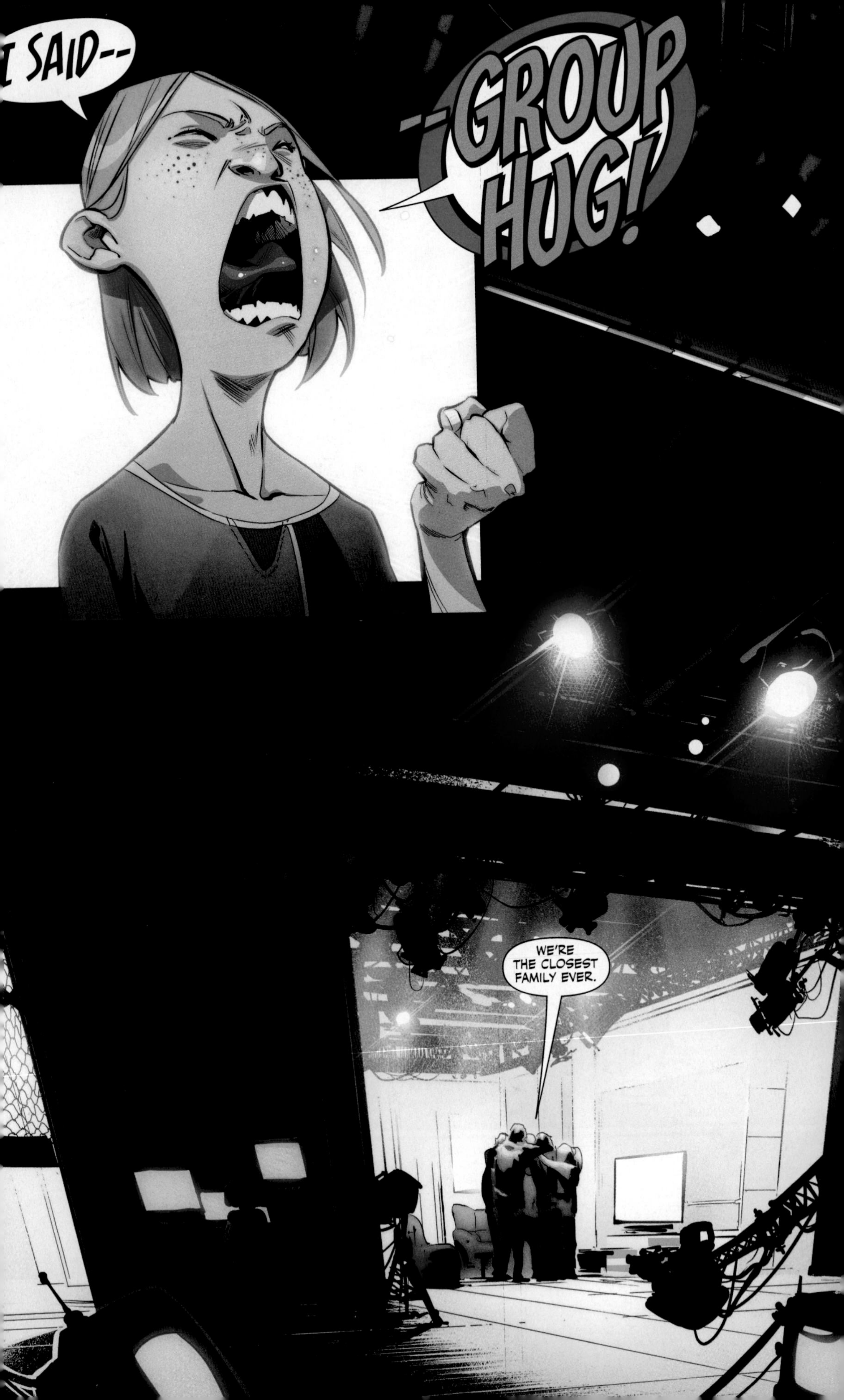
I SAID--
--GROUP HUG!
WE'RE THE CLOSEST FAMILY EVER.

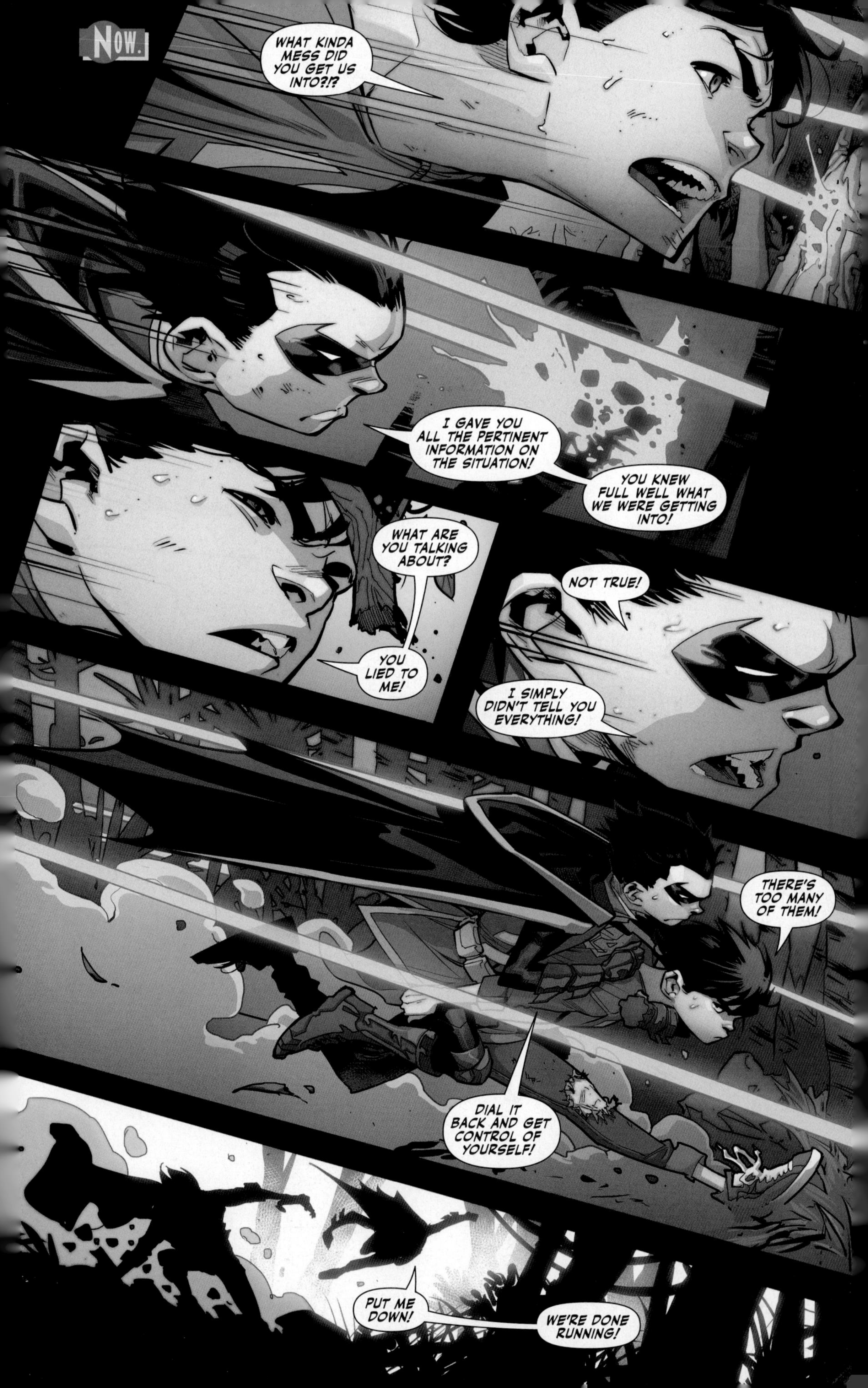
NOW.
WHAT KINDA MESS DID YOU GET US INTO?!?
I GAVE YOU ALL THE PERTINENT INFORMATION ON THE SITUATION!
YOU KNEW FULL WELL WHAT WE WERE GETTING INTO!
WHAT ARE YOU TALKING ABOUT?
YOU LIED TO ME!
NOT TRUE!
I SIMPLY DIDN'T TELL YOU EVERYTHING!
THERE'S TOO MANY OF THEM!
DIAL IT BACK AND GET CONTROL OF YOURSELF!
PUT ME DOWN!
WE'RE DONE RUNNING!

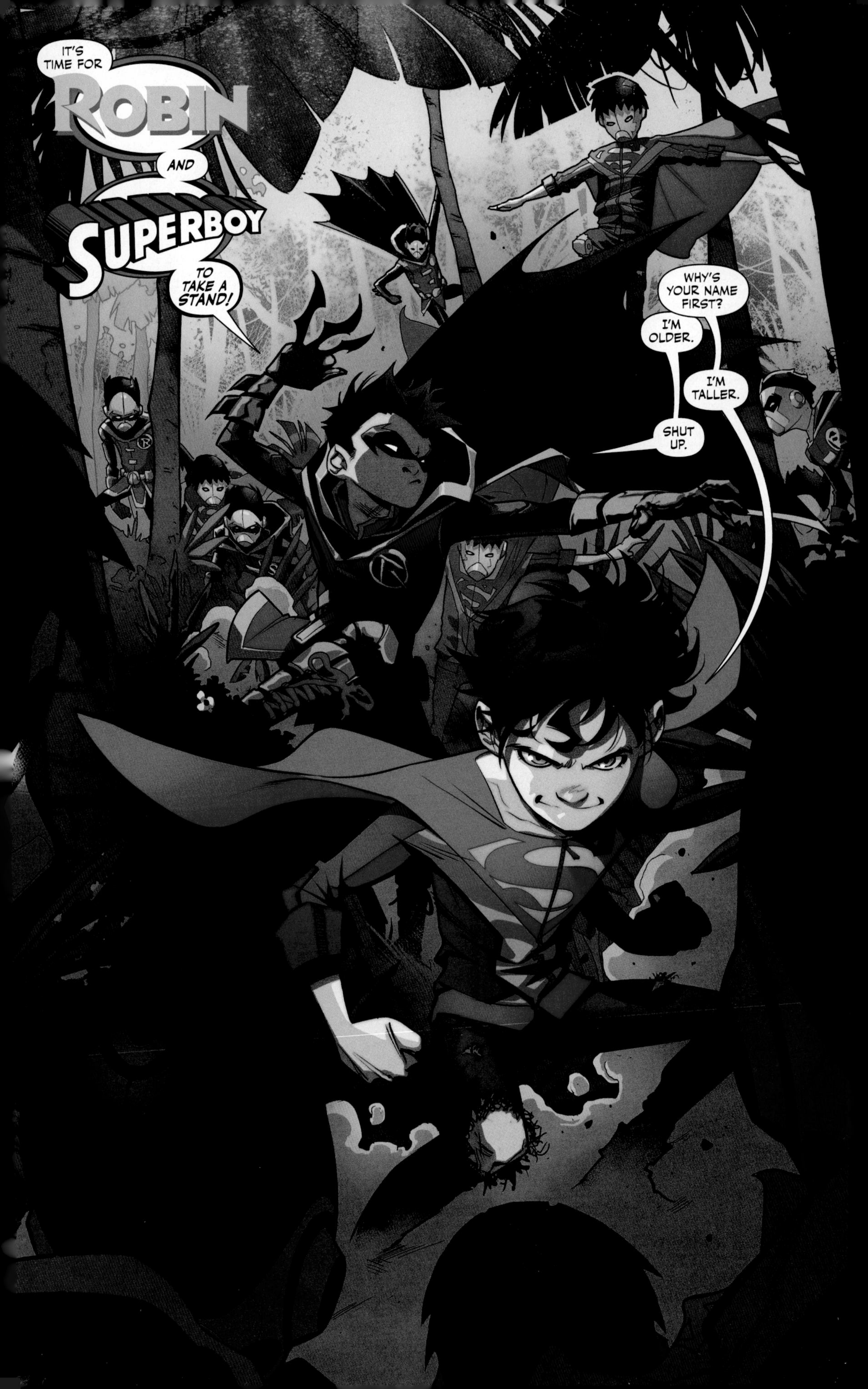
IT'S TIME FOR
ROBIN
AND
SUPERBOY
TO TAKE A STAND!
WHY'S YOUR NAME FIRST?
I'M OLDER.
I'M TALLER.
SHUT UP.

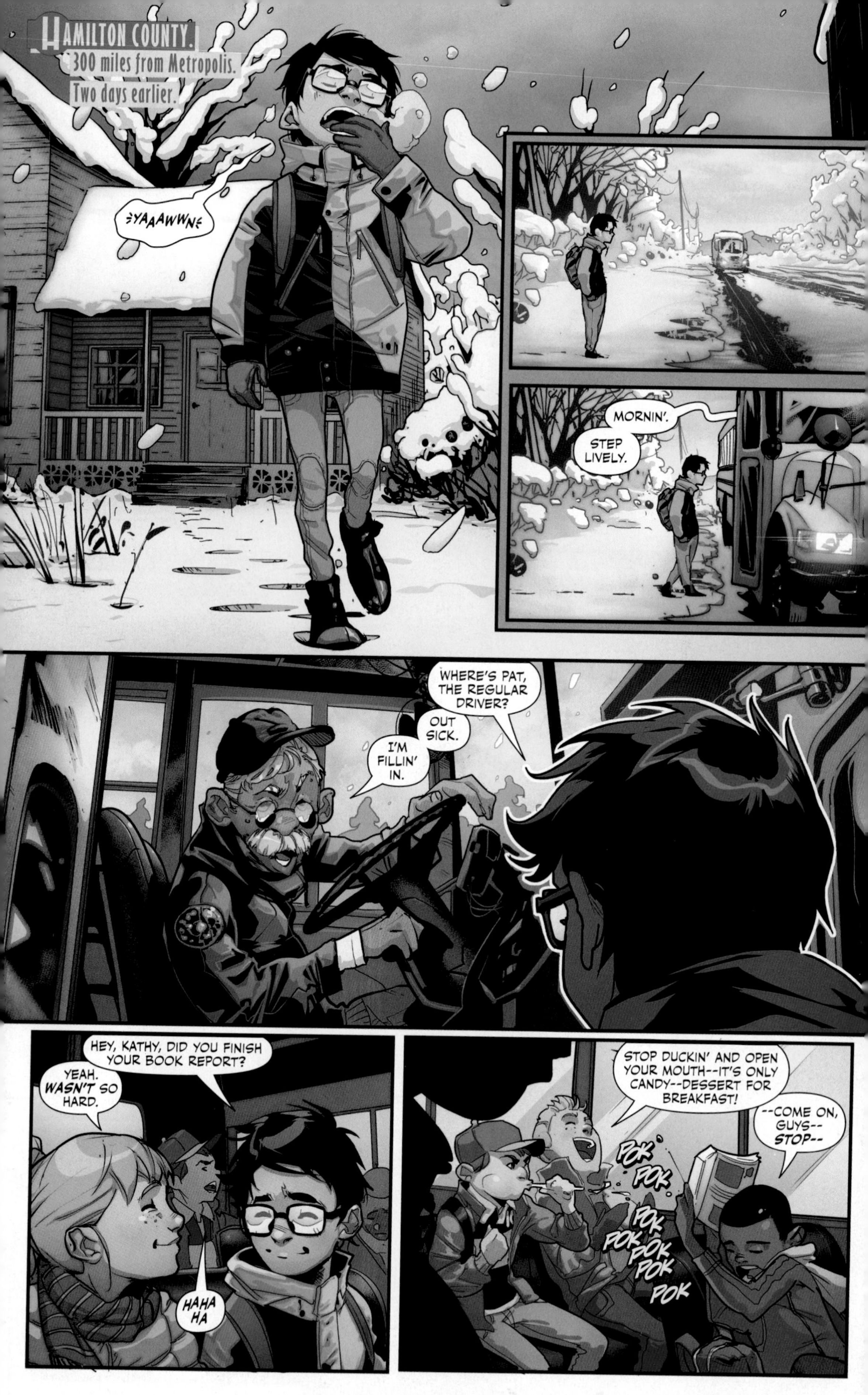
HAMILTON COUNTY.
300 miles from Metropolis.
Two days earlier.
YAAAWWN
MORNIN'.
STEP LIVELY.
WHERE'S PAT, THE REGULAR DRIVER?
OUT SICK.
I'M FILLIN' IN.
HEY, KATHY, DID YOU FINISH YOUR BOOK REPORT?
YEAH. WASN'T SO HARD.
HAHA HA
STOP DUCKIN' AND OPEN YOUR MOUTH--IT'S ONLY CANDY--DESSERT FOR BREAKFAST!
--COME ON, GUYS-- STOP--
POK POK
POK POK POK POK POK

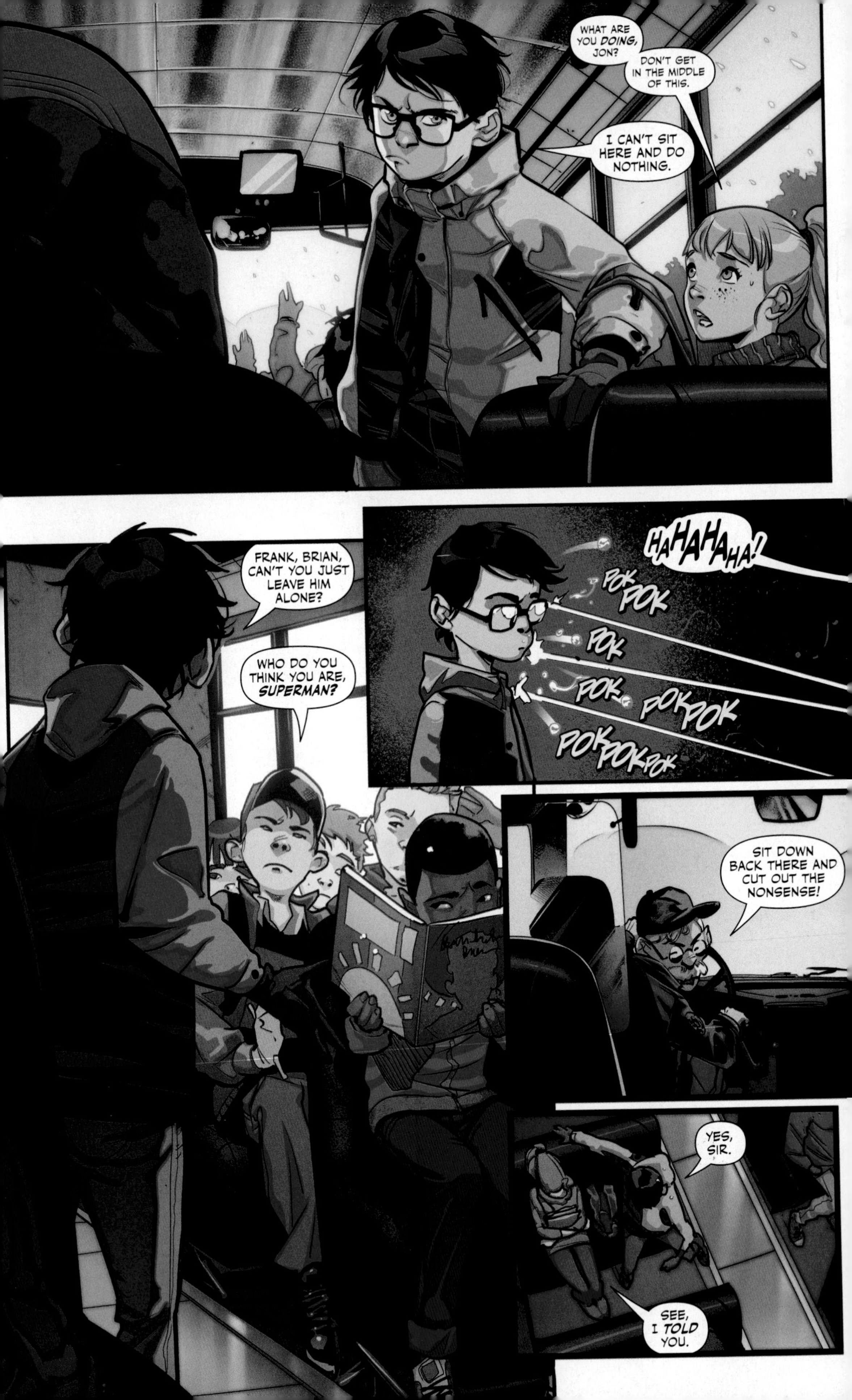
WHAT ARE YOU *DOING*, JON?
DON'T GET IN THE MIDDLE OF THIS.
I CAN'T SIT HERE AND DO NOTHING.
FRANK, BRIAN, CAN'T YOU JUST LEAVE HIM ALONE?
WHO DO YOU THINK YOU ARE, ***SUPERMAN?***
HAHAHAHA!
POK POK
POK
POK
POK POK
POK POK POK
SIT DOWN BACK THERE AND CUT OUT THE NONSENSE!
YES, SIR.
SEE, I *TOLD* YOU.

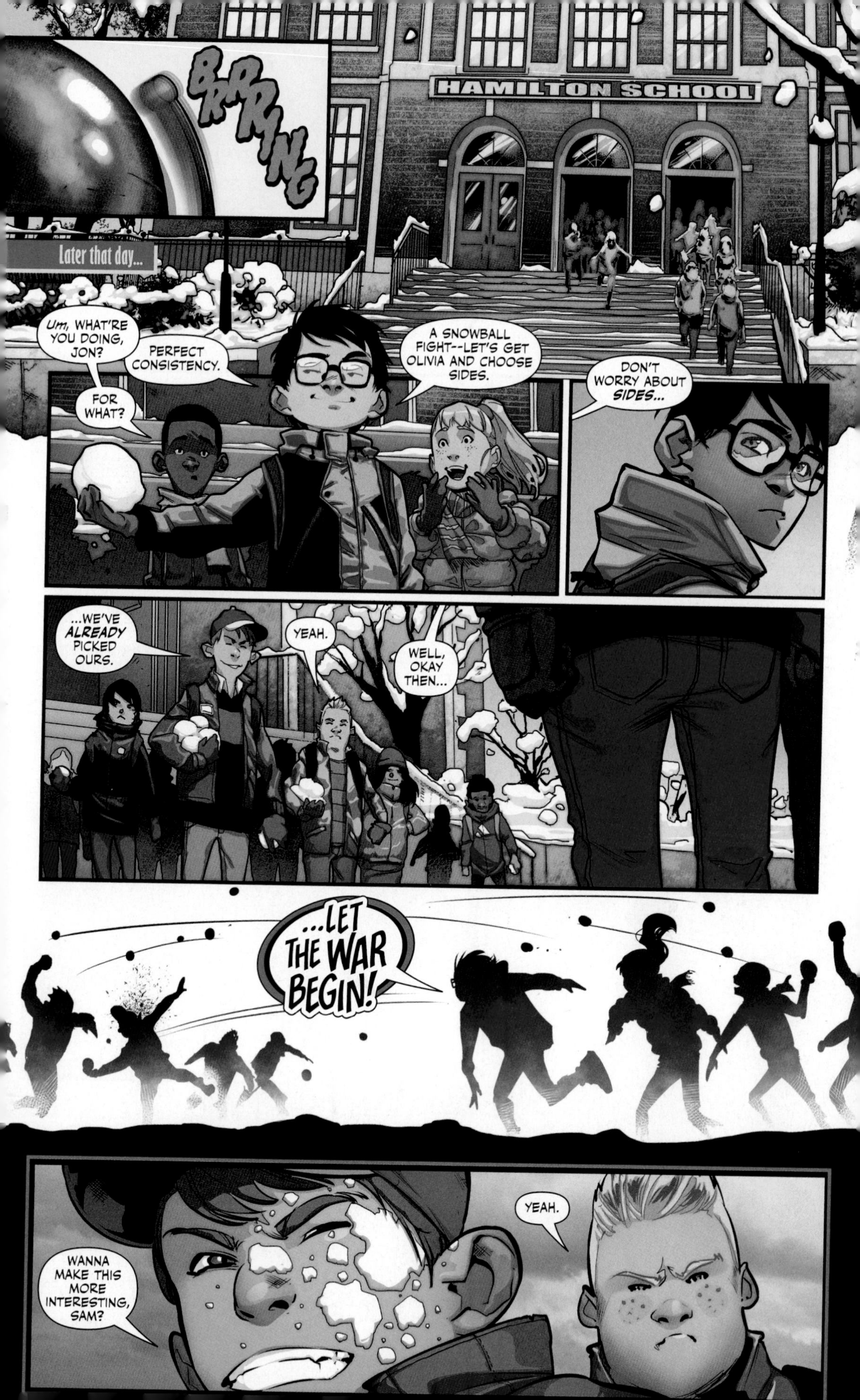
BRRRING
HAMILTON SCHOOL
Later that day...
Um, WHAT'RE YOU DOING, JON?
PERFECT CONSISTENCY.
FOR WHAT?
A SNOWBALL FIGHT--LET'S GET OLIVIA AND CHOOSE SIDES.
DON'T WORRY ABOUT SIDES...
...WE'VE ALREADY PICKED OURS.
YEAH.
WELL, OKAY THEN...
...LET THE WAR BEGIN!
WANNA MAKE THIS MORE INTERESTING, SAM?
YEAH.

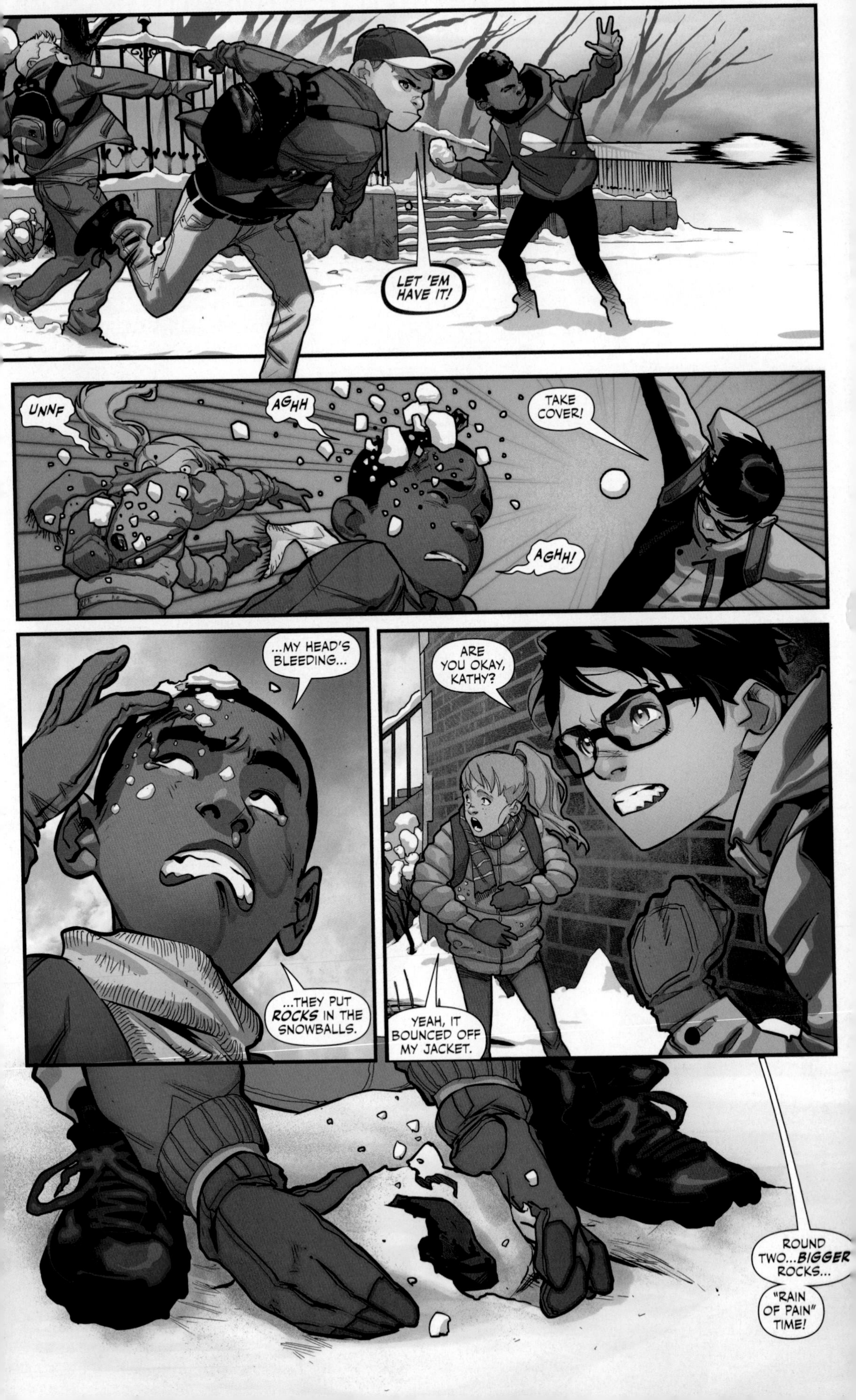
LET 'EM HAVE IT!
UNNF
AGHH
TAKE COVER!
AGHH!
...MY HEAD'S BLEEDING...
...THEY PUT ROCKS IN THE SNOWBALLS.
ARE YOU OKAY, KATHY?
YEAH, IT BOUNCED OFF MY JACKET.
ROUND TWO...BIGGER ROCKS...
"RAIN OF PAIN" TIME!

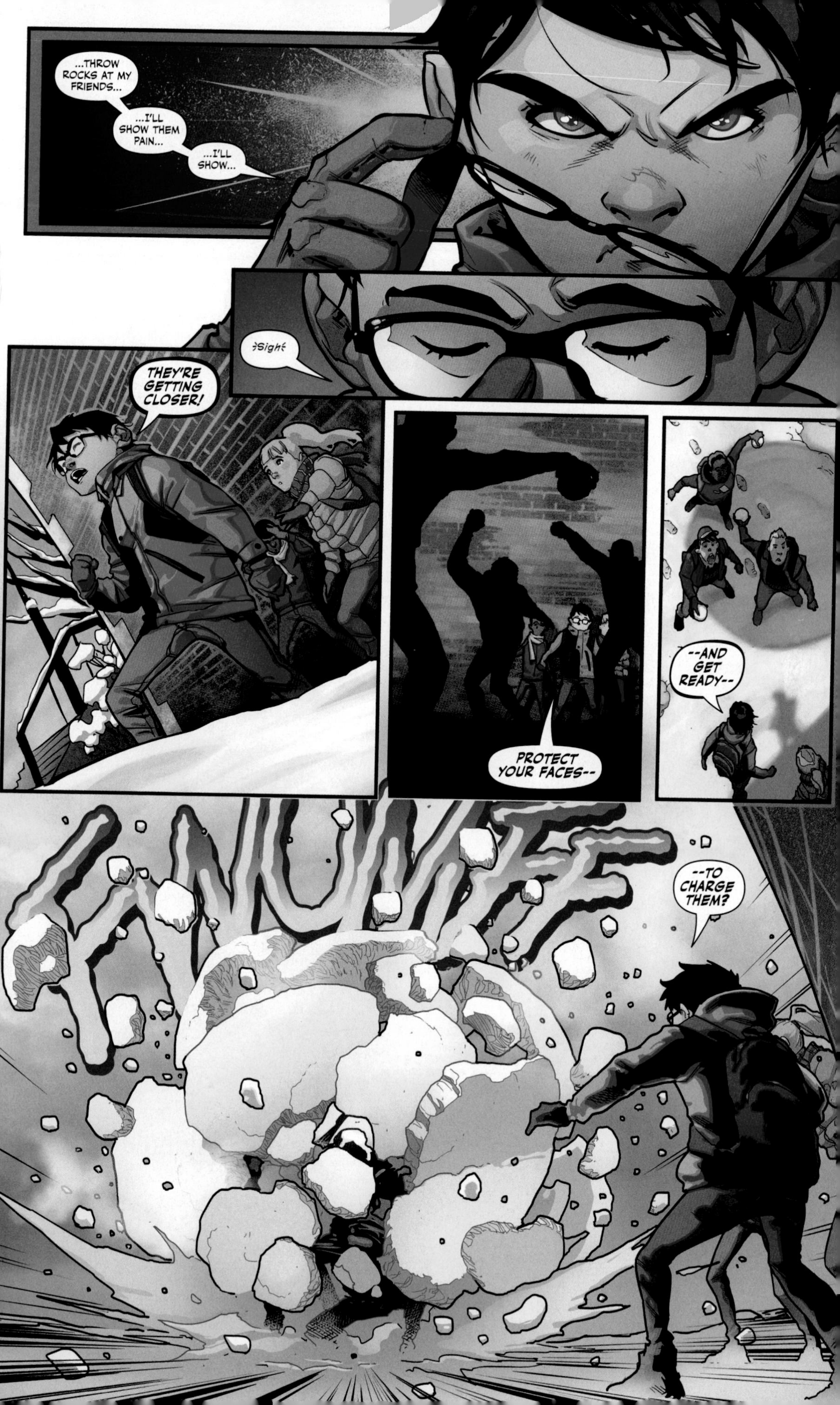
...THROW ROCKS AT MY FRIENDS...
...I'LL SHOW THEM PAIN...
...I'LL SHOW...
Sigh
THEY'RE GETTING CLOSER!
PROTECT YOUR FACES--
--AND GET READY--
--TO CHARGE THEM?

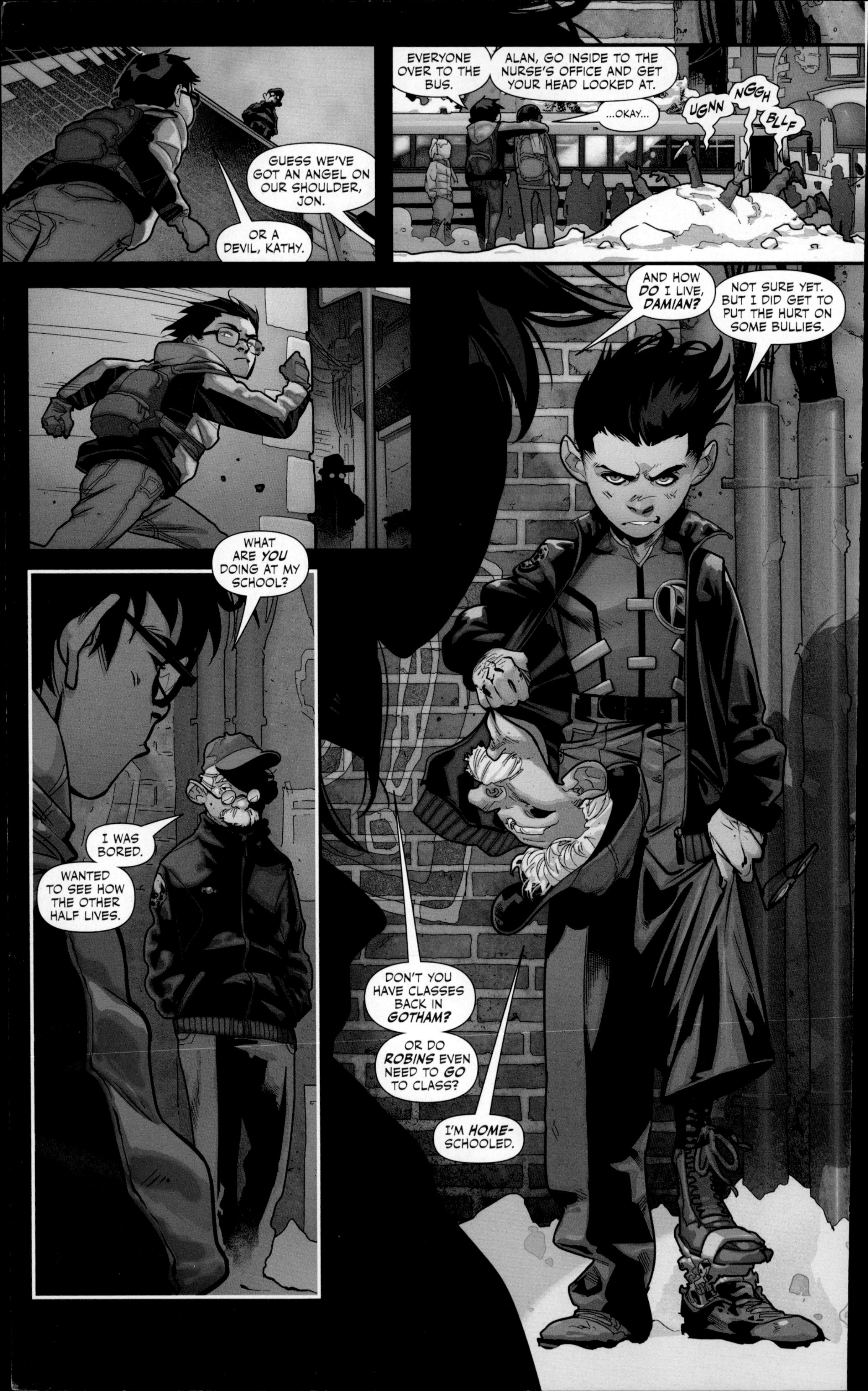
GUESS WE'VE GOT AN ANGEL ON OUR SHOULDER, JON.
OR A DEVIL, KATHY.
EVERYONE OVER TO THE BUS.
ALAN, GO INSIDE TO THE NURSE'S OFFICE AND GET YOUR HEAD LOOKED AT.
...OKAY...
UGNN
NGGH
BLLF
WHAT ARE *YOU* DOING AT MY SCHOOL?
I WAS BORED.
WANTED TO SEE HOW THE OTHER HALF LIVES.
AND HOW *DO* I LIVE, *DAMIAN?*
NOT SURE YET. BUT I DID GET TO PUT THE HURT ON SOME BULLIES.
DON'T YOU HAVE CLASSES BACK IN *GOTHAM?*
OR DO *ROBINS* EVEN NEED TO *GO* TO CLASS?
I'M *HOME*-SCHOOLED.

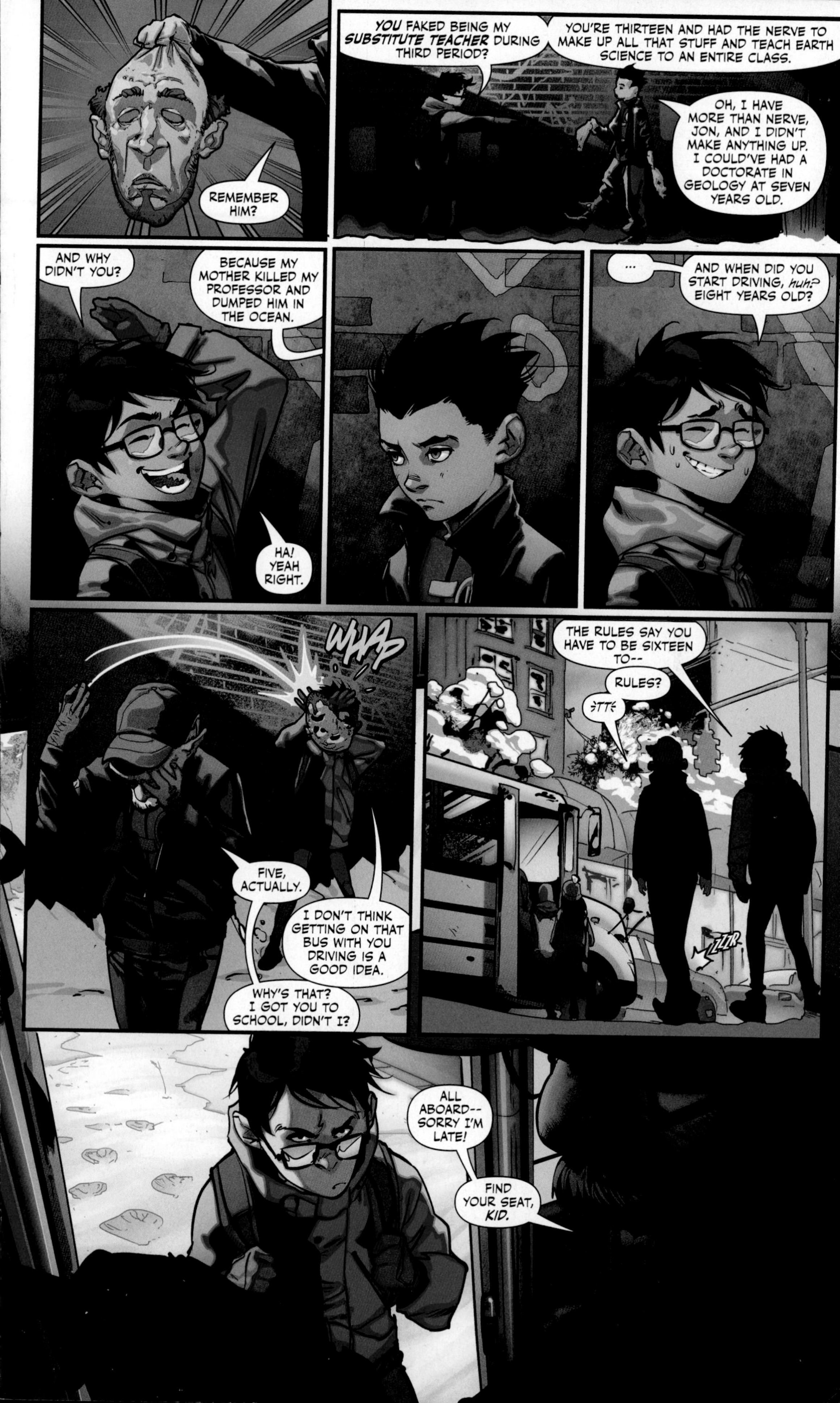
REMEMBER HIM?
YOU FAKED BEING MY SUBSTITUTE TEACHER DURING THIRD PERIOD?
YOU'RE THIRTEEN AND HAD THE NERVE TO MAKE UP ALL THAT STUFF AND TEACH EARTH SCIENCE TO AN ENTIRE CLASS.
OH, I HAVE MORE THAN NERVE, JON, AND I DIDN'T MAKE ANYTHING UP. I COULD'VE HAD A DOCTORATE IN GEOLOGY AT SEVEN YEARS OLD.
AND WHY DIDN'T YOU?
BECAUSE MY MOTHER KILLED MY PROFESSOR AND DUMPED HIM IN THE OCEAN.
HA! YEAH RIGHT.
...
AND WHEN DID YOU START DRIVING, *huh?* EIGHT YEARS OLD?
WHAP
FIVE, ACTUALLY.
I DON'T THINK GETTING ON THAT BUS WITH YOU DRIVING IS A GOOD IDEA.
WHY'S THAT? I GOT YOU TO SCHOOL, DIDN'T I?
THE RULES SAY YOU HAVE TO BE SIXTEEN TO--
RULES?
TT
ZZZR
ALL ABOARD-- SORRY I'M LATE!
FIND YOUR SEAT, *KID.*

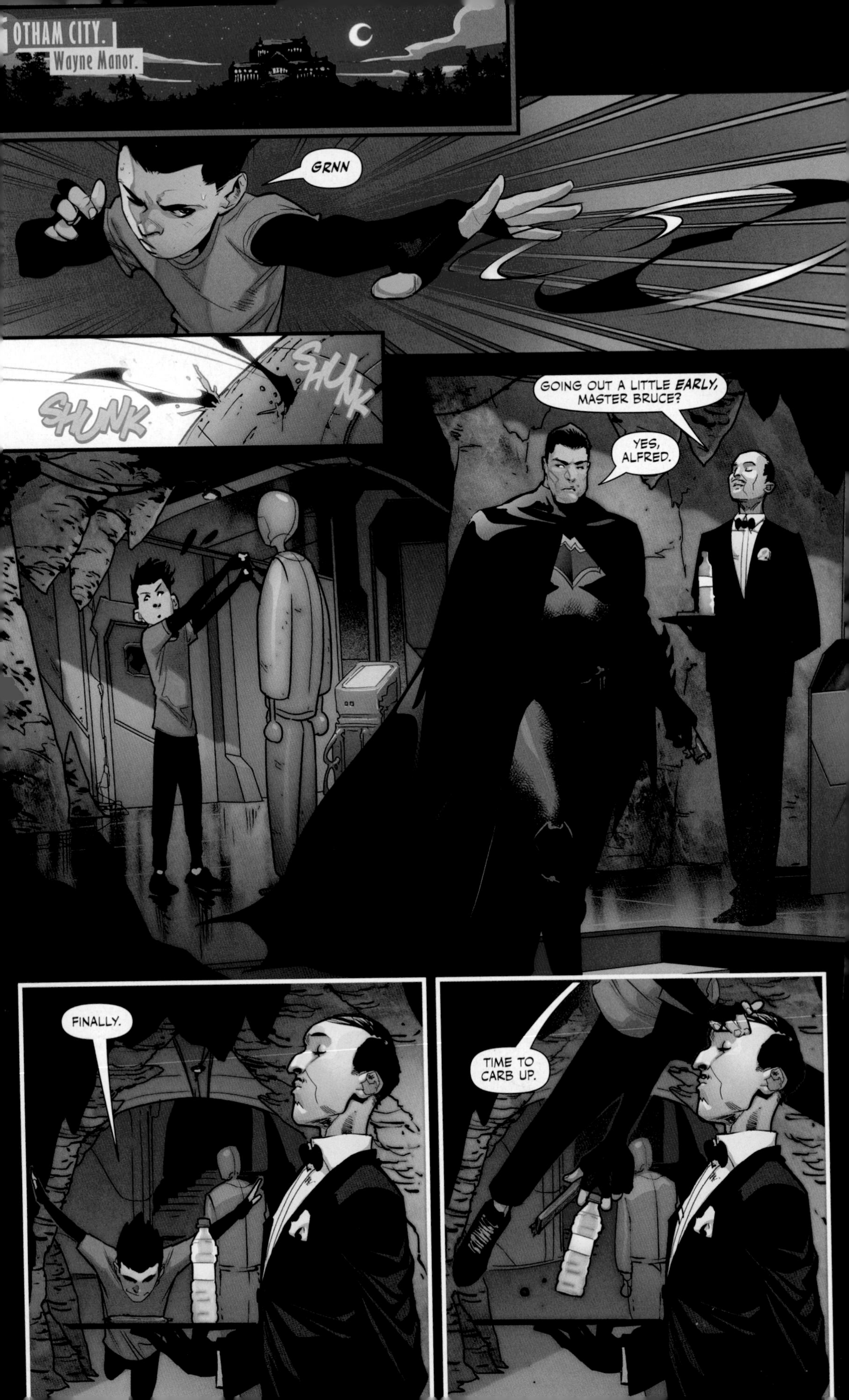

OTHAM CITY.
Wayne Manor.
GRNN
SHUNK
SHUNK
GOING OUT A LITTLE EARLY, MASTER BRUCE?
YES, ALFRED.
FINALLY.
TIME TO CARB UP.

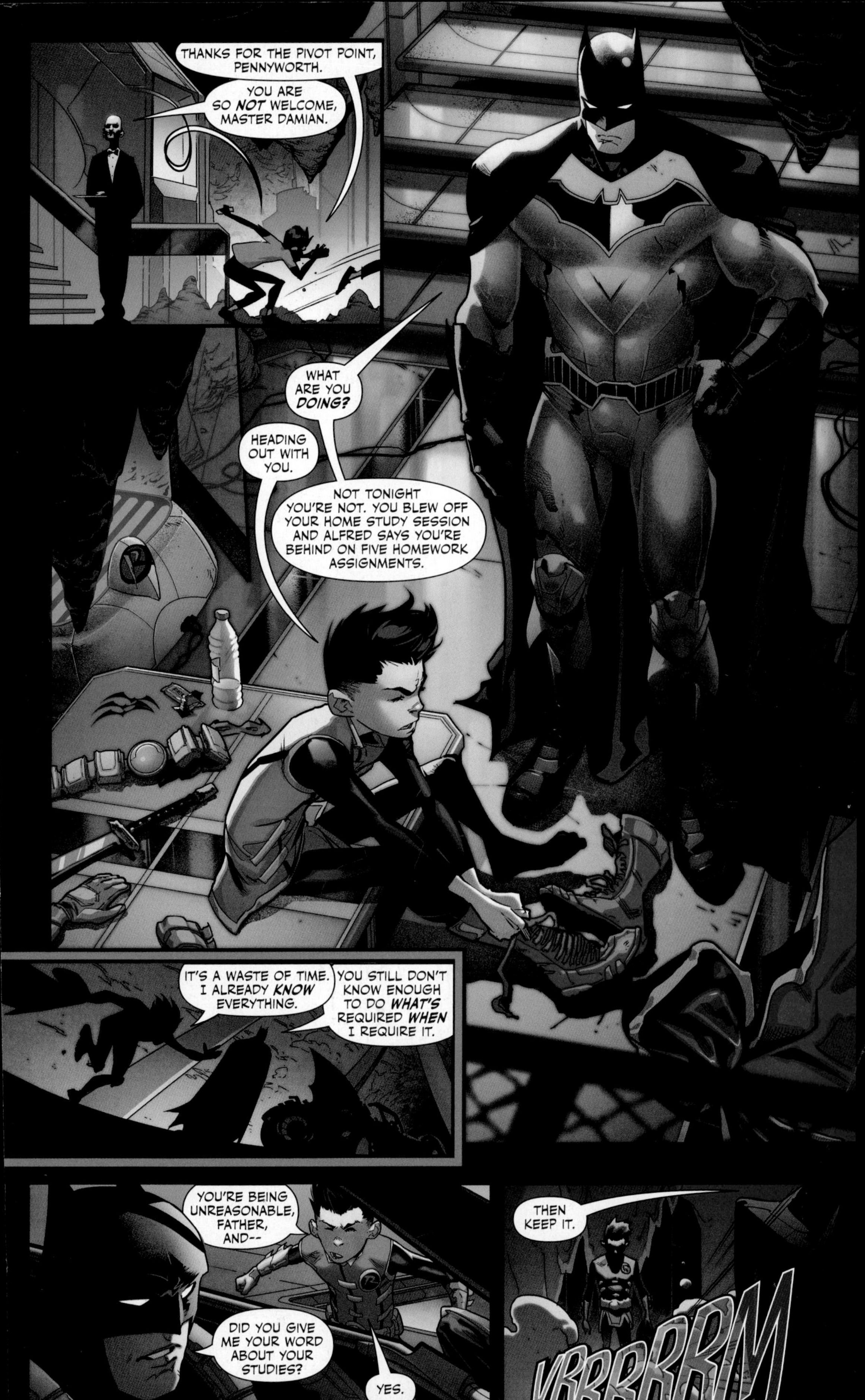
THANKS FOR THE PIVOT POINT, PENNYWORTH.
YOU ARE SO NOT WELCOME, MASTER DAMIAN.
WHAT ARE YOU DOING?
HEADING OUT WITH YOU.
NOT TONIGHT YOU'RE NOT. YOU BLEW OFF YOUR HOME STUDY SESSION AND ALFRED SAYS YOU'RE BEHIND ON FIVE HOMEWORK ASSIGNMENTS.
IT'S A WASTE OF TIME. I ALREADY KNOW EVERYTHING.
YOU STILL DON'T KNOW ENOUGH TO DO WHAT'S REQUIRED WHEN I REQUIRE IT.
YOU'RE BEING UNREASONABLE, FATHER, AND--
DID YOU GIVE ME YOUR WORD ABOUT YOUR STUDIES?
YES.
THEN KEEP IT.
VRRRRRRM

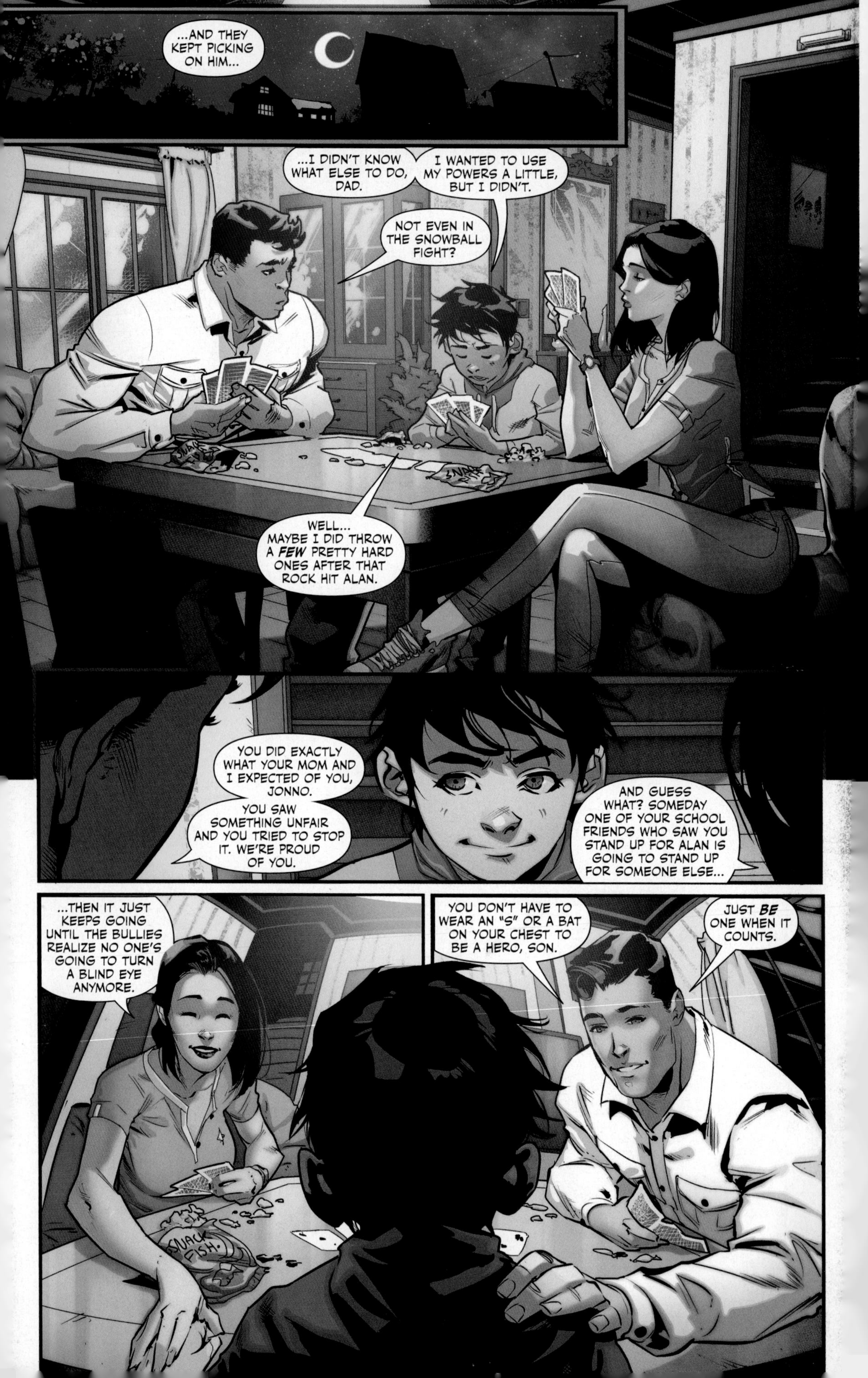
...AND THEY KEPT PICKING ON HIM...
...I DIDN'T KNOW WHAT ELSE TO DO, DAD.
I WANTED TO USE MY POWERS A LITTLE, BUT I DIDN'T.
NOT EVEN IN THE SNOWBALL FIGHT?
WELL... MAYBE I DID THROW A FEW PRETTY HARD ONES AFTER THAT ROCK HIT ALAN.
YOU DID EXACTLY WHAT YOUR MOM AND I EXPECTED OF YOU, JONNO.
YOU SAW SOMETHING UNFAIR AND YOU TRIED TO STOP IT. WE'RE PROUD OF YOU.
AND GUESS WHAT? SOMEDAY ONE OF YOUR SCHOOL FRIENDS WHO SAW YOU STAND UP FOR ALAN IS GOING TO STAND UP FOR SOMEONE ELSE...
...THEN IT JUST KEEPS GOING UNTIL THE BULLIES REALIZE NO ONE'S GOING TO TURN A BLIND EYE ANYMORE.
YOU DON'T HAVE TO WEAR AN "S" OR A BAT ON YOUR CHEST TO BE A HERO, SON.
JUST BE ONE WHEN IT COUNTS.
SNACK FISH

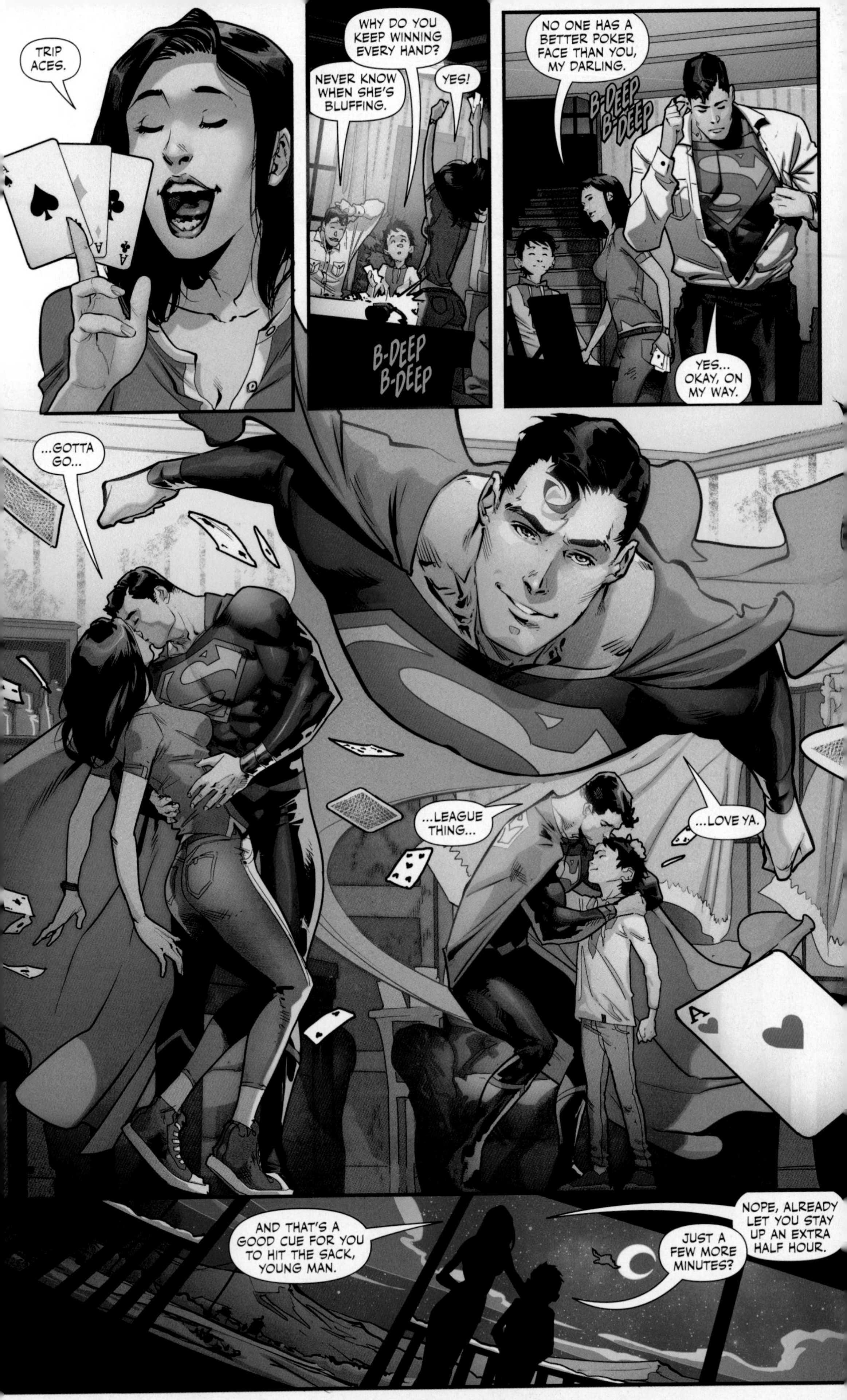
TRIP ACES.
WHY DO YOU KEEP WINNING EVERY HAND?
NEVER KNOW WHEN SHE'S BLUFFING.
YES!
B-DEEP B-DEEP
NO ONE HAS A BETTER POKER FACE THAN YOU, MY DARLING.
B-DEEP B-DEEP
YES... OKAY, ON MY WAY.
...GOTTA GO...
...LEAGUE THING...
...LOVE YA.
AND THAT'S A GOOD CUE FOR YOU TO HIT THE SACK, YOUNG MAN.
JUST A FEW MORE MINUTES?
NOPE, ALREADY LET YOU STAY UP AN EXTRA HALF HOUR.

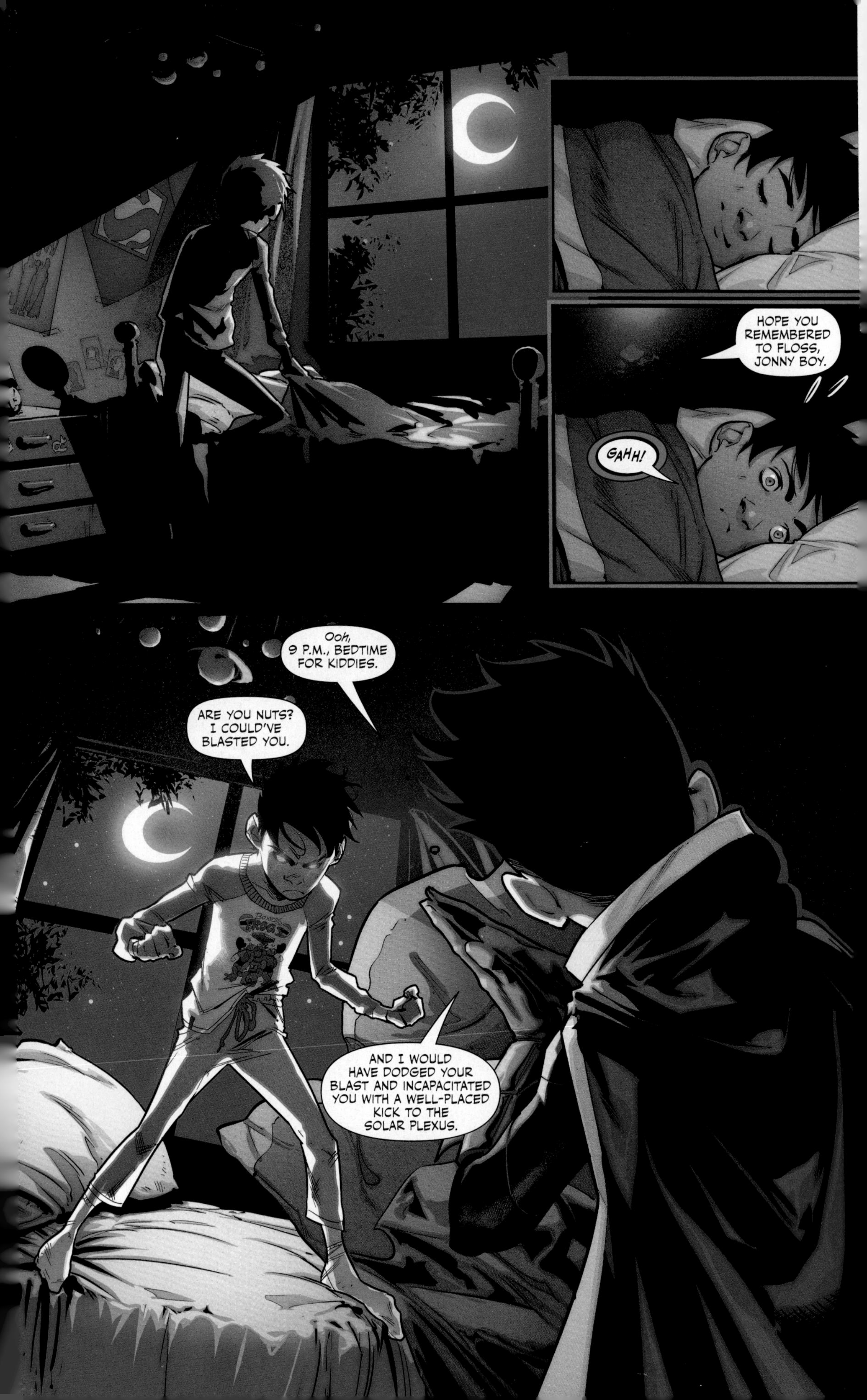
HOPE YOU REMEMBERED TO FLOSS, JONNY BOY.
GAHH!
Ooh, 9 P.M., BEDTIME FOR KIDDIES.
ARE YOU NUTS? I COULD'VE BLASTED YOU.
AND I WOULD HAVE DODGED YOUR BLAST AND INCAPACITATED YOU WITH A WELL-PLACED KICK TO THE SOLAR PLEXUS.

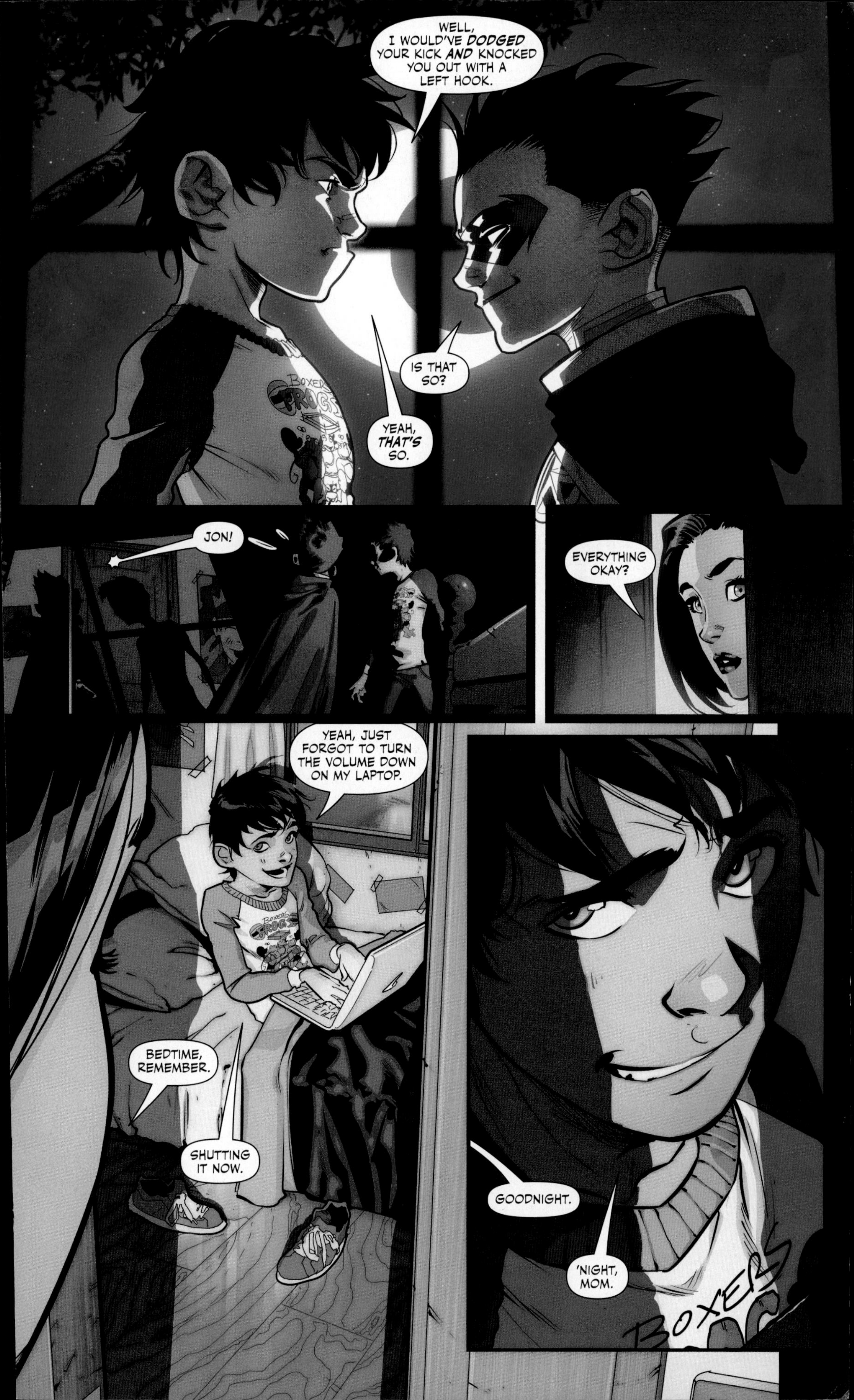
WELL, I WOULD'VE *DODGED* YOUR KICK *AND* KNOCKED YOU OUT WITH A LEFT HOOK.
IS THAT SO?
YEAH, *THAT'S* SO.
JON!
EVERYTHING OKAY?
YEAH, JUST FORGOT TO TURN THE VOLUME DOWN ON MY LAPTOP.
BEDTIME, REMEMBER.
SHUTTING IT NOW.
GOODNIGHT.
'NIGHT, MOM.

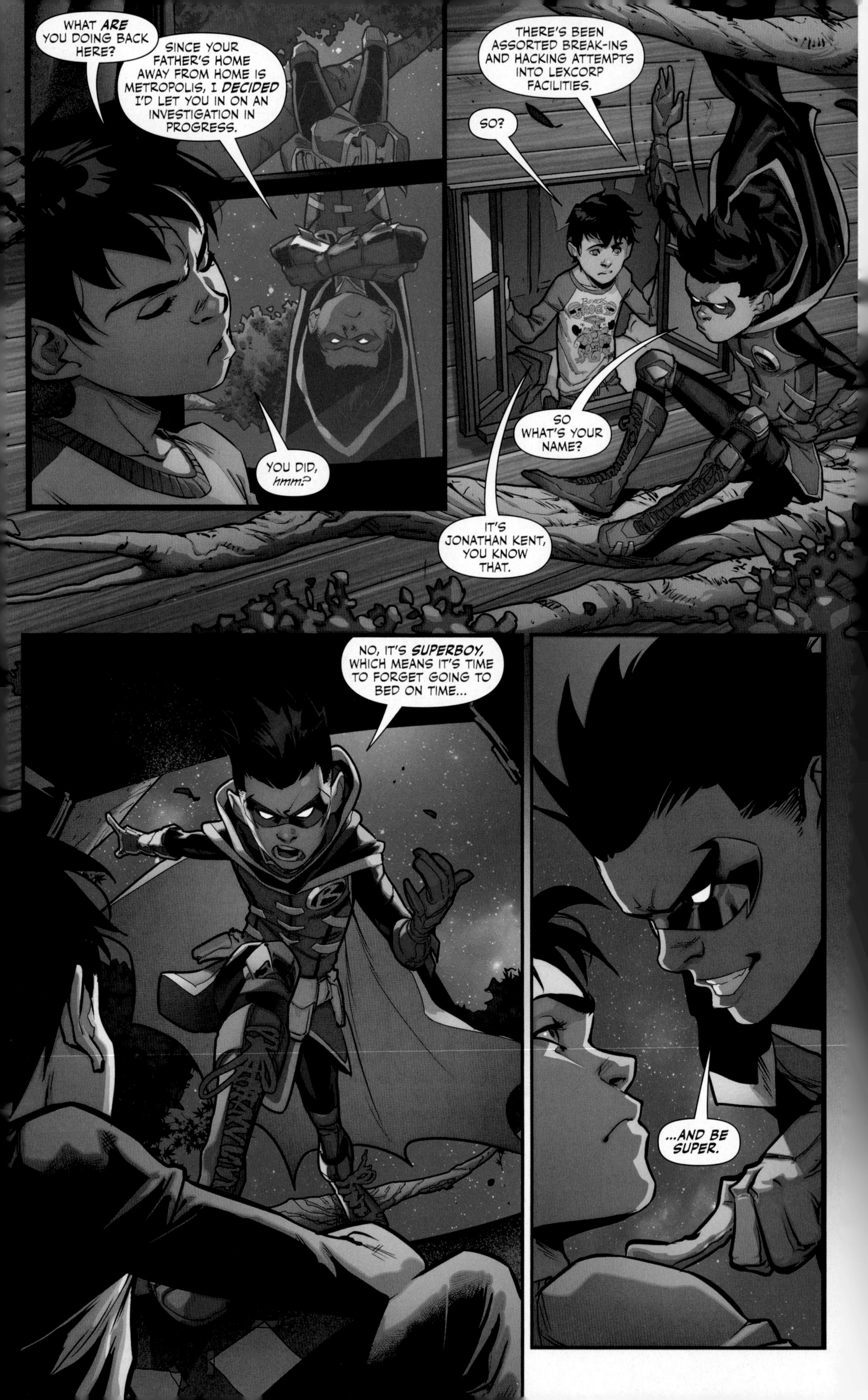
WHAT ARE YOU DOING BACK HERE?
SINCE YOUR FATHER'S HOME AWAY FROM HOME IS METROPOLIS, I DECIDED I'D LET YOU IN ON AN INVESTIGATION IN PROGRESS.
YOU DID, hmm?
THERE'S BEEN ASSORTED BREAK-INS AND HACKING ATTEMPTS INTO LEXCORP FACILITIES.
SO?
SO WHAT'S YOUR NAME?
IT'S JONATHAN KENT, YOU KNOW THAT.
NO, IT'S SUPERBOY, WHICH MEANS IT'S TIME TO FORGET GOING TO BED ON TIME...
...AND BE SUPER.

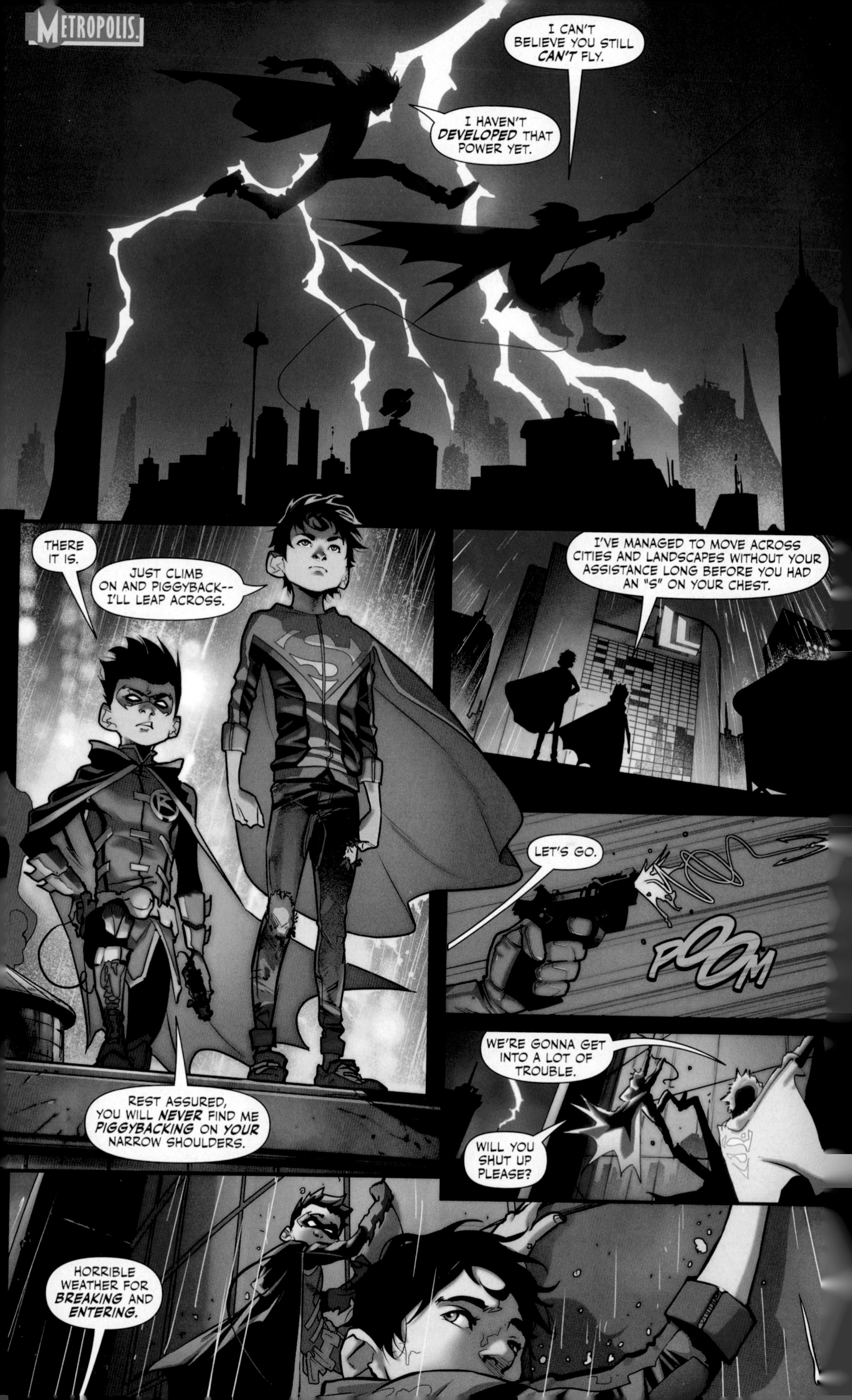
METROPOLIS.
I CAN'T BELIEVE YOU STILL *CAN'T* FLY.
I HAVEN'T *DEVELOPED* THAT POWER YET.
THERE IT IS.
JUST CLIMB ON AND PIGGYBACK-- I'LL LEAP ACROSS.
REST ASSURED, YOU WILL *NEVER* FIND ME *PIGGYBACKING* ON *YOUR* NARROW SHOULDERS.
I'VE MANAGED TO MOVE ACROSS CITIES AND LANDSCAPES WITHOUT YOUR ASSISTANCE LONG BEFORE YOU HAD AN "S" ON YOUR CHEST.
LET'S GO.
POOM
WE'RE GONNA GET INTO A LOT OF TROUBLE.
WILL YOU SHUT UP PLEASE?
HORRIBLE WEATHER FOR *BREAKING* AND *ENTERING.*

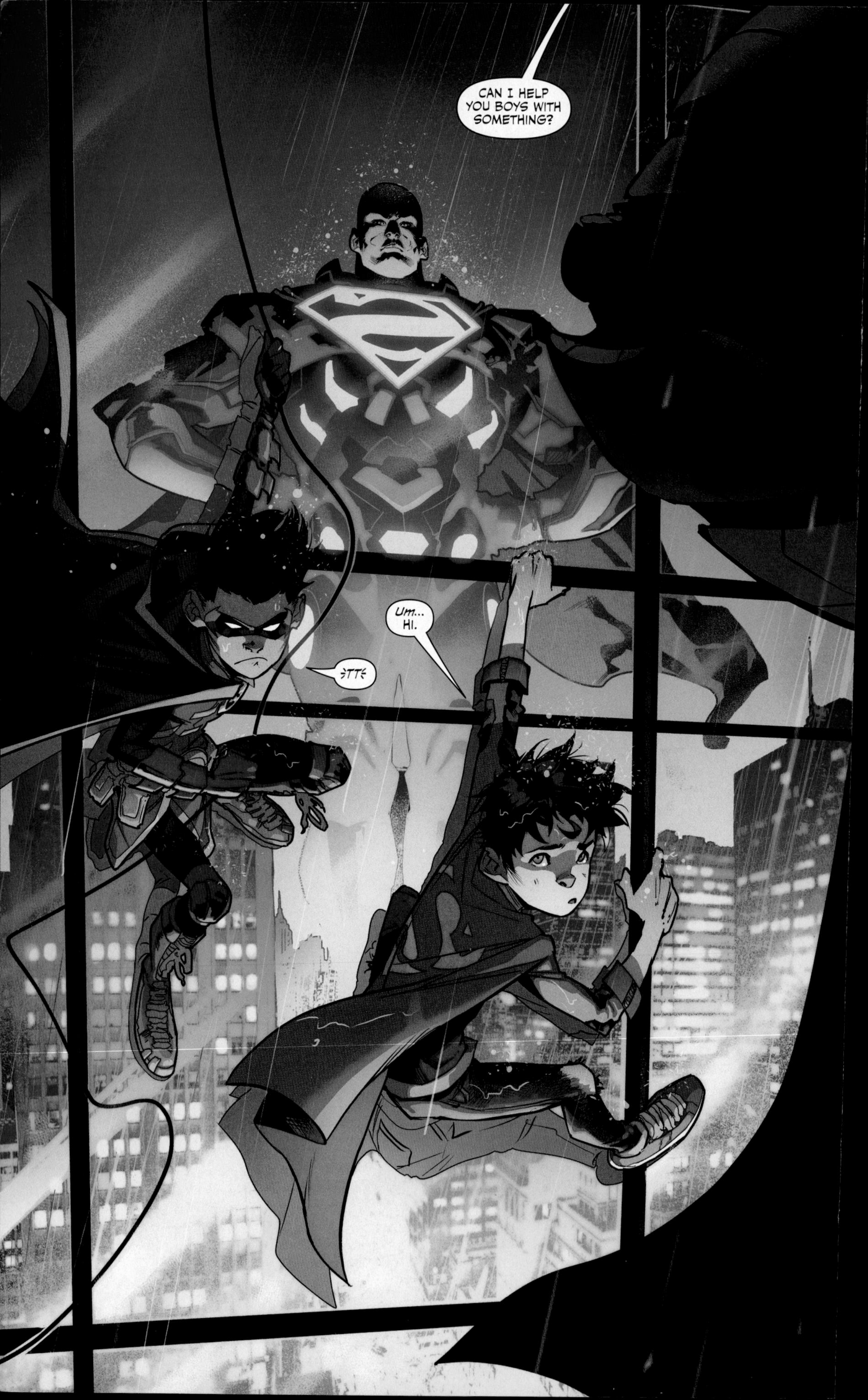
CAN I HELP YOU BOYS WITH SOMETHING?
UM... HI.
TT

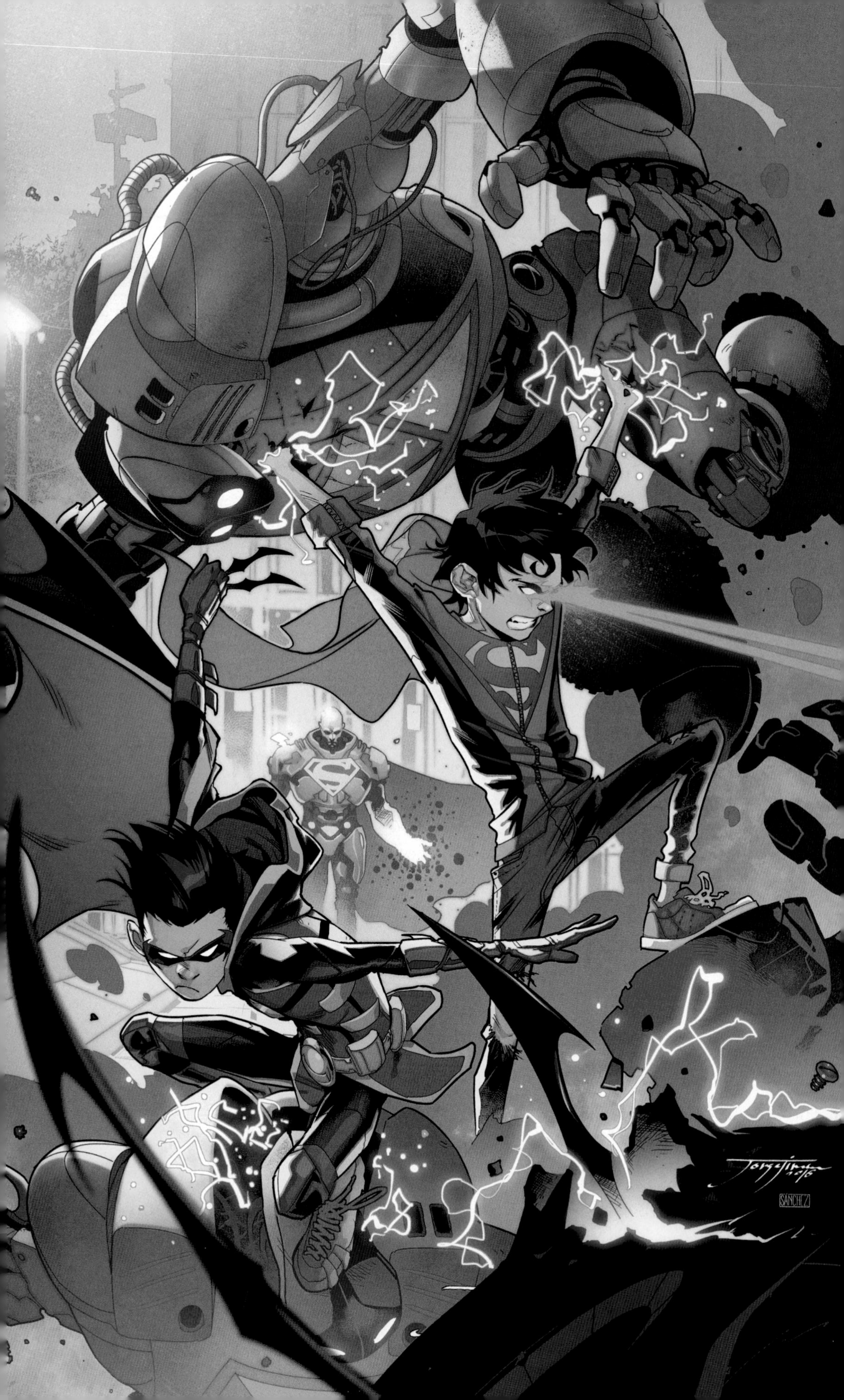
SÁNCHEZ

WHEN I GROW UP... PART TWO: LEX AND FRIENDS

JORGE JIMENEZ artist ✶ ALEJANDRO SANCHEZ colorist

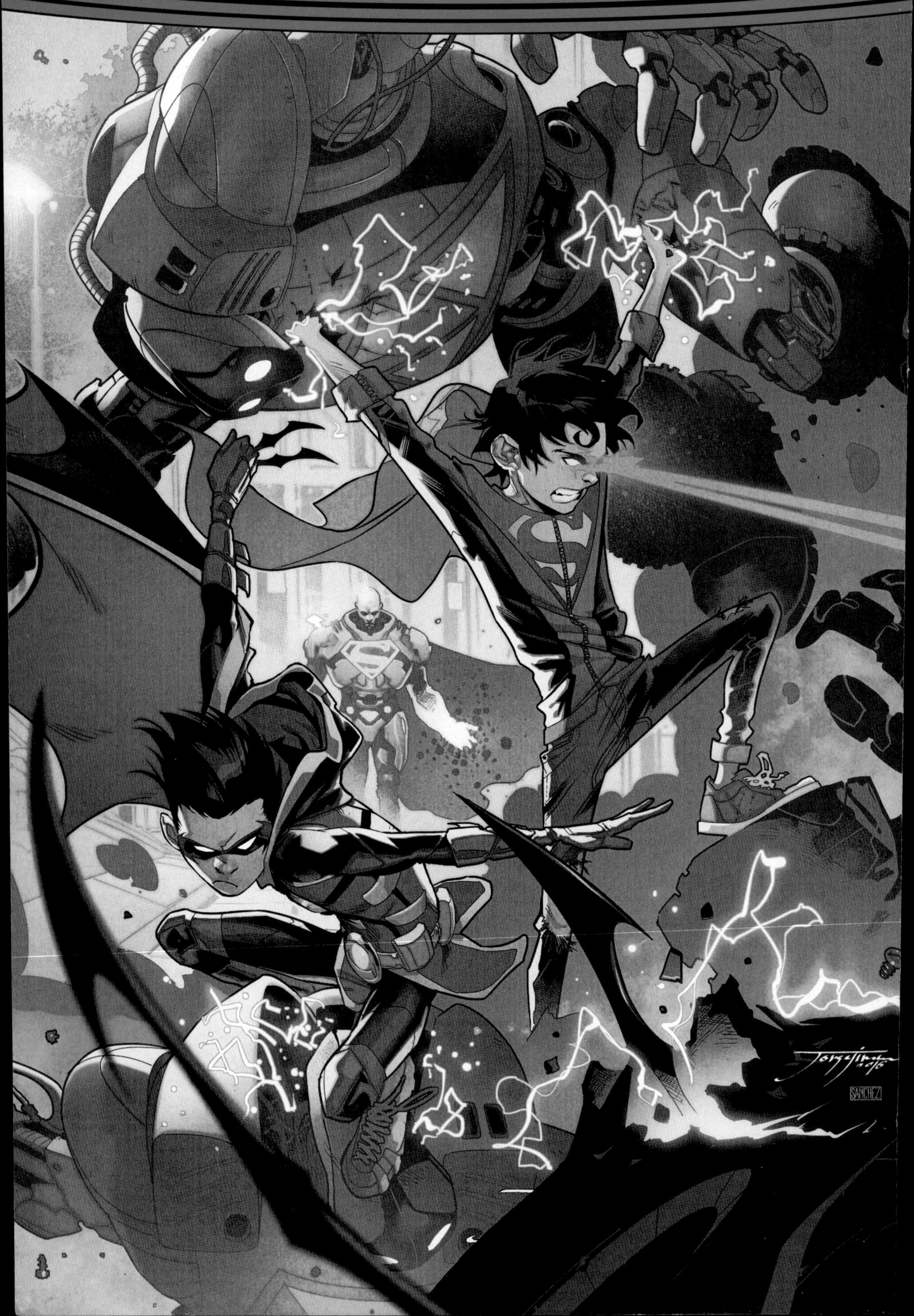
SÁNCHEZ

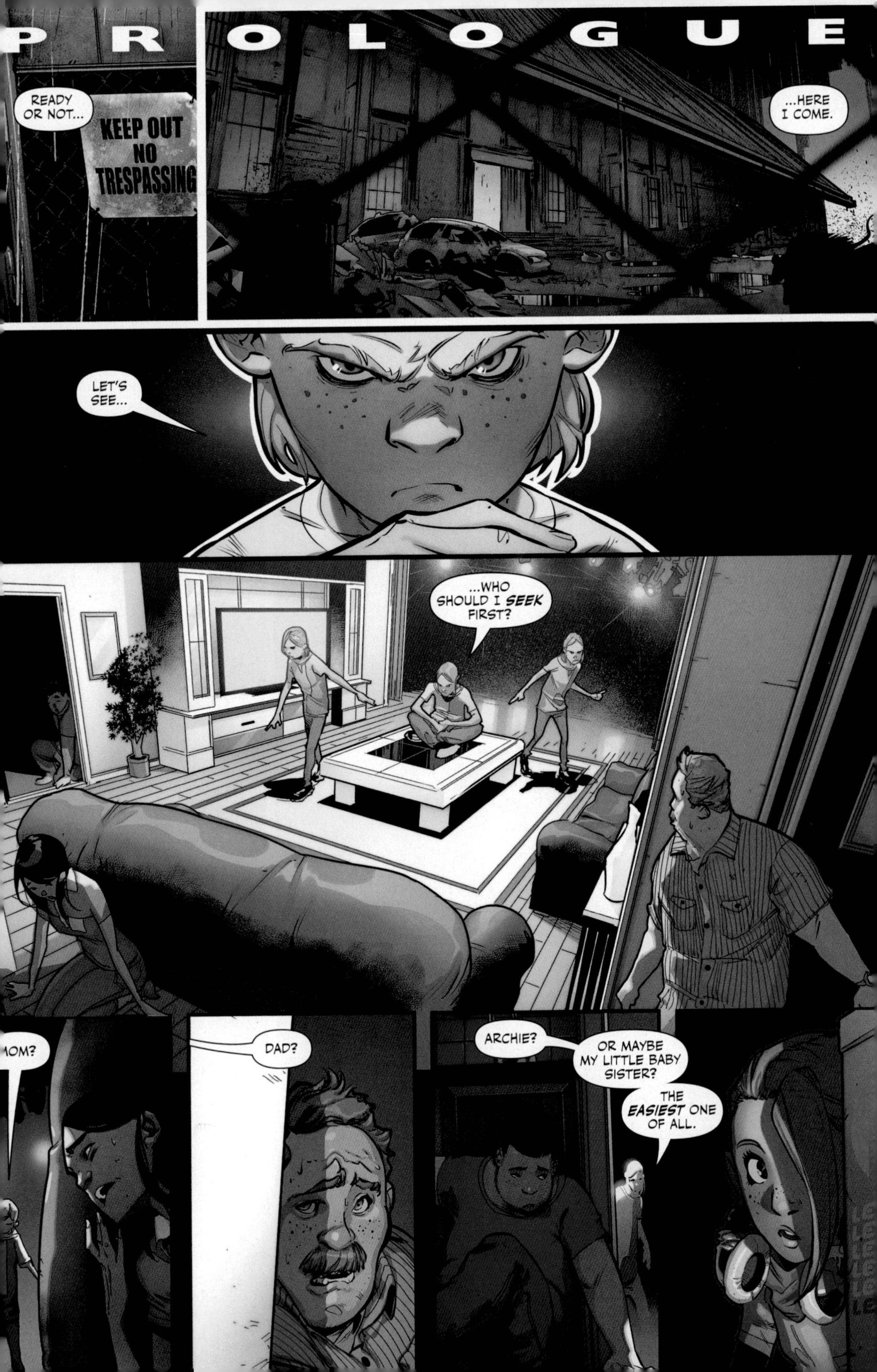
PROLOGUE
READY OR NOT...
KEEP OUT NO TRESPASSING
...HERE I COME.
LET'S SEE...
...WHO SHOULD I SEEK FIRST?
MOM?
DAD?
ARCHIE?
OR MAYBE MY LITTLE BABY SISTER?
THE EASIEST ONE OF ALL.

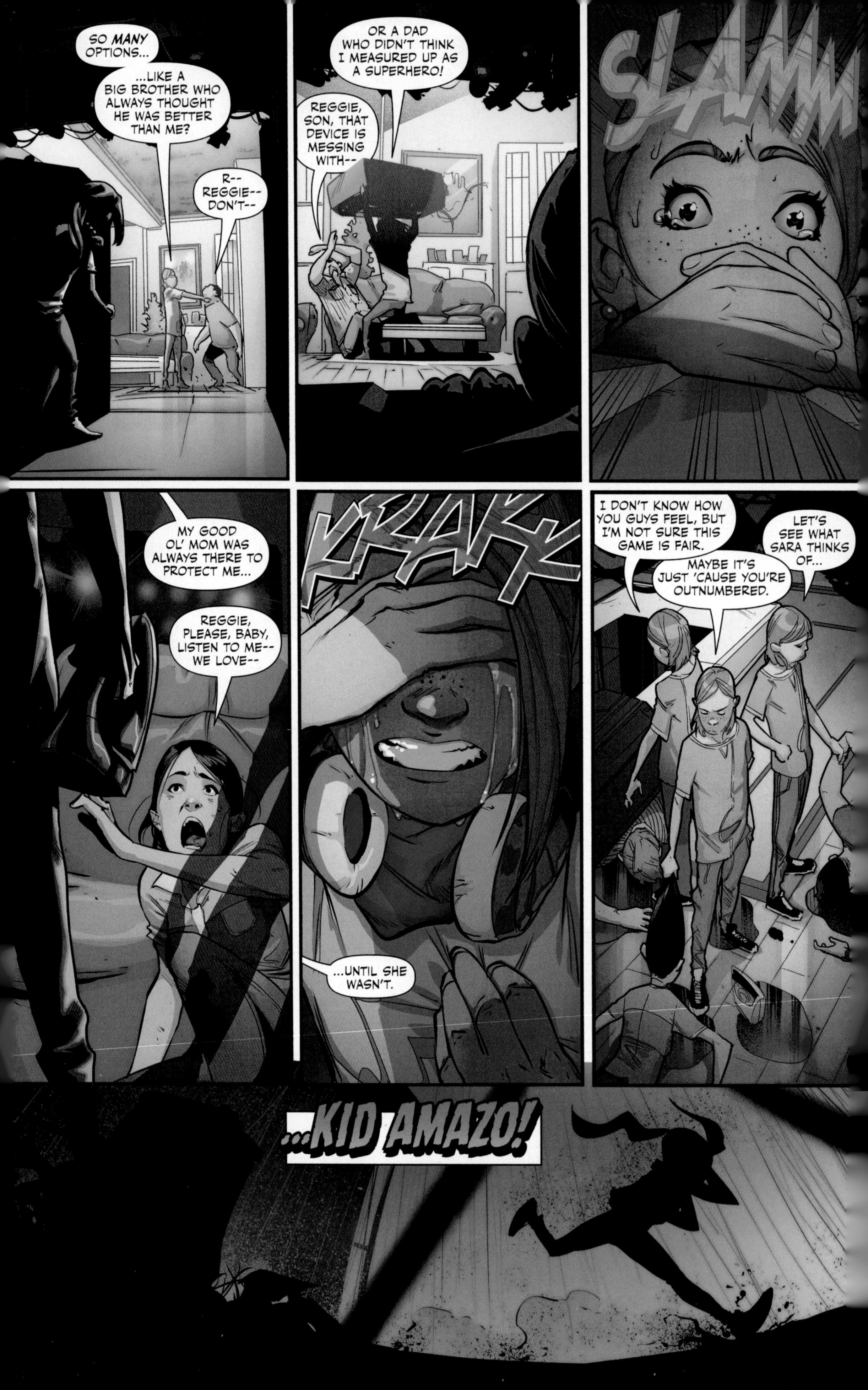
SO MANY OPTIONS...
...LIKE A BIG BROTHER WHO ALWAYS THOUGHT HE WAS BETTER THAN ME?
R-- REGGIE-- DON'T--
OR A DAD WHO DIDN'T THINK I MEASURED UP AS A SUPERHERO!
REGGIE, SON, THAT DEVICE IS MESSING WITH--
SLAMM
MY GOOD OL' MOM WAS ALWAYS THERE TO PROTECT ME...
REGGIE, PLEASE, BABY, LISTEN TO ME-- WE LOVE--
KRAK
...UNTIL SHE WASN'T.
I DON'T KNOW HOW YOU GUYS FEEL, BUT I'M NOT SURE THIS GAME IS FAIR.
MAYBE IT'S JUST 'CAUSE YOU'RE OUTNUMBERED.
LET'S SEE WHAT SARA THINKS OF...
...KID AMAZO!

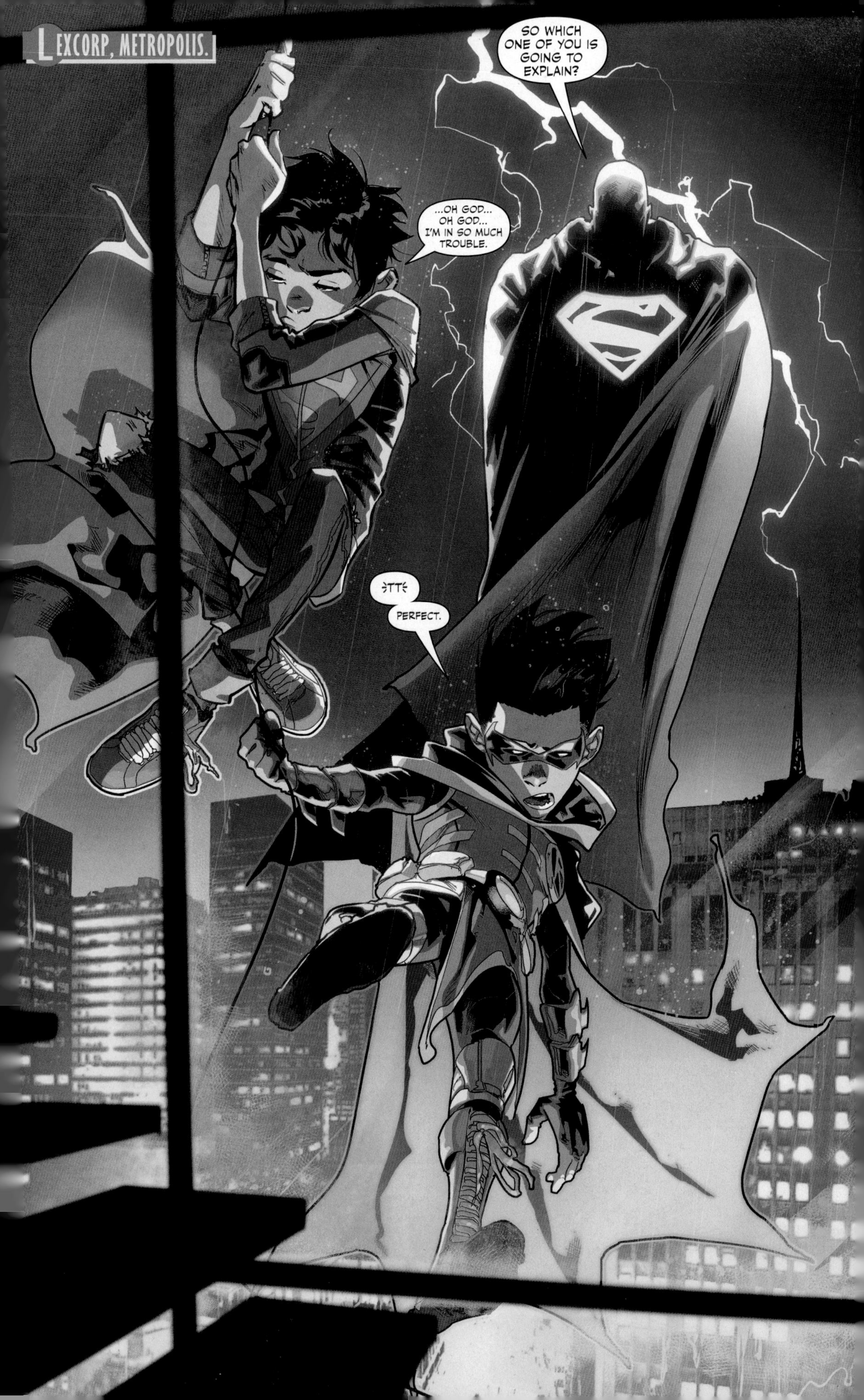
LEXCORP, METROPOLIS.
SO WHICH ONE OF YOU IS GOING TO EXPLAIN?
...OH GOD... OH GOD... I'M IN SO MUCH TROUBLE.
TT
PERFECT.

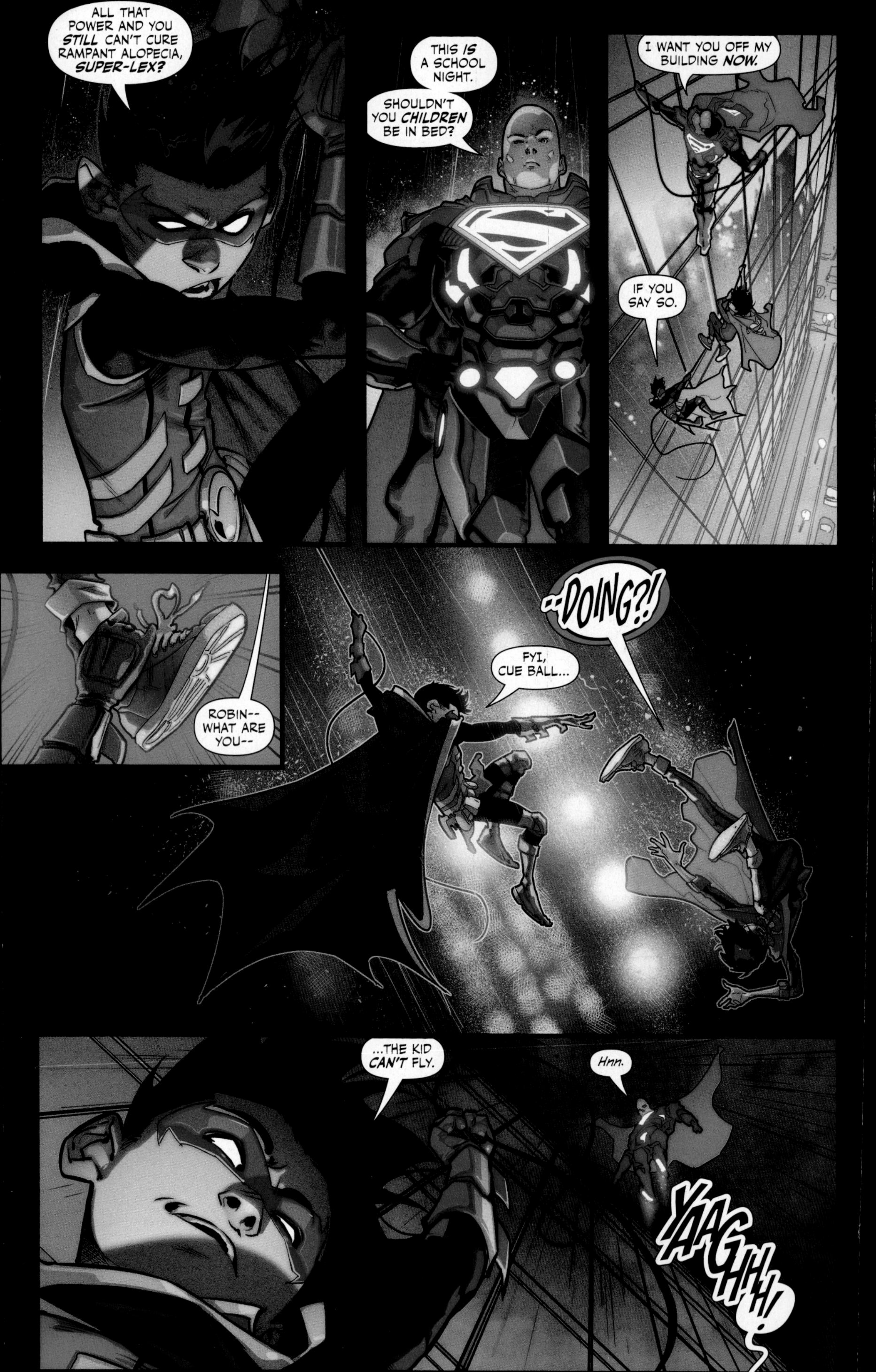
ALL THAT POWER AND YOU STILL CAN'T CURE RAMPANT ALOPECIA, SUPER-LEX?
THIS IS A SCHOOL NIGHT.
SHOULDN'T YOU CHILDREN BE IN BED?
I WANT YOU OFF MY BUILDING NOW.
IF YOU SAY SO.
ROBIN-- WHAT ARE YOU--
--DOING?!
FYI, CUE BALL...
...THE KID CAN'T FLY.
Hnn.
YAAGHHH!

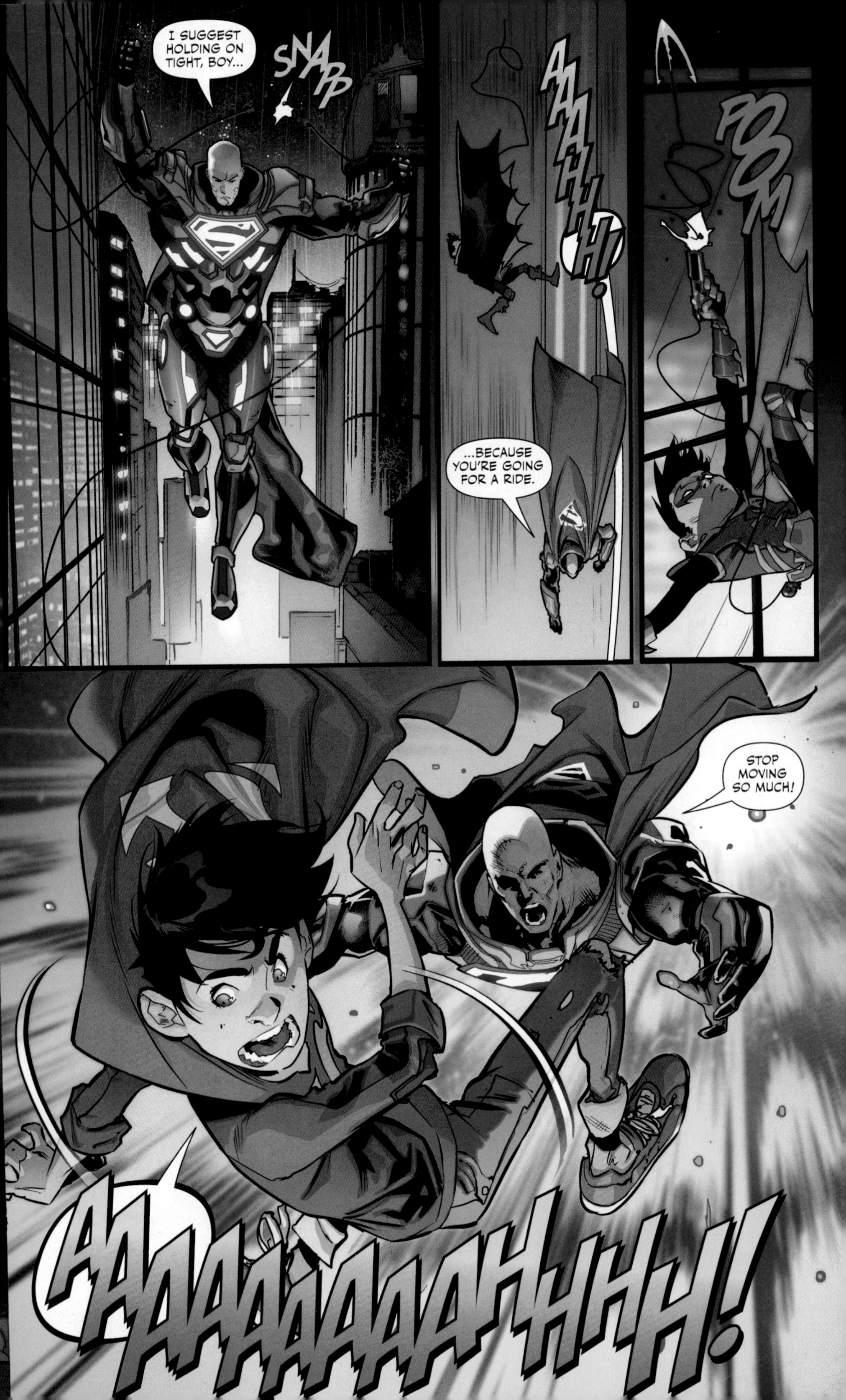
I SUGGEST HOLDING ON TIGHT, BOY...
SNAPP
AAAAHHH!
...BECAUSE YOU'RE GOING FOR A RIDE.
POOM
STOP MOVING SO MUCH!
AAAAAAAAAHHHH!

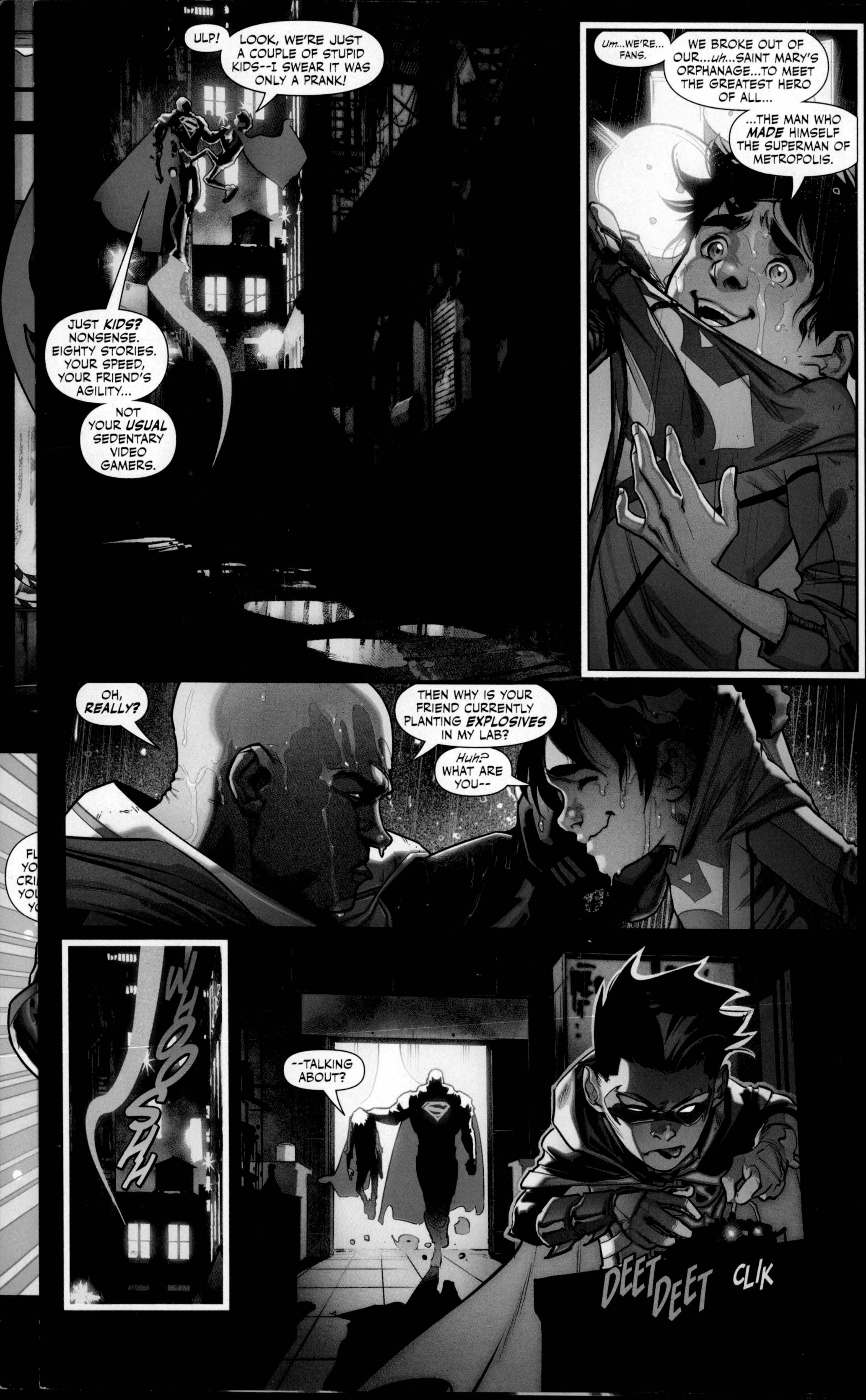

ULP!
LOOK, WE'RE JUST A COUPLE OF STUPID KIDS--I SWEAR IT WAS ONLY A PRANK!
JUST KIDS? NONSENSE. EIGHTY STORIES. YOUR SPEED, YOUR FRIEND'S AGILITY...
NOT YOUR USUAL SEDENTARY VIDEO GAMERS.
Um...WE'RE... FANS.
WE BROKE OUT OF OUR...uh...SAINT MARY'S ORPHANAGE...TO MEET THE GREATEST HERO OF ALL...
...THE MAN WHO MADE HIMSELF THE SUPERMAN OF METROPOLIS.
OH, REALLY?
THEN WHY IS YOUR FRIEND CURRENTLY PLANTING EXPLOSIVES IN MY LAB?
Huh? WHAT ARE YOU--
WHOOSHH
--TALKING ABOUT?
DEET DEET
CLIK

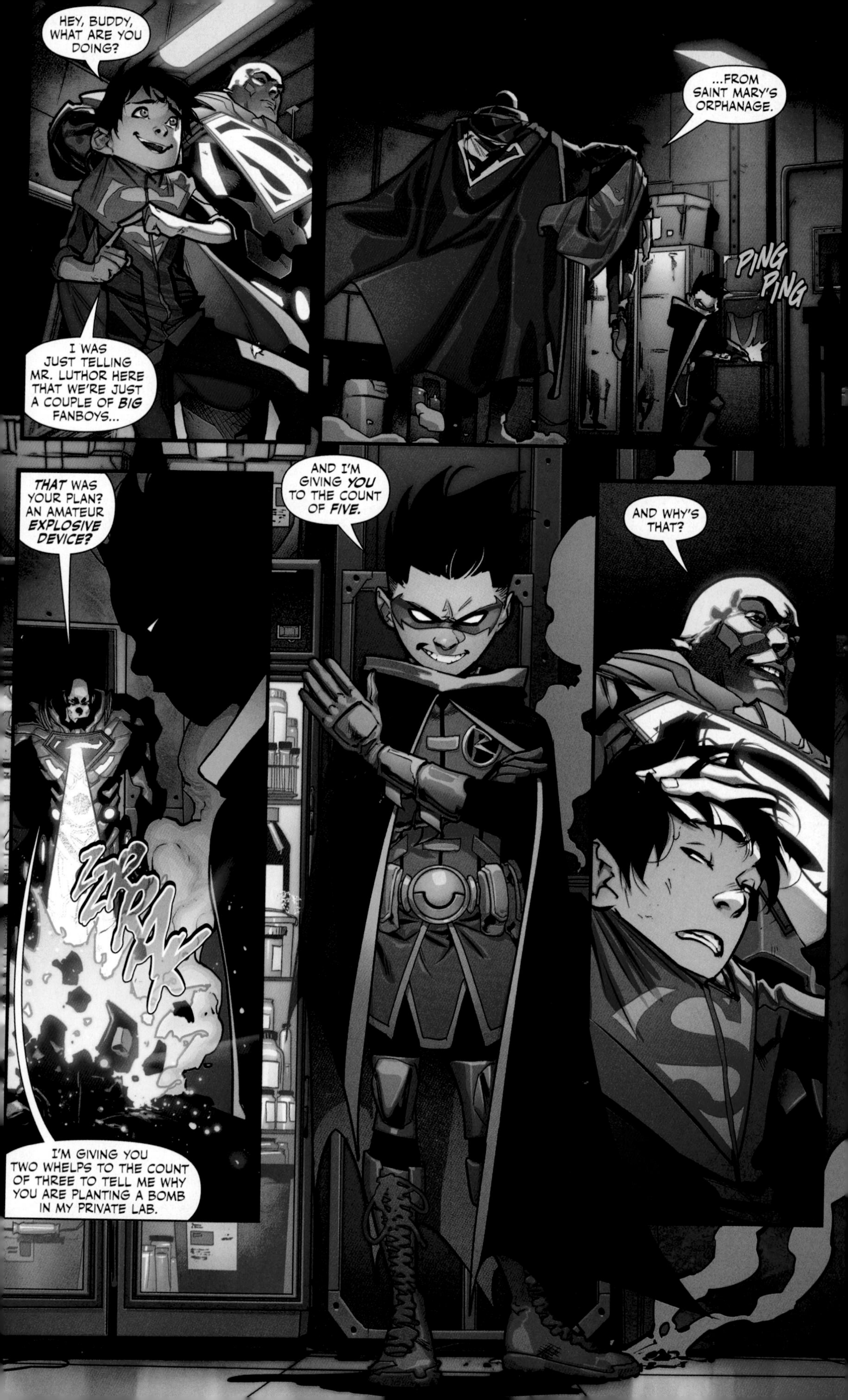
HEY, BUDDY, WHAT ARE YOU DOING?
I WAS JUST TELLING MR. LUTHOR HERE THAT WE'RE JUST A COUPLE OF *BIG* FANBOYS...
...FROM SAINT MARY'S ORPHANAGE.
PING PING
THAT WAS YOUR PLAN? AN AMATEUR *EXPLOSIVE DEVICE?*
ZZRAK
I'M GIVING YOU TWO WHELPS TO THE COUNT OF THREE TO TELL ME WHY YOU ARE PLANTING A BOMB IN MY PRIVATE LAB.
AND I'M GIVING *YOU* TO THE COUNT OF *FIVE.*
AND WHY'S THAT?

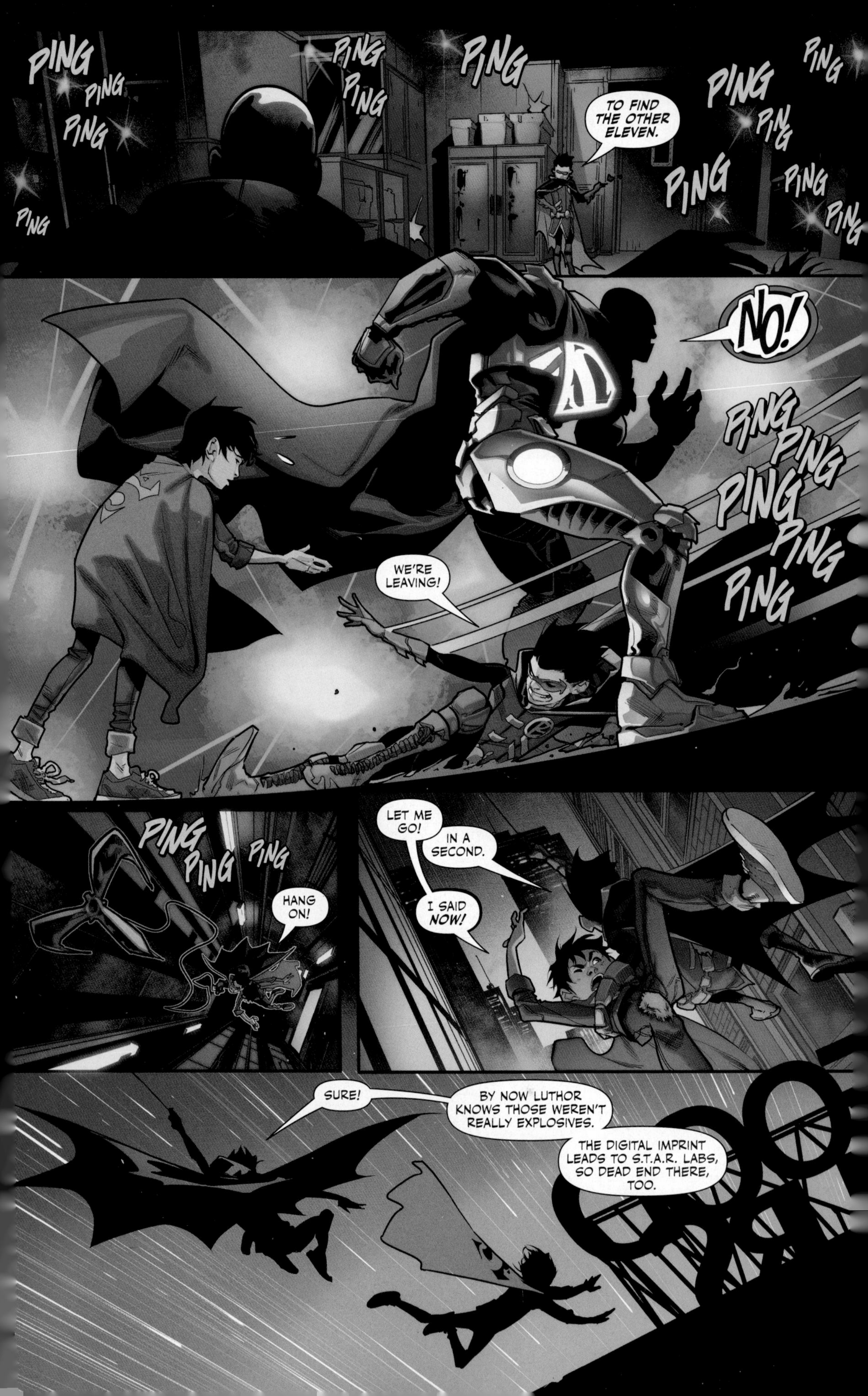

PING
PING
PING
PING
PING
PING
PING
TO FIND THE OTHER ELEVEN.
PING
PING
PING
PING
PING
PING
NO!
PING PING PING PING PING
WE'RE LEAVING!
PING PING PING
HANG ON!
LET ME GO!
IN A SECOND.
I SAID NOW!
SURE!
BY NOW LUTHOR KNOWS THOSE WEREN'T REALLY EXPLOSIVES.
THE DIGITAL IMPRINT LEADS TO S.T.A.R. LABS, SO DEAD END THERE, TOO.

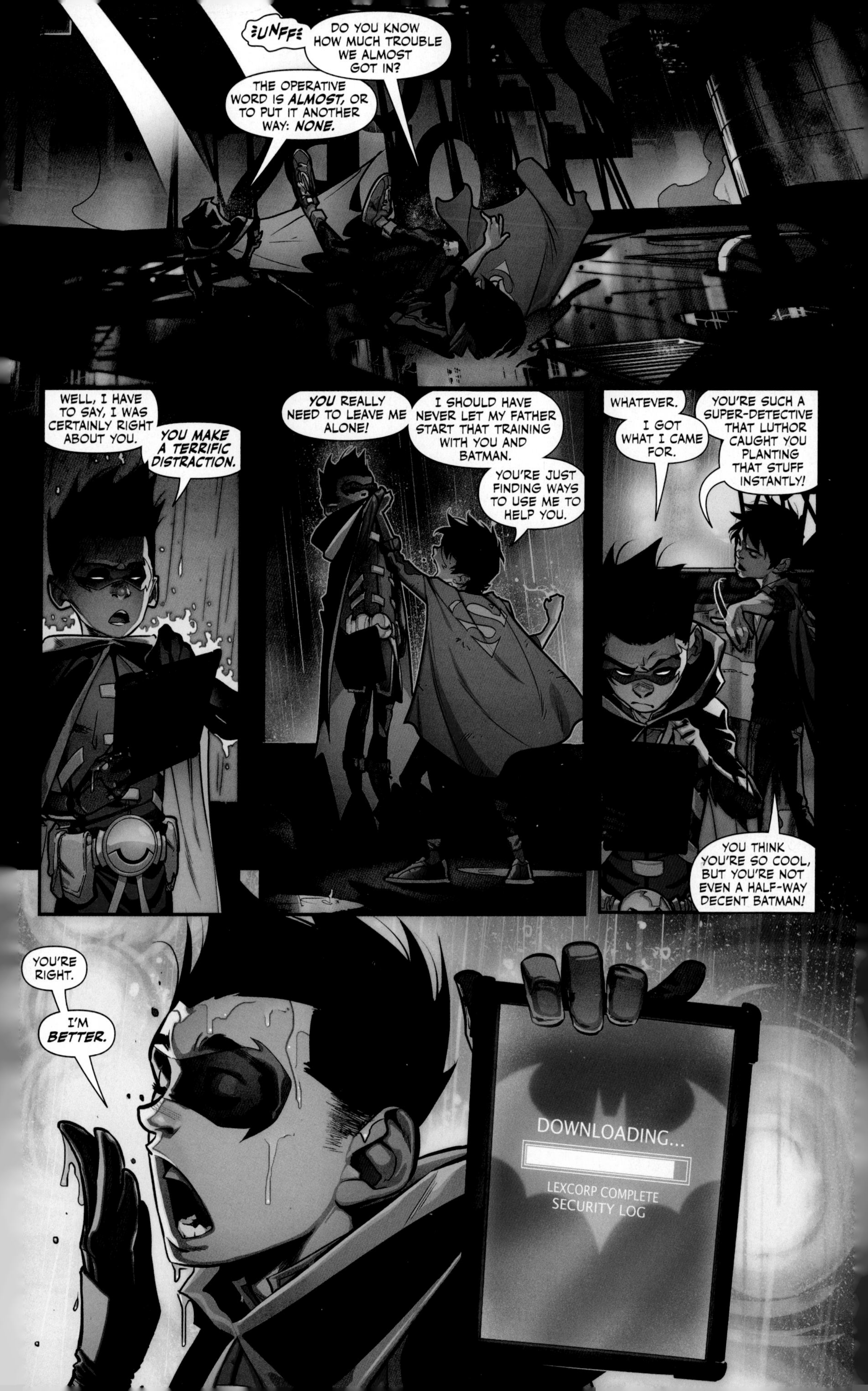
UNFF
DO YOU KNOW HOW MUCH TROUBLE WE ALMOST GOT IN?
THE OPERATIVE WORD IS ALMOST, OR TO PUT IT ANOTHER WAY: NONE.
WELL, I HAVE TO SAY, I WAS CERTAINLY RIGHT ABOUT YOU.
YOU MAKE A TERRIFIC DISTRACTION.
YOU REALLY NEED TO LEAVE ME ALONE!
I SHOULD HAVE NEVER LET MY FATHER START THAT TRAINING WITH YOU AND BATMAN.
YOU'RE JUST FINDING WAYS TO USE ME TO HELP YOU.
WHATEVER.
I GOT WHAT I CAME FOR.
YOU'RE SUCH A SUPER-DETECTIVE THAT LUTHOR CAUGHT YOU PLANTING THAT STUFF INSTANTLY!
YOU THINK YOU'RE SO COOL, BUT YOU'RE NOT EVEN A HALF-WAY DECENT BATMAN!
YOU'RE RIGHT.
I'M BETTER.
DOWNLOADING...
LEXCORP COMPLETE SECURITY LOG

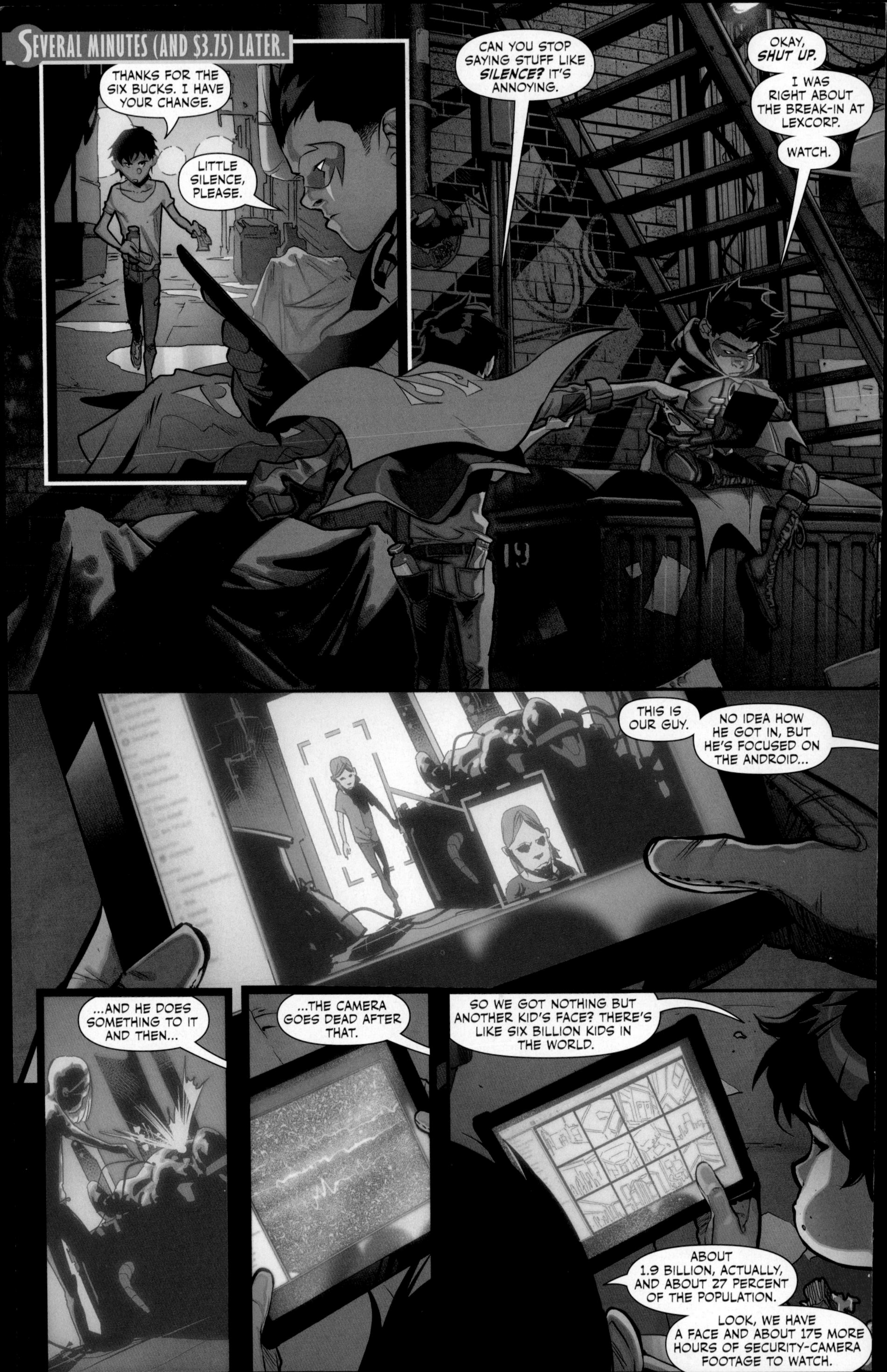
SEVERAL MINUTES (AND $3.75) LATER.
THANKS FOR THE SIX BUCKS. I HAVE YOUR CHANGE.
LITTLE SILENCE, PLEASE.
CAN YOU STOP SAYING STUFF LIKE SILENCE? IT'S ANNOYING.
OKAY, SHUT UP.
I WAS RIGHT ABOUT THE BREAK-IN AT LEXCORP.
WATCH.
THIS IS OUR GUY.
NO IDEA HOW HE GOT IN, BUT HE'S FOCUSED ON THE ANDROID...
...AND HE DOES SOMETHING TO IT AND THEN...
...THE CAMERA GOES DEAD AFTER THAT.
SO WE GOT NOTHING BUT ANOTHER KID'S FACE? THERE'S LIKE SIX BILLION KIDS IN THE WORLD.
ABOUT 1.9 BILLION, ACTUALLY, AND ABOUT 27 PERCENT OF THE POPULATION.
LOOK, WE HAVE A FACE AND ABOUT 175 MORE HOURS OF SECURITY-CAMERA FOOTAGE TO WATCH.

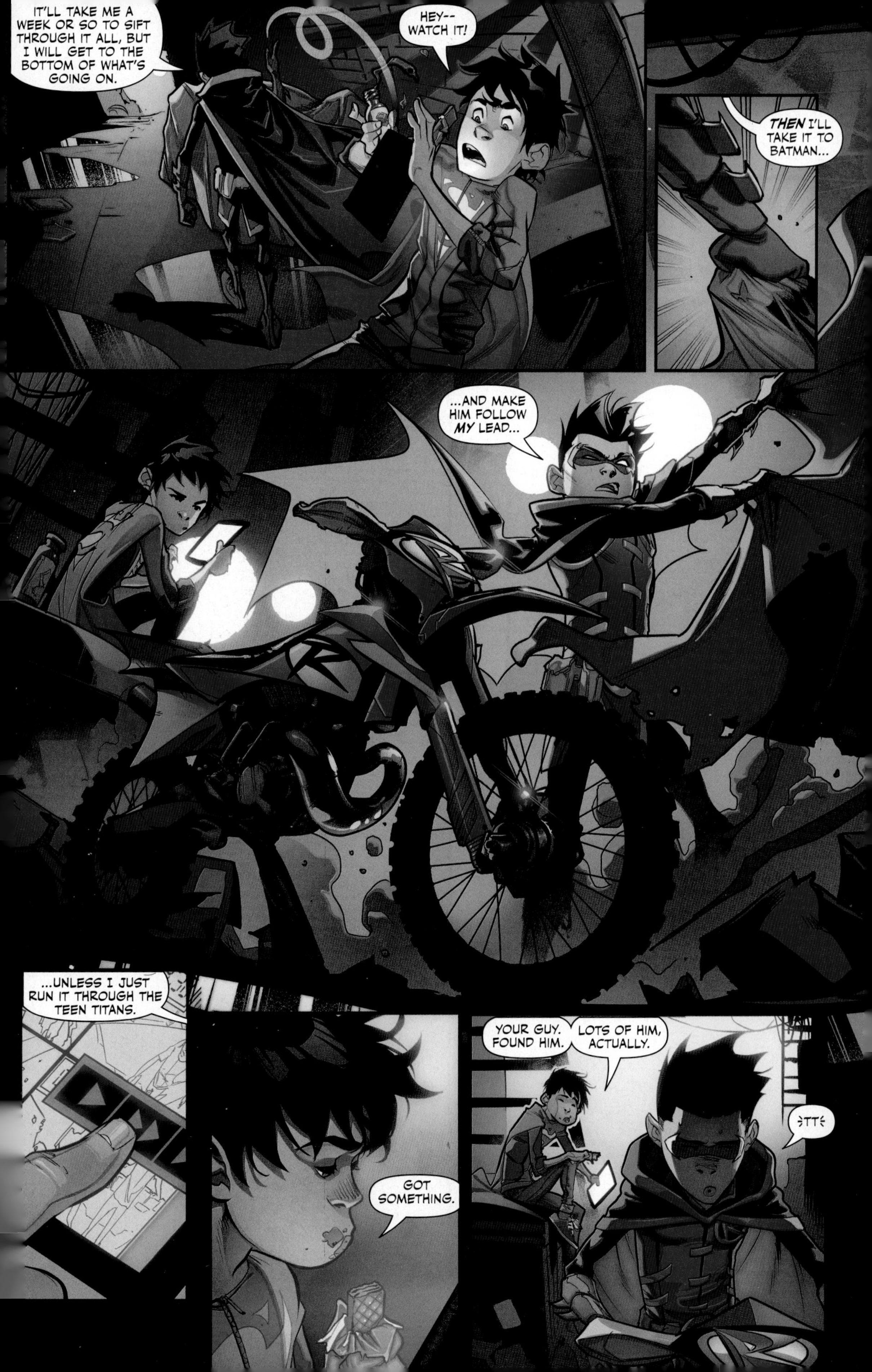
IT'LL TAKE ME A WEEK OR SO TO SIFT THROUGH IT ALL, BUT I WILL GET TO THE BOTTOM OF WHAT'S GOING ON.
HEY-- WATCH IT!
THEN I'LL TAKE IT TO BATMAN...
...AND MAKE HIM FOLLOW MY LEAD...
...UNLESS I JUST RUN IT THROUGH THE TEEN TITANS.
GOT SOMETHING.
YOUR GUY. FOUND HIM.
LOTS OF HIM, ACTUALLY.
TT

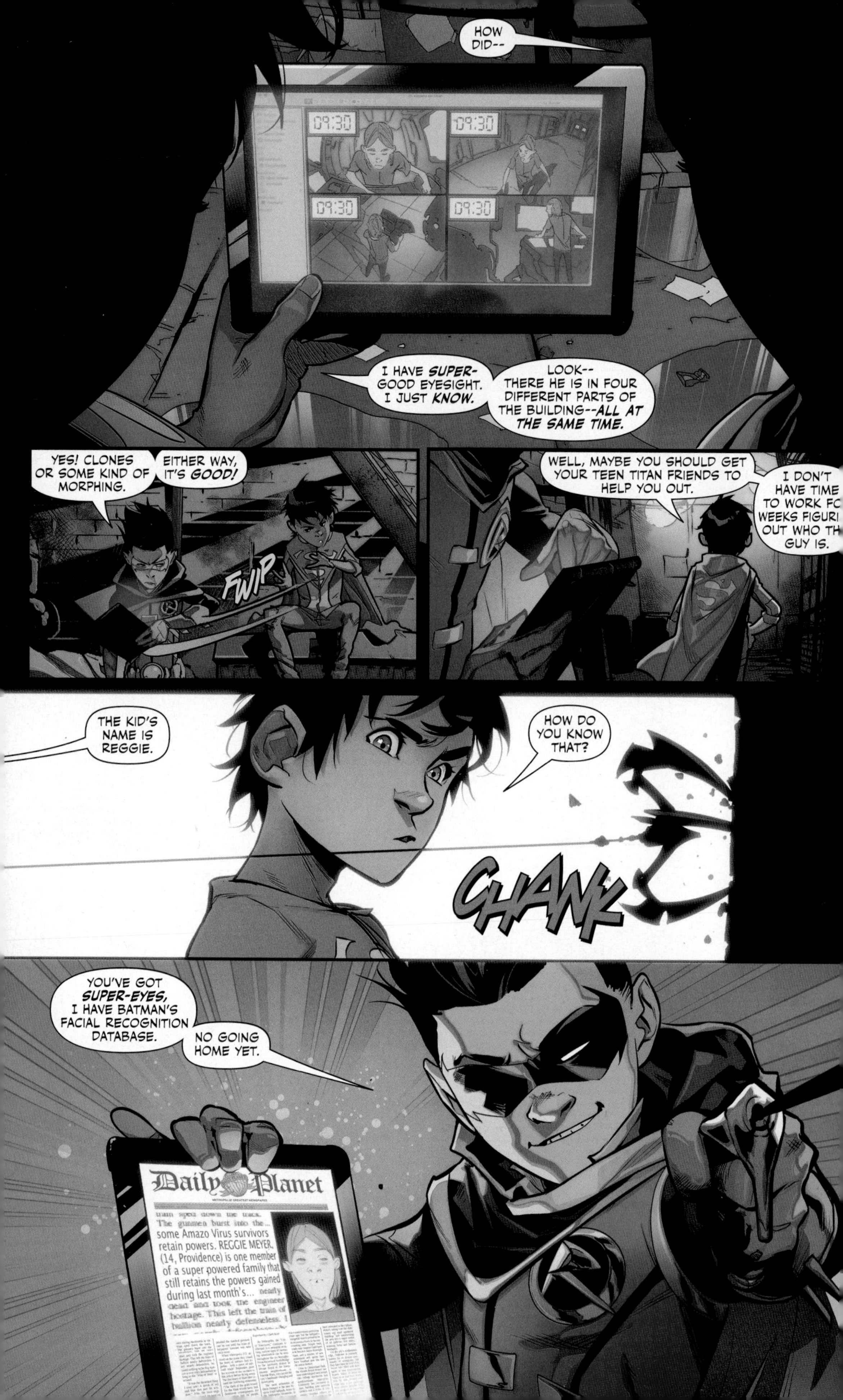
HOW DID--
I HAVE SUPER-GOOD EYESIGHT. I JUST KNOW.
LOOK-- THERE HE IS IN FOUR DIFFERENT PARTS OF THE BUILDING--ALL AT THE SAME TIME.
YES! CLONES OR SOME KIND OF MORPHING.
EITHER WAY, IT'S GOOD!
FWIP
WELL, MAYBE YOU SHOULD GET YOUR TEEN TITAN FRIENDS TO HELP YOU OUT.
I DON'T HAVE TIME TO WORK FC WEEKS FIGURI OUT WHO TH GUY IS.
THE KID'S NAME IS REGGIE.
HOW DO YOU KNOW THAT?
CHANK
YOU'VE GOT SUPER-EYES, I HAVE BATMAN'S FACIAL RECOGNITION DATABASE.
NO GOING HOME YET.
Daily Planet
The gunmen burst into the... some Amazo Virus survivors retain powers. REGGIE MEYER, (14, Providence) is one member of a super powered family that still retains the powers gained during last month's...

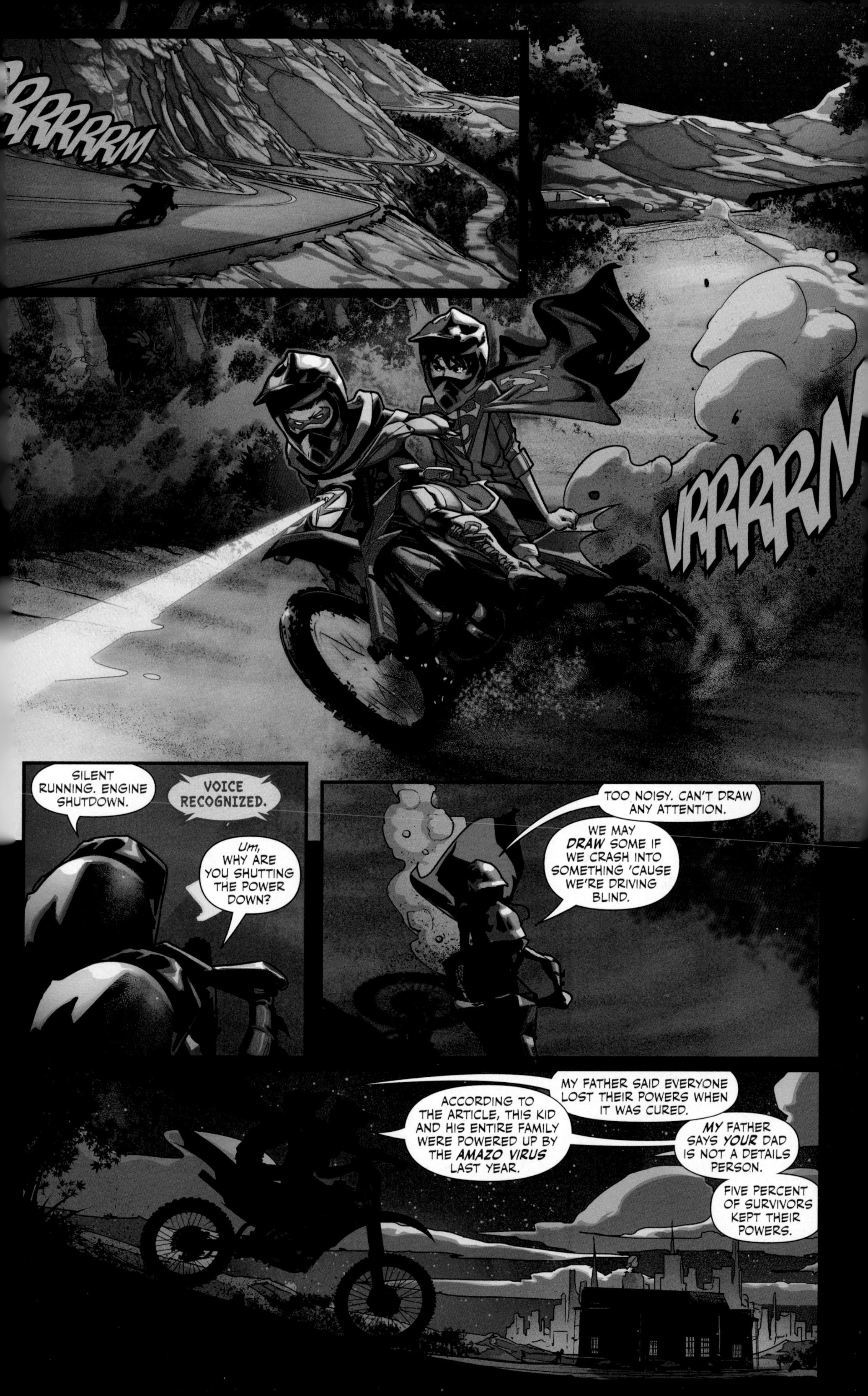
RRRRRRM
VRRRRN
SILENT RUNNING. ENGINE SHUTDOWN.
VOICE RECOGNIZED.
Um, WHY ARE YOU SHUTTING THE POWER DOWN?
TOO NOISY. CAN'T DRAW ANY ATTENTION.
WE MAY DRAW SOME IF WE CRASH INTO SOMETHING 'CAUSE WE'RE DRIVING BLIND.
ACCORDING TO THE ARTICLE, THIS KID AND HIS ENTIRE FAMILY WERE POWERED UP BY THE AMAZO VIRUS LAST YEAR.
MY FATHER SAID EVERYONE LOST THEIR POWERS WHEN IT WAS CURED.
MY FATHER SAYS YOUR DAD IS NOT A DETAILS PERSON.
FIVE PERCENT OF SURVIVORS KEPT THEIR POWERS.

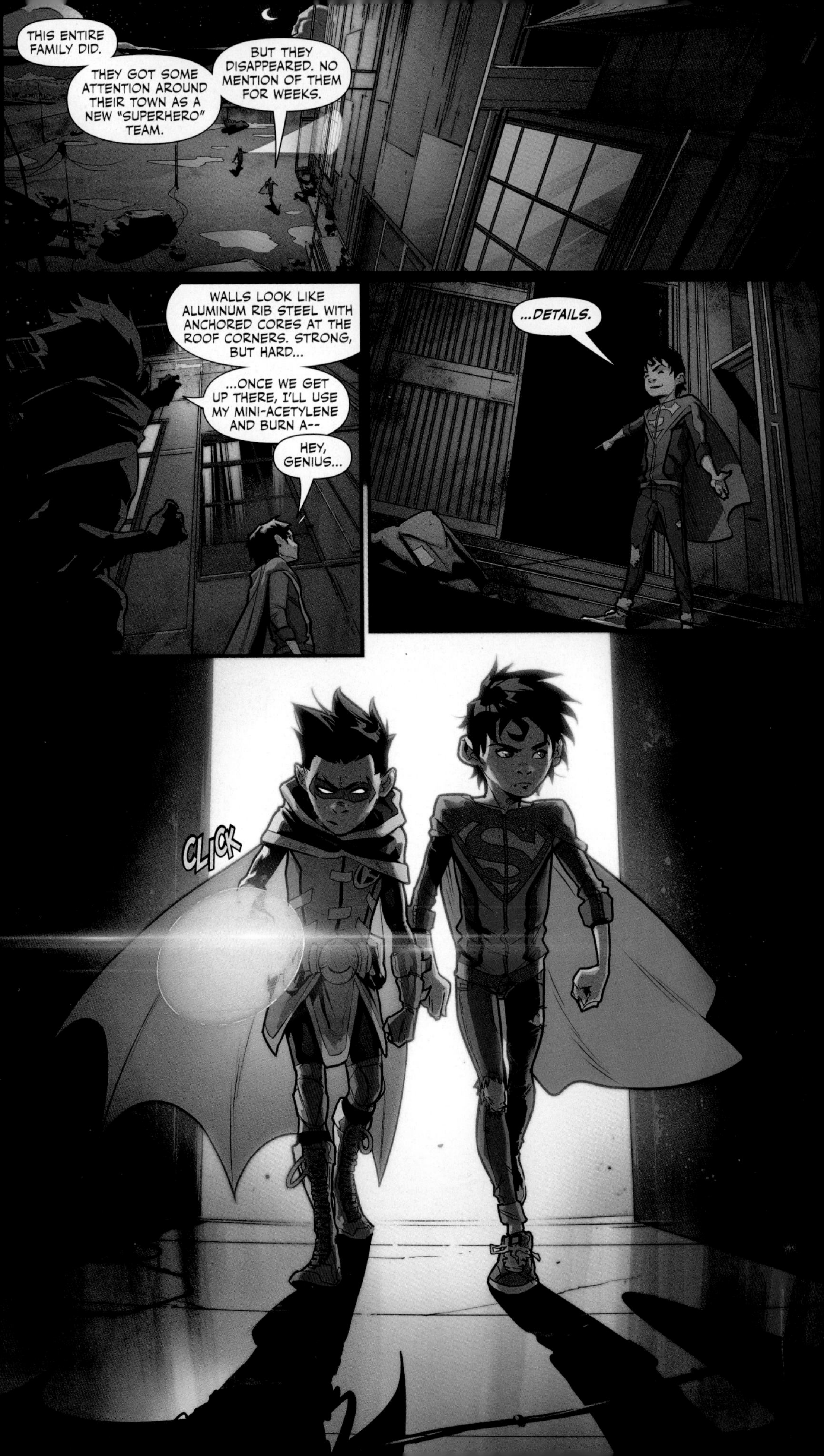
THIS ENTIRE FAMILY DID.
THEY GOT SOME ATTENTION AROUND THEIR TOWN AS A NEW "SUPERHERO" TEAM.
BUT THEY DISAPPEARED. NO MENTION OF THEM FOR WEEKS.
WALLS LOOK LIKE ALUMINUM RIB STEEL WITH ANCHORED CORES AT THE ROOF CORNERS. STRONG, BUT HARD...
...ONCE WE GET UP THERE, I'LL USE MY MINI-ACETYLENE AND BURN A--
HEY, GENIUS...
...DETAILS.
CLICK

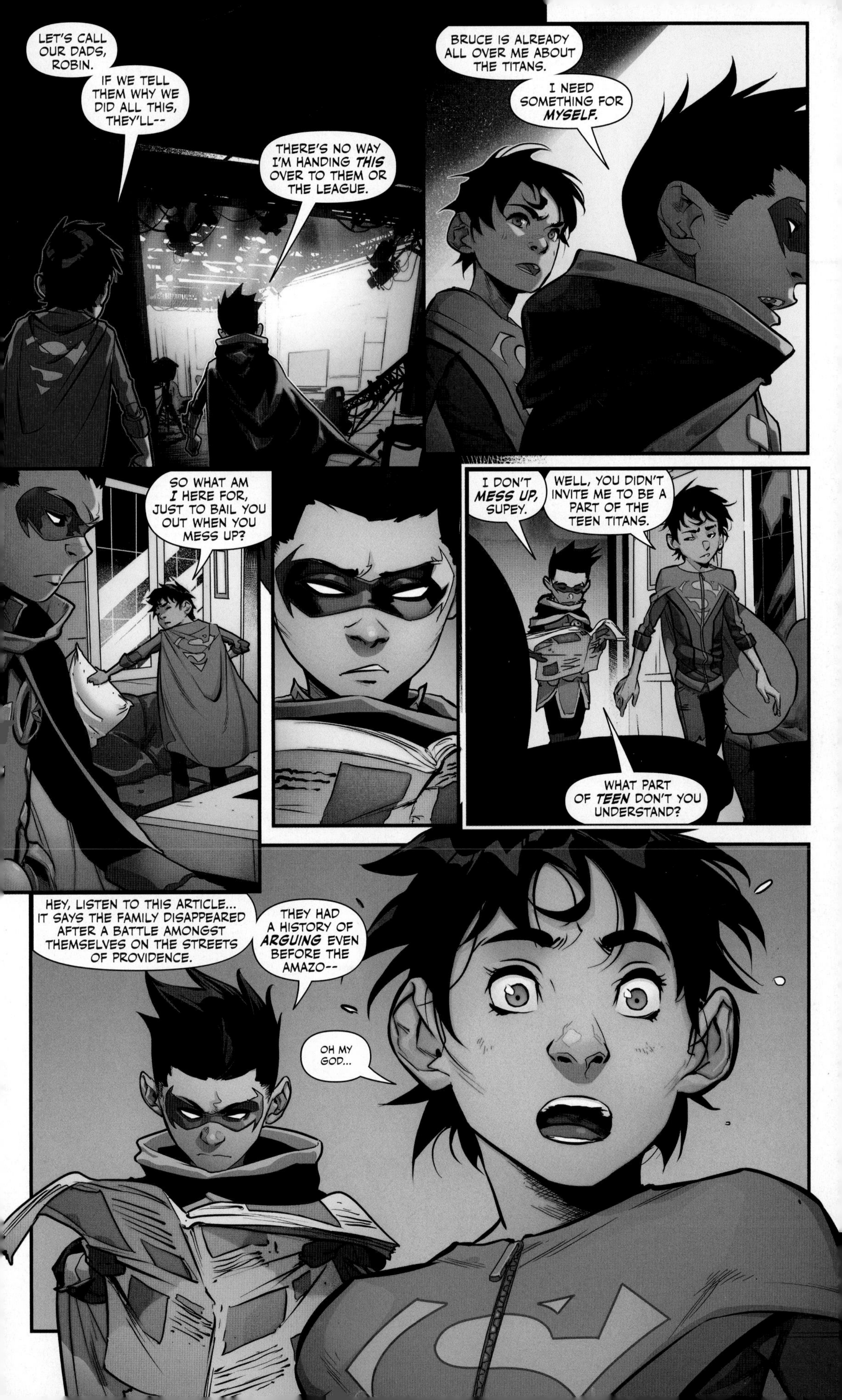

LET'S CALL OUR DADS, ROBIN.
IF WE TELL THEM WHY WE DID ALL THIS, THEY'LL--
THERE'S NO WAY I'M HANDING *THIS* OVER TO THEM OR THE LEAGUE.
BRUCE IS ALREADY ALL OVER ME ABOUT THE TITANS.
I NEED SOMETHING FOR *MYSELF*.
SO WHAT AM *I* HERE FOR, JUST TO BAIL YOU OUT WHEN YOU MESS UP?
I DON'T *MESS UP*, SUPEY.
WELL, YOU DIDN'T INVITE ME TO BE A PART OF THE TEEN TITANS.
WHAT PART OF *TEEN* DON'T YOU UNDERSTAND?
HEY, LISTEN TO THIS ARTICLE... IT SAYS THE FAMILY DISAPPEARED AFTER A BATTLE AMONGST THEMSELVES ON THE STREETS OF PROVIDENCE.
THEY HAD A HISTORY OF *ARGUING* EVEN BEFORE THE AMAZO--
OH MY GOD...

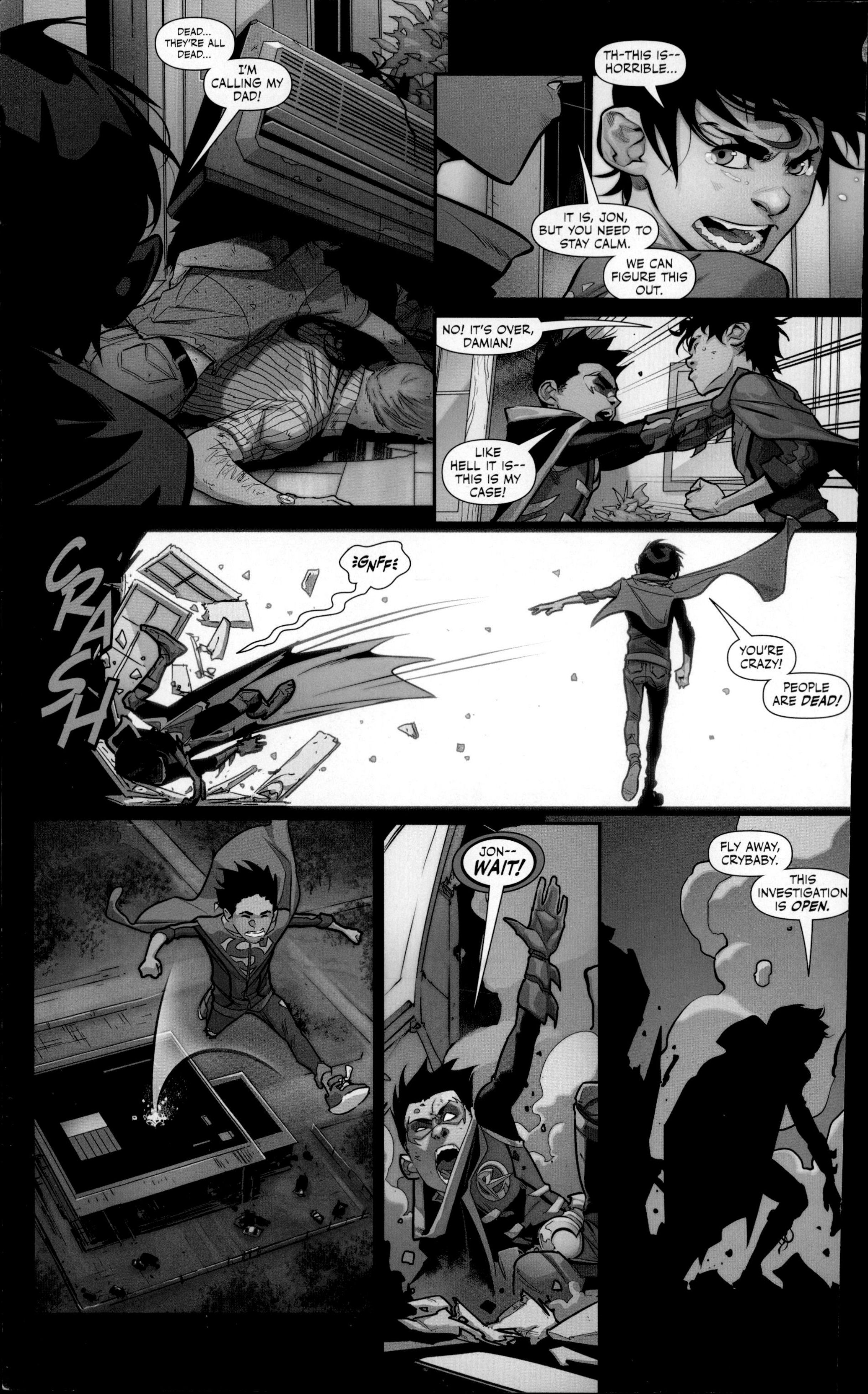
DEAD... THEY'RE ALL DEAD...
I'M CALLING MY DAD!
TH-THIS IS-- HORRIBLE...
IT IS, JON, BUT YOU NEED TO STAY CALM.
WE CAN FIGURE THIS OUT.
NO! IT'S OVER, DAMIAN!
LIKE HELL IT IS-- THIS IS MY CASE!
CRASH
GNFF
YOU'RE CRAZY!
PEOPLE ARE DEAD!
JON-- WAIT!
FLY AWAY, CRYBABY.
THIS INVESTIGATION IS OPEN.

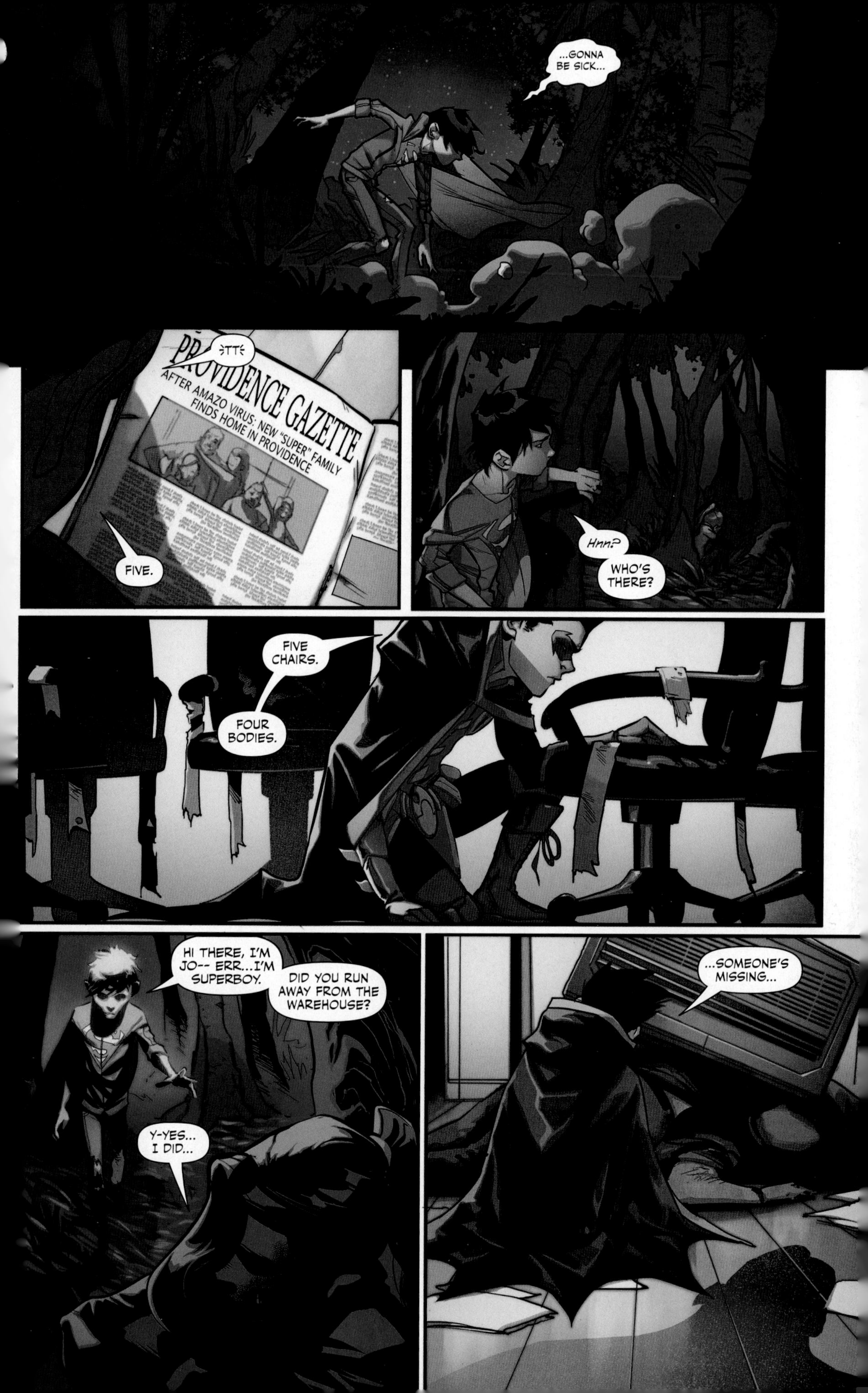
...GONNA BE SICK...
TT
PROVIDENCE GAZETTE
AFTER AMAZO VIRUS: NEW "SUPER" FAMILY FINDS HOME IN PROVIDENCE
FIVE.
Hnn?
WHO'S THERE?
FIVE CHAIRS.
FOUR BODIES.
HI THERE, I'M JO-- ERR...I'M SUPERBOY.
DID YOU RUN AWAY FROM THE WAREHOUSE?
Y-YES... I DID...
...SOMEONE'S MISSING...

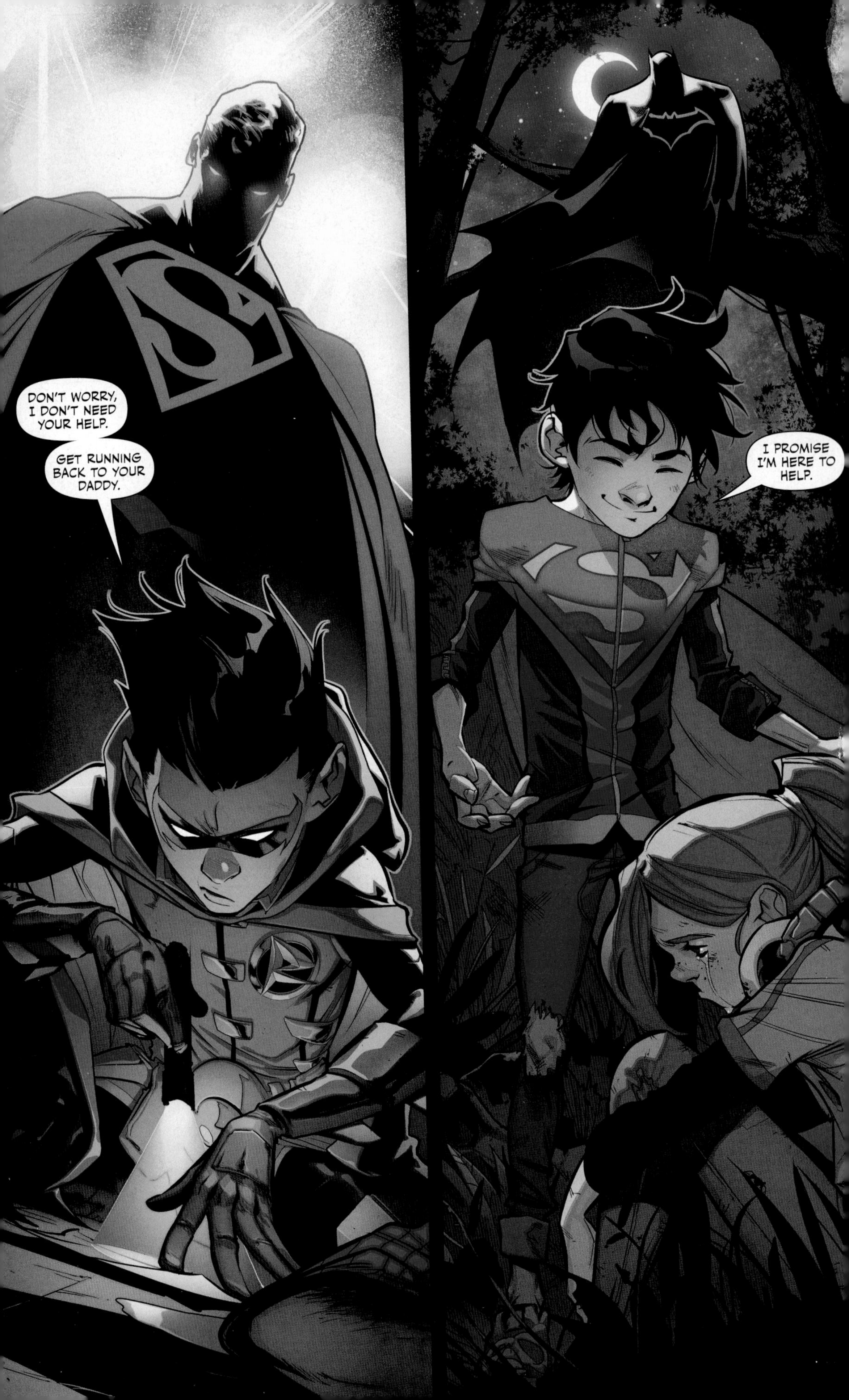
DON'T WORRY, I DON'T NEED YOUR HELP.
GET RUNNING BACK TO YOUR DADDY.
I PROMISE I'M HERE TO HELP.

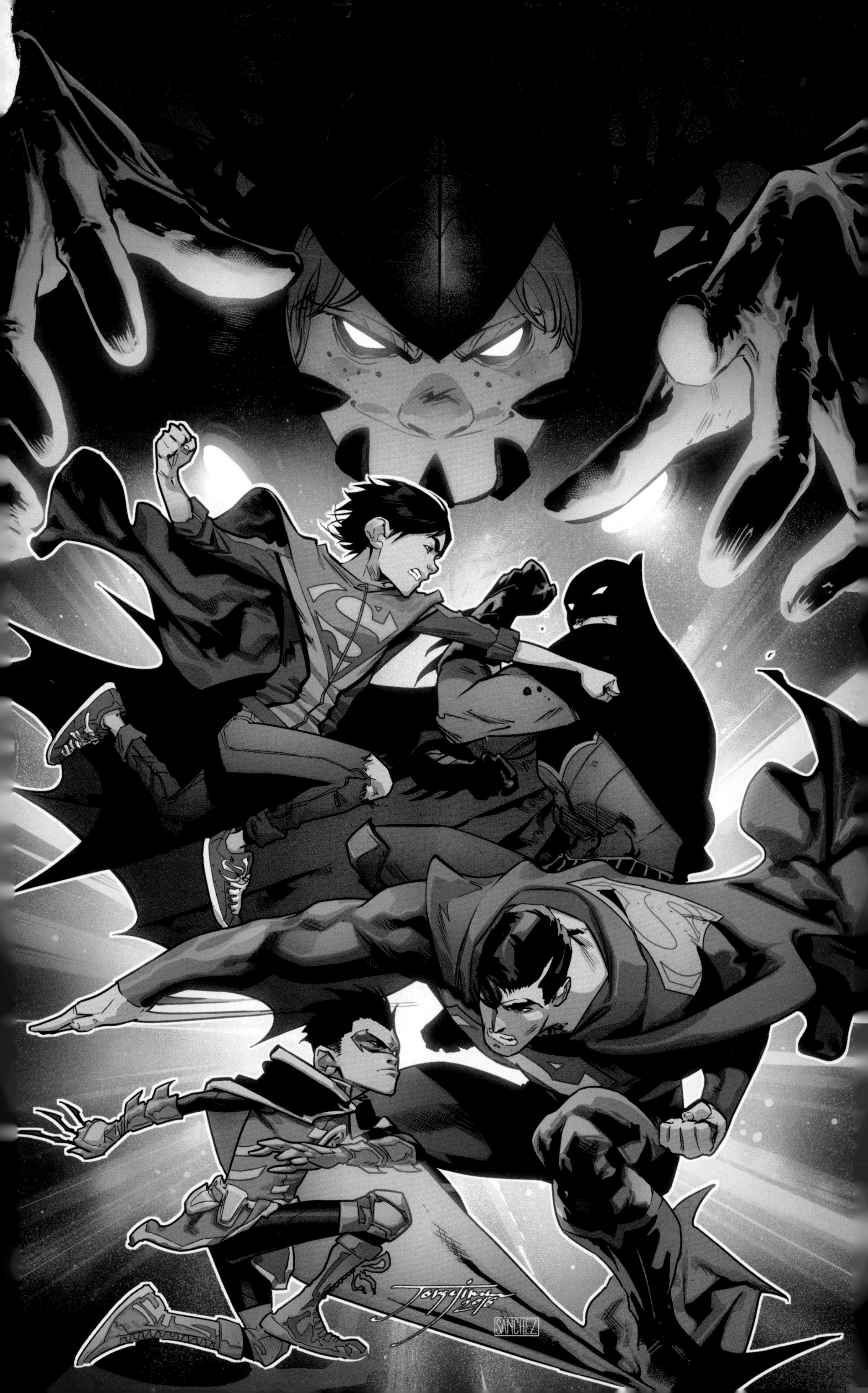
SANCHEZ

WHEN I GROW UP… PART THREE: SIBLING RIVALRY

JORGE JIMENEZ artist * ALEJANDRO SANCHEZ colorist

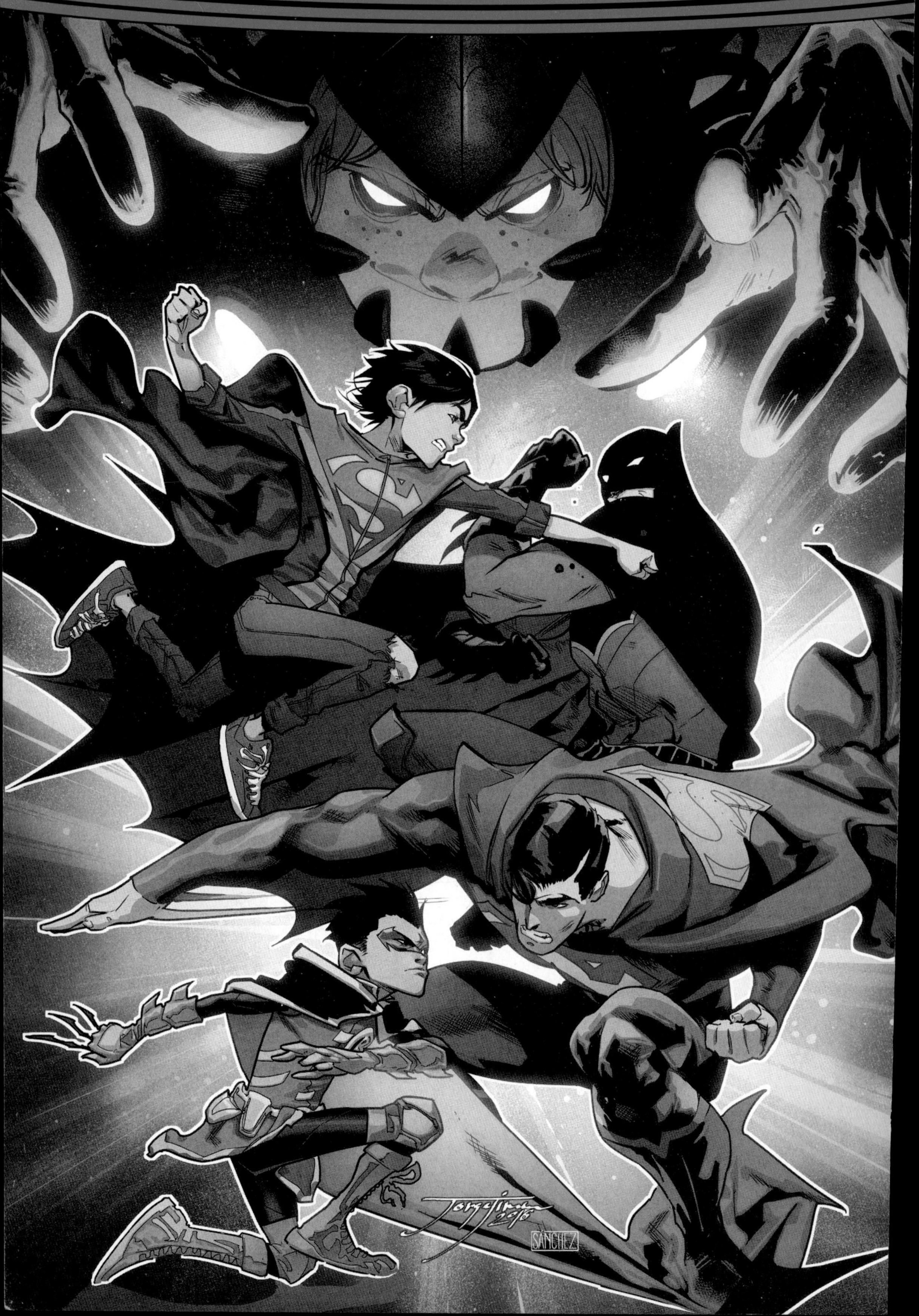
SANCHEZ

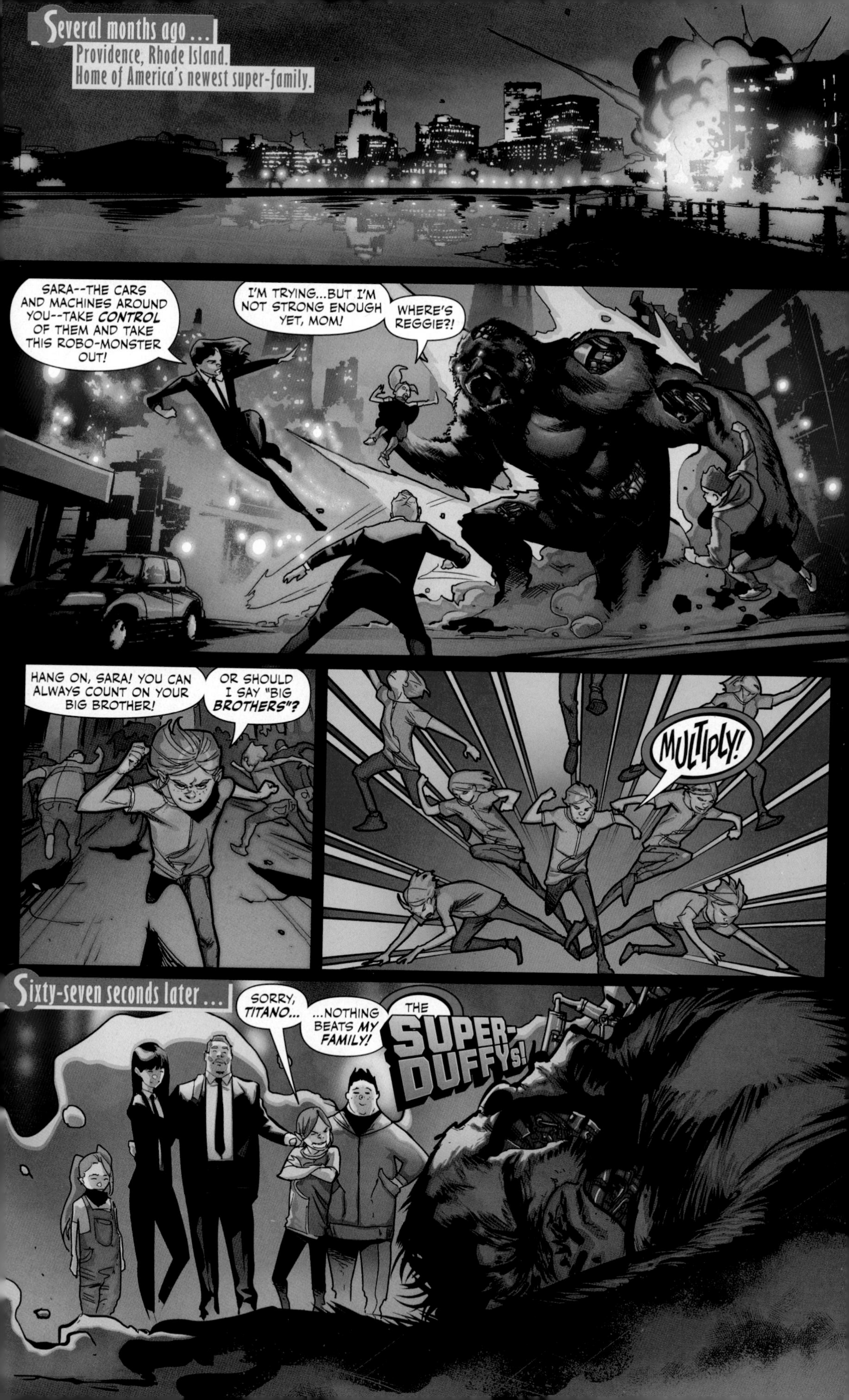
Several months ago . . .
Providence, Rhode Island.
Home of America's newest super-family.
SARA--THE CARS AND MACHINES AROUND YOU--TAKE CONTROL OF THEM AND TAKE THIS ROBO-MONSTER OUT!
I'M TRYING...BUT I'M NOT STRONG ENOUGH YET, MOM!
WHERE'S REGGIE?!
HANG ON, SARA! YOU CAN ALWAYS COUNT ON YOUR BIG BROTHER!
OR SHOULD I SAY "BIG BROTHERS"?
MULTIPLY!
Sixty-seven seconds later . . .
SORRY, TITANO...
...NOTHING BEATS MY FAMILY!
THE SUPER-DUFFYS!

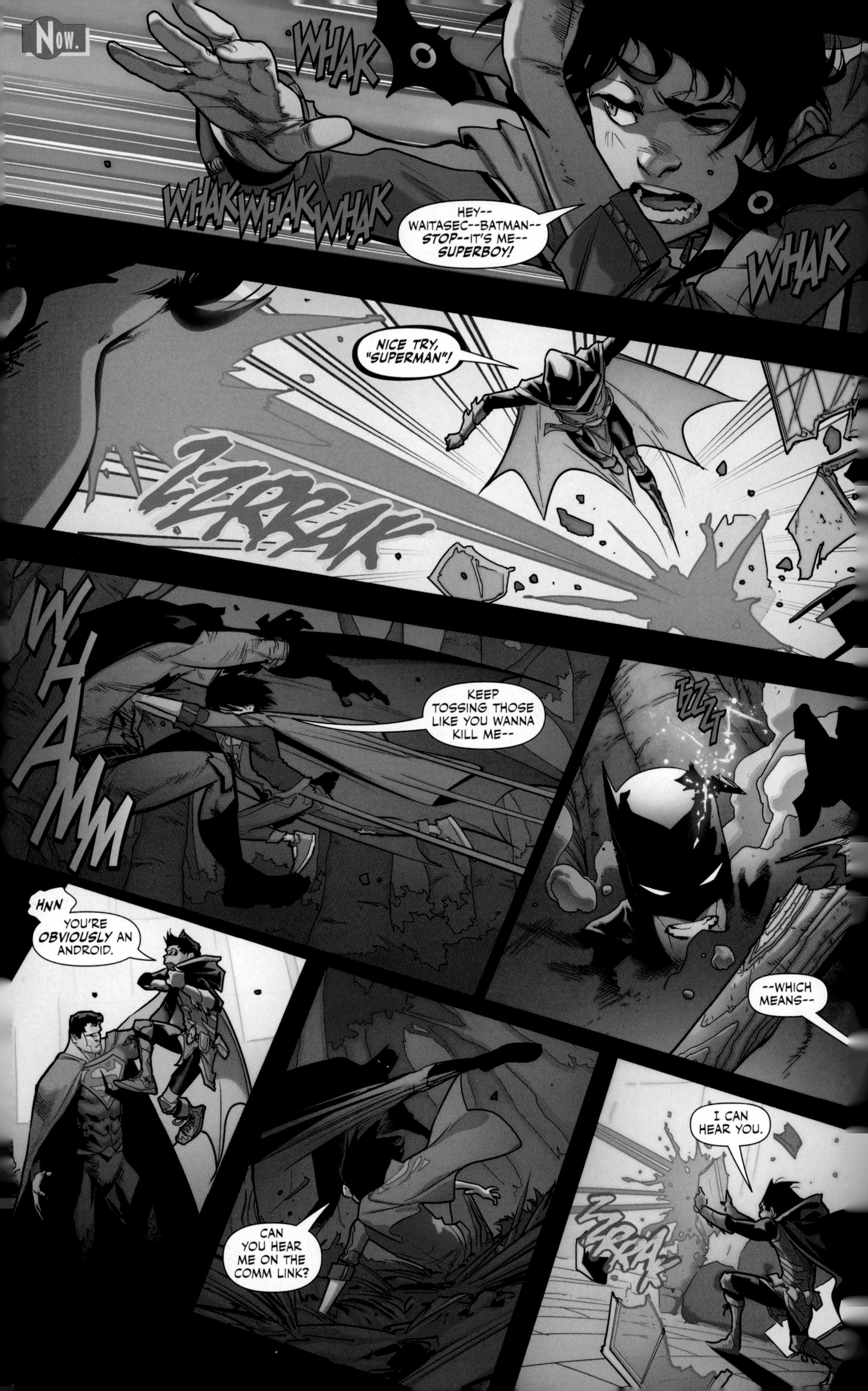
NOW.
WHAK
WHAKWHAKWHAK
HEY--
WAITASEC--BATMAN--
STOP--IT'S ME--
SUPERBOY!
WHAK
NICE TRY, "SUPERMAN"!
ZZRRAK
WHAMM
KEEP TOSSING THOSE LIKE YOU WANNA KILL ME--
TZZZT
--WHICH MEANS--
HNN
YOU'RE OBVIOUSLY AN ANDROID.
CAN YOU HEAR ME ON THE COMM LINK?
I CAN HEAR YOU.
ZRRAK

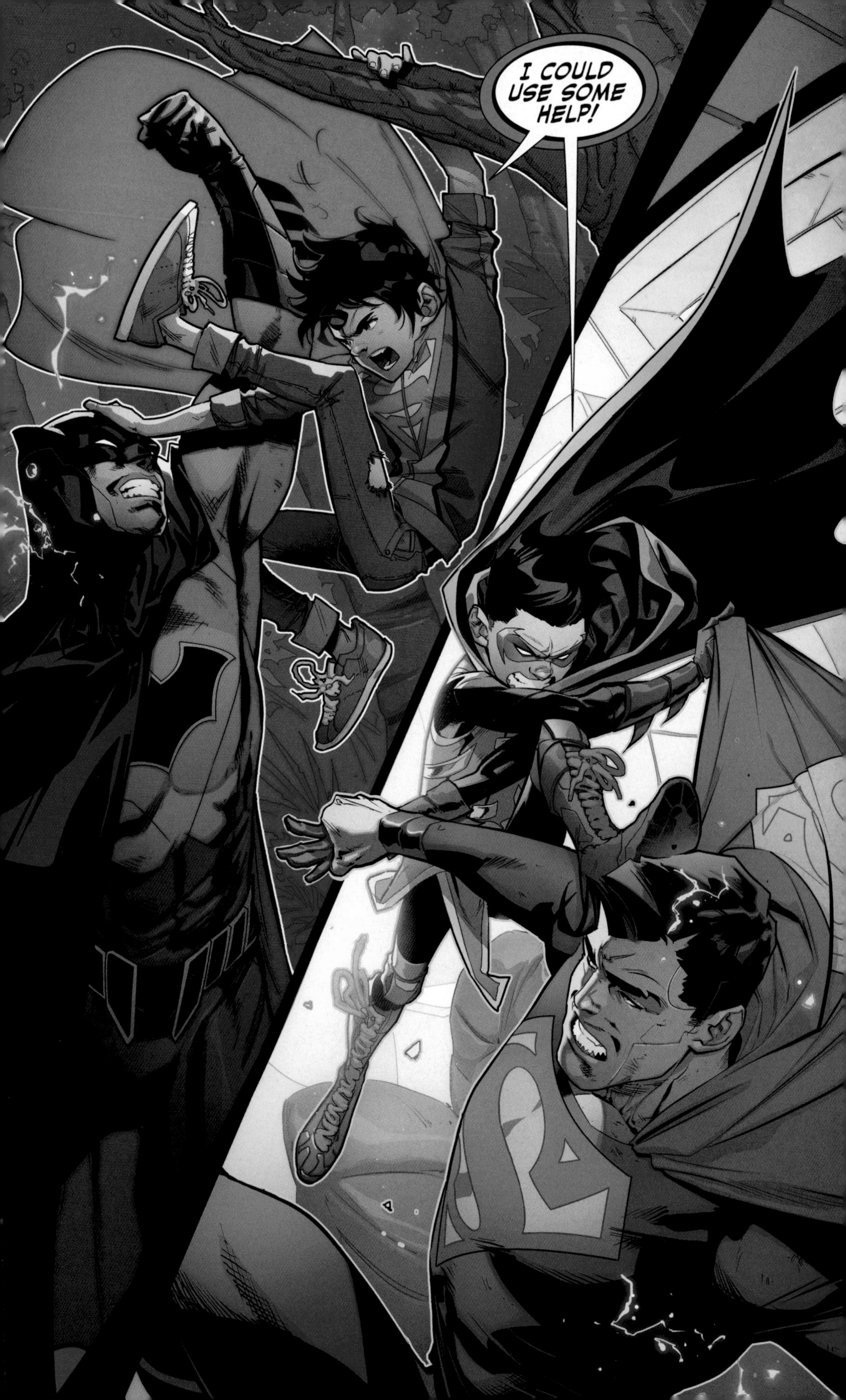
I COULD USE SOME HELP!

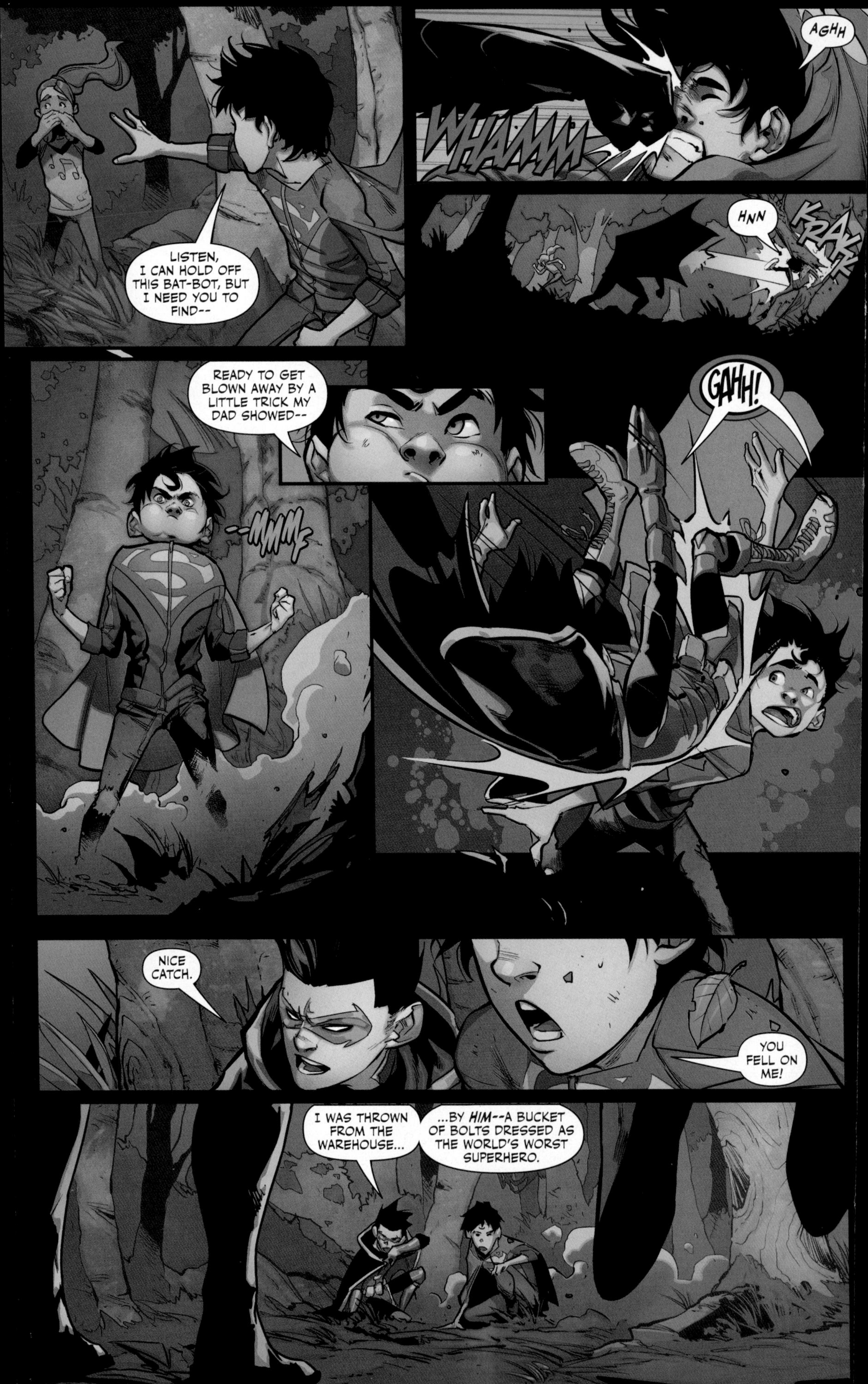

LISTEN, I CAN HOLD OFF THIS BAT-BOT, BUT I NEED YOU TO FIND--
AGHH
WHAMMM
HNN
KRAK
READY TO GET BLOWN AWAY BY A LITTLE TRICK MY DAD SHOWED--
--MMMF
GAHH!
NICE CATCH.
YOU FELL ON ME!
I WAS THROWN FROM THE WAREHOUSE...
...BY *HIM*--A BUCKET OF BOLTS DRESSED AS THE WORLD'S WORST SUPERHERO.

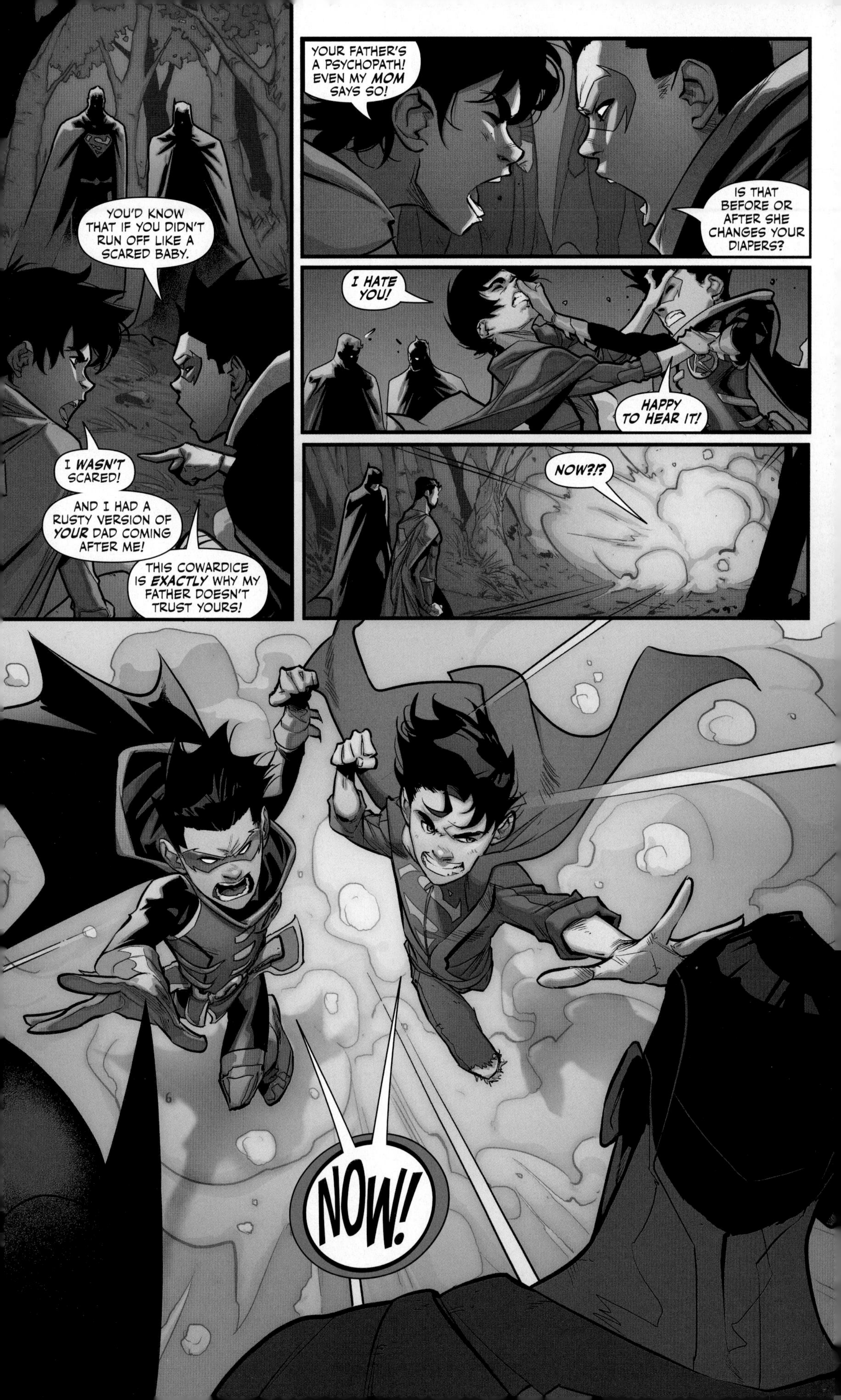

YOU'D KNOW THAT IF YOU DIDN'T RUN OFF LIKE A SCARED BABY.
I WASN'T SCARED!
AND I HAD A RUSTY VERSION OF YOUR DAD COMING AFTER ME!
THIS COWARDICE IS EXACTLY WHY MY FATHER DOESN'T TRUST YOURS!
YOUR FATHER'S A PSYCHOPATH! EVEN MY MOM SAYS SO!
IS THAT BEFORE OR AFTER SHE CHANGES YOUR DIAPERS?
I HATE YOU!
HAPPY TO HEAR IT!
NOW?!?
NOW!

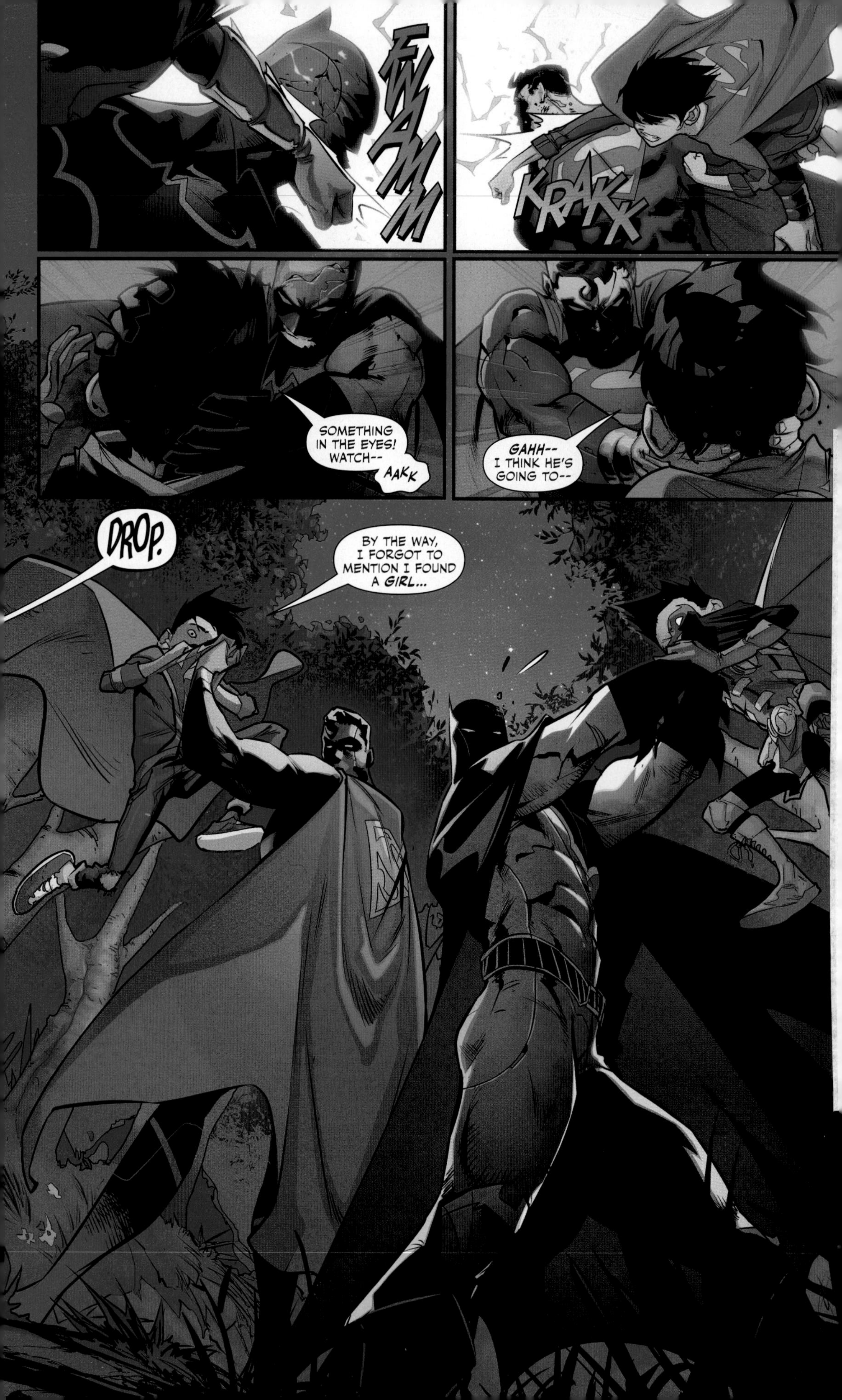
FWAMM
KRAKK
SOMETHING IN THE EYES! WATCH--
AAKK
GAHH-- I THINK HE'S GOING TO--
DROP.
BY THE WAY, I FORGOT TO MENTION I FOUND A GIRL...

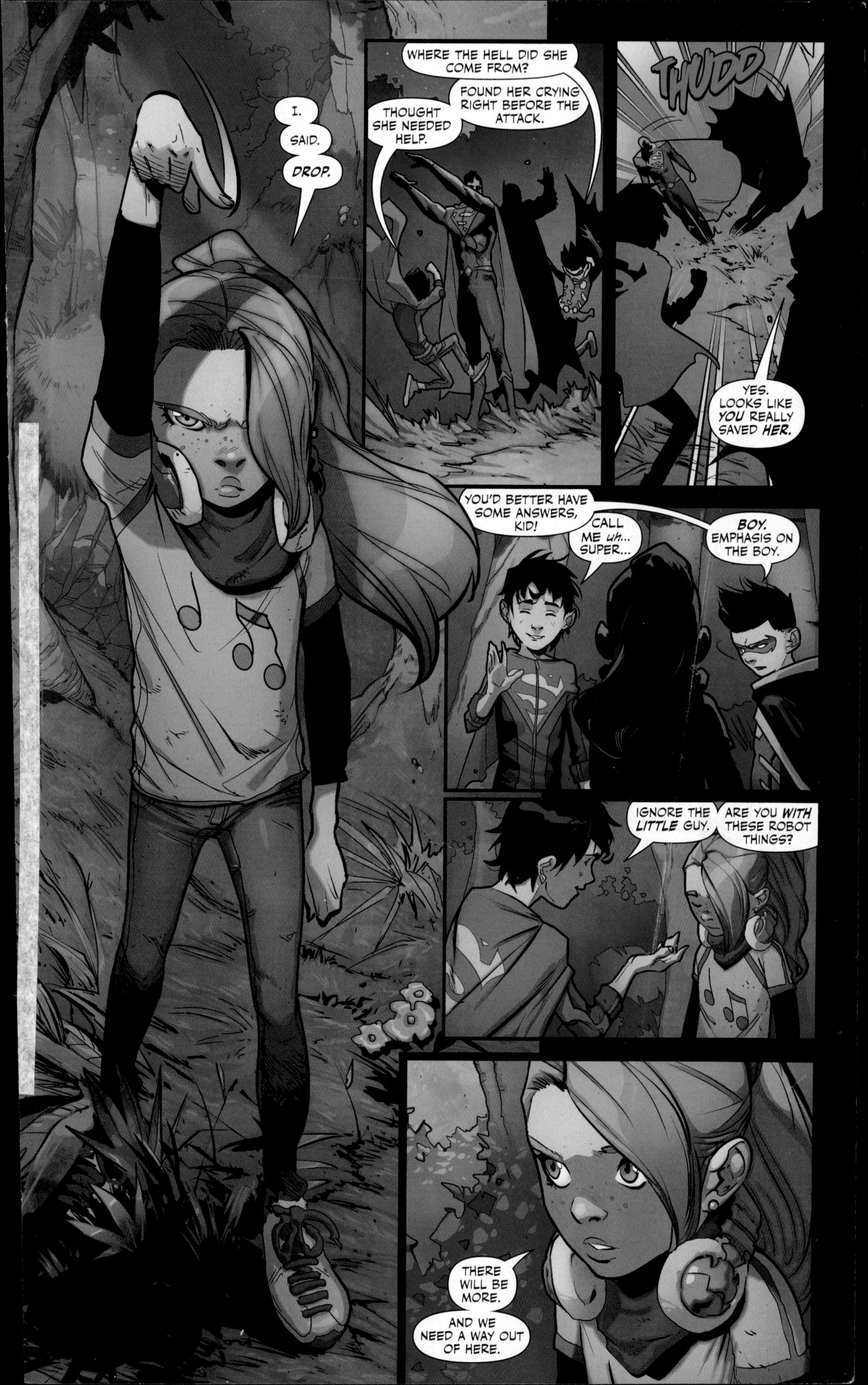
I.
SAID.
DROP.
WHERE THE HELL DID SHE COME FROM?
FOUND HER CRYING RIGHT BEFORE THE ATTACK.
THOUGHT SHE NEEDED HELP.
THUDD
YES. LOOKS LIKE *YOU* REALLY SAVED *HER.*
YOU'D BETTER HAVE SOME ANSWERS, KID!
CALL ME *uh*... SUPER...
BOY. EMPHASIS ON THE BOY.
IGNORE THE *LITTLE* GUY.
ARE YOU *WITH* THESE ROBOT THINGS?
THERE WILL BE MORE.
AND WE NEED A WAY OUT OF HERE.

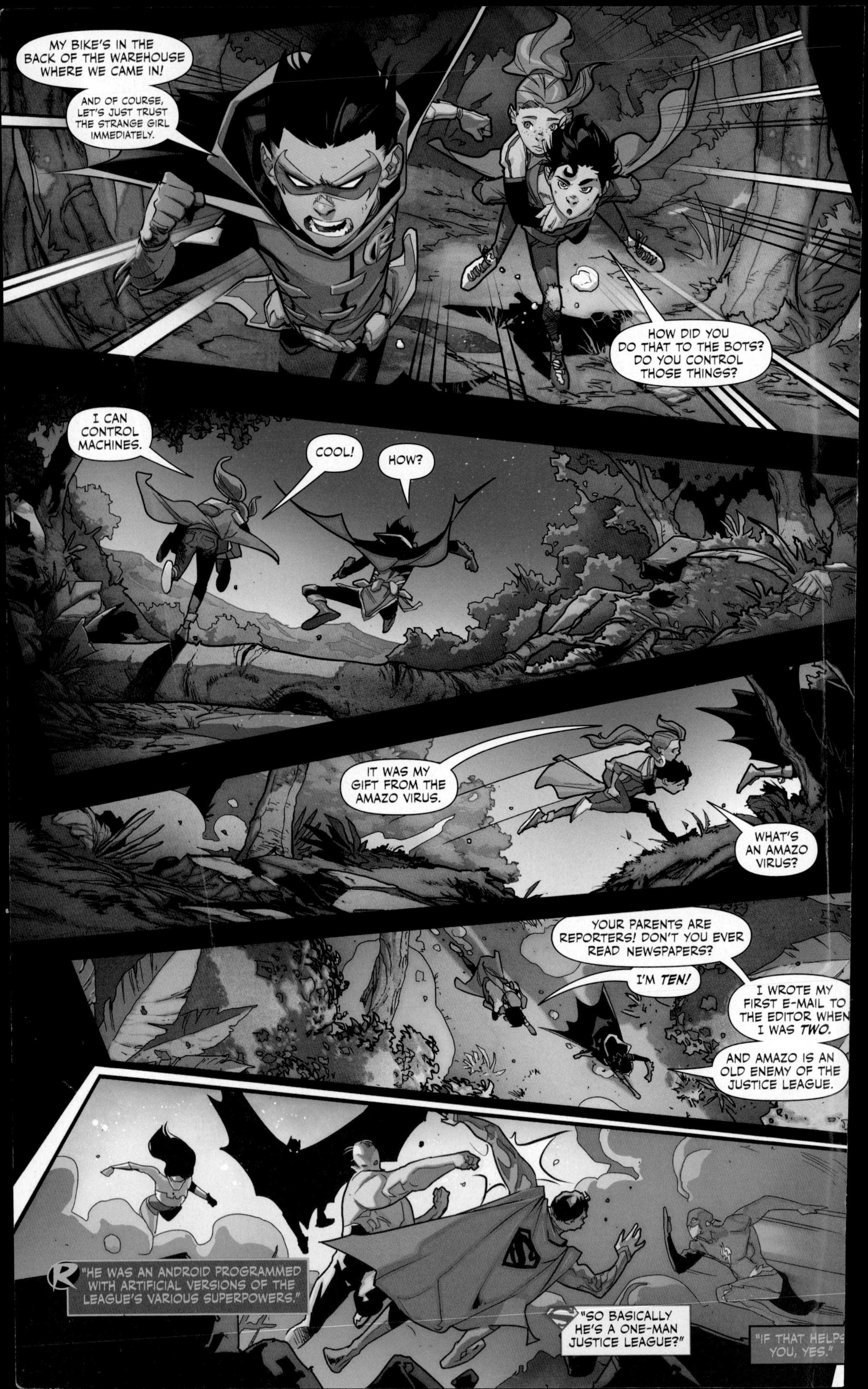
MY BIKE'S IN THE BACK OF THE WAREHOUSE WHERE WE CAME IN!
AND OF COURSE, LET'S JUST TRUST THE STRANGE GIRL IMMEDIATELY.
HOW DID YOU DO THAT TO THE BOTS? DO YOU CONTROL THOSE THINGS?
I CAN CONTROL MACHINES.
COOL!
HOW?
IT WAS MY GIFT FROM THE AMAZO VIRUS.
WHAT'S AN AMAZO VIRUS?
YOUR PARENTS ARE REPORTERS! DON'T YOU EVER READ NEWSPAPERS?
I'M TEN!
I WROTE MY FIRST E-MAIL TO THE EDITOR WHEN I WAS TWO.
AND AMAZO IS AN OLD ENEMY OF THE JUSTICE LEAGUE.
"HE WAS AN ANDROID PROGRAMMED WITH ARTIFICIAL VERSIONS OF THE LEAGUE'S VARIOUS SUPERPOWERS."
"SO BASICALLY HE'S A ONE-MAN JUSTICE LEAGUE?"
"IF THAT HELPS YOU, YES."

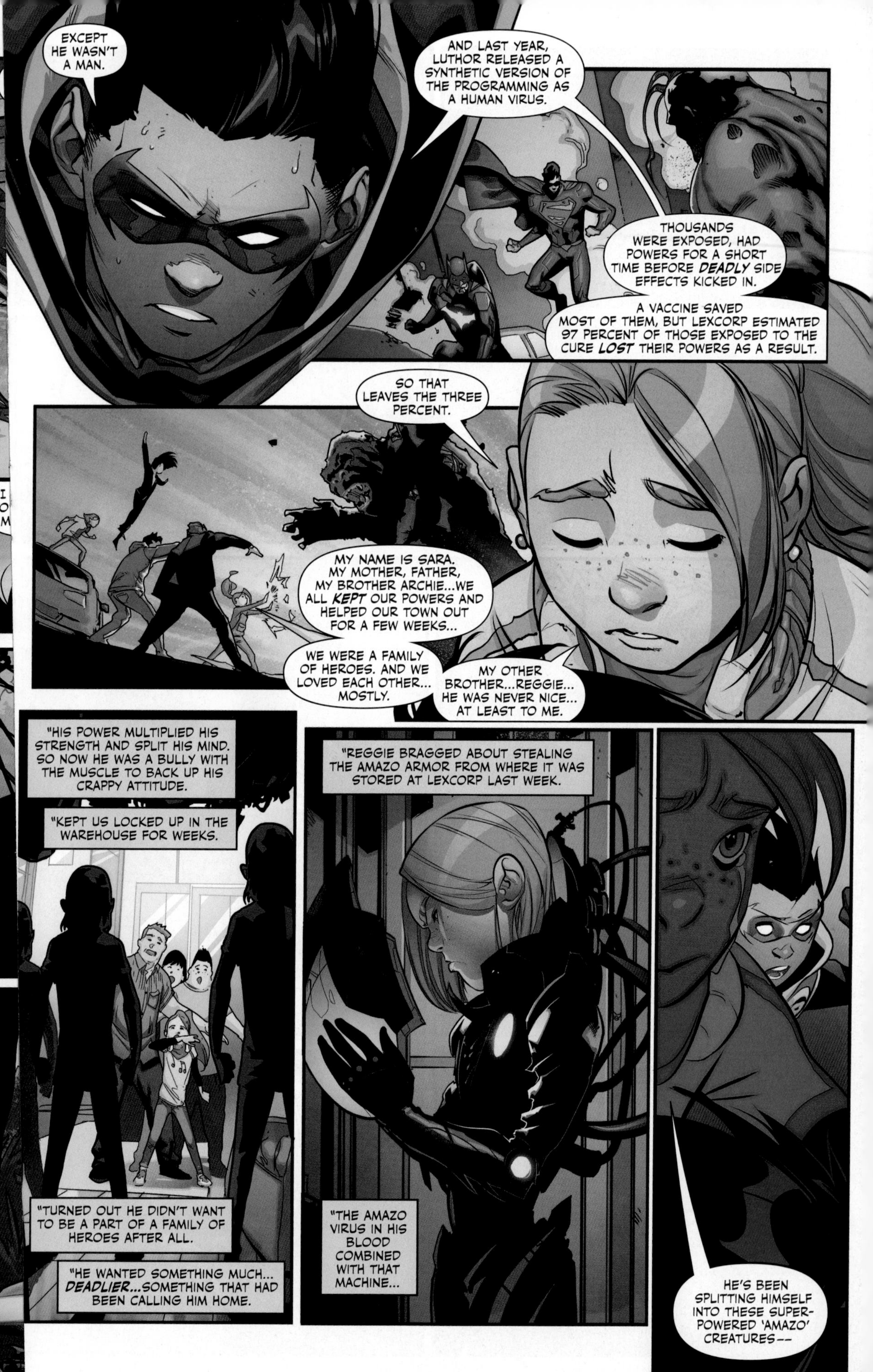

EXCEPT HE WASN'T A MAN.
AND LAST YEAR, LUTHOR RELEASED A SYNTHETIC VERSION OF THE PROGRAMMING AS A HUMAN VIRUS.
THOUSANDS WERE EXPOSED, HAD POWERS FOR A SHORT TIME BEFORE DEADLY SIDE EFFECTS KICKED IN.
A VACCINE SAVED MOST OF THEM, BUT LEXCORP ESTIMATED 97 PERCENT OF THOSE EXPOSED TO THE CURE LOST THEIR POWERS AS A RESULT.
SO THAT LEAVES THE THREE PERCENT.
MY NAME IS SARA. MY MOTHER, FATHER, MY BROTHER ARCHIE...WE ALL KEPT OUR POWERS AND HELPED OUR TOWN OUT FOR A FEW WEEKS...
WE WERE A FAMILY OF HEROES. AND WE LOVED EACH OTHER... MOSTLY.
MY OTHER BROTHER...REGGIE... HE WAS NEVER NICE... AT LEAST TO ME.
"HIS POWER MULTIPLIED HIS STRENGTH AND SPLIT HIS MIND. SO NOW HE WAS A BULLY WITH THE MUSCLE TO BACK UP HIS CRAPPY ATTITUDE.
"KEPT US LOCKED UP IN THE WAREHOUSE FOR WEEKS.
"TURNED OUT HE DIDN'T WANT TO BE A PART OF A FAMILY OF HEROES AFTER ALL.
"HE WANTED SOMETHING MUCH... DEADLIER...SOMETHING THAT HAD BEEN CALLING HIM HOME.
"REGGIE BRAGGED ABOUT STEALING THE AMAZO ARMOR FROM WHERE IT WAS STORED AT LEXCORP LAST WEEK.
"THE AMAZO VIRUS IN HIS BLOOD COMBINED WITH THAT MACHINE...
HE'S BEEN SPLITTING HIMSELF INTO THESE SUPER-POWERED 'AMAZO' CREATURES--

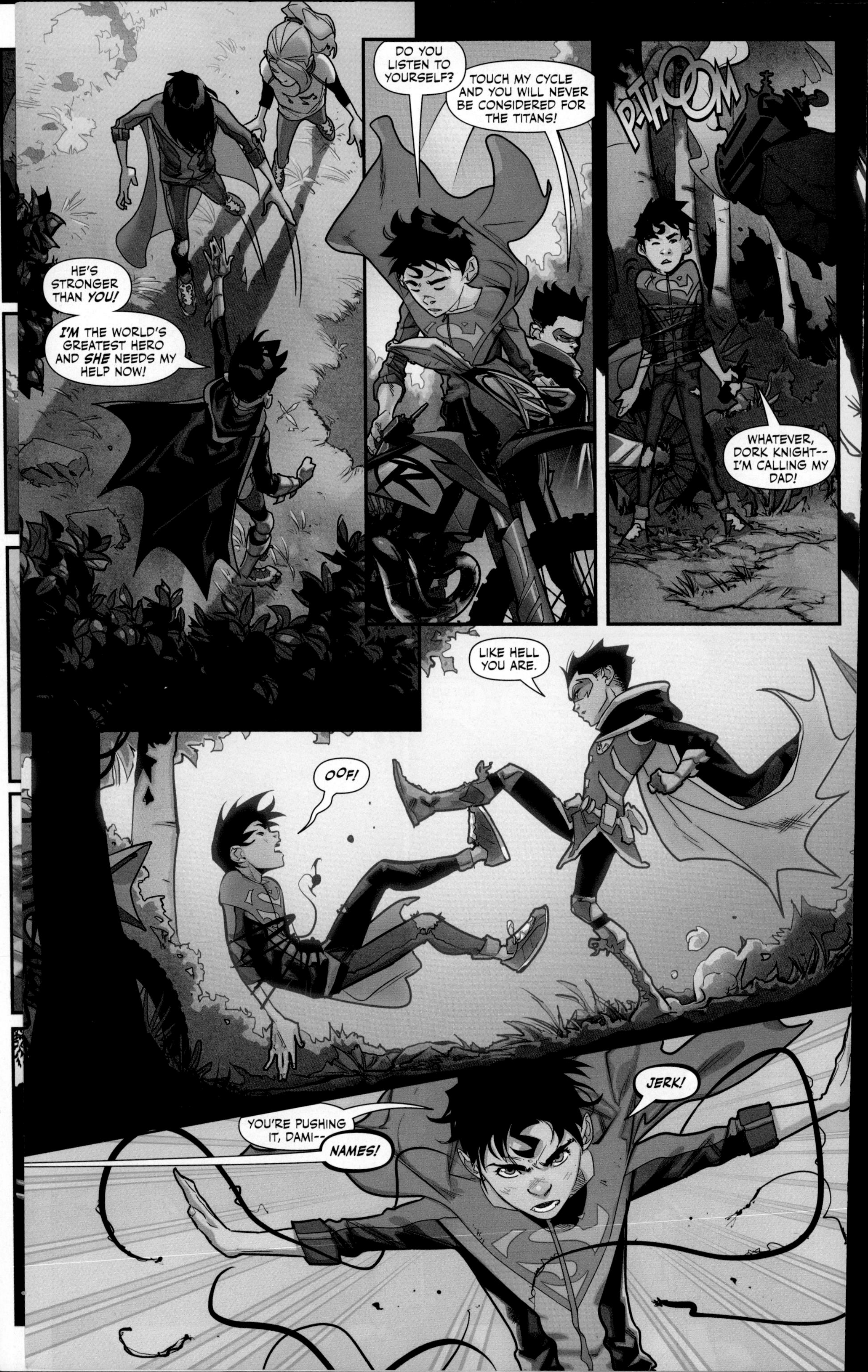
HE'S STRONGER THAN YOU!
I'M THE WORLD'S GREATEST HERO AND SHE NEEDS MY HELP NOW!
DO YOU LISTEN TO YOURSELF?
TOUCH MY CYCLE AND YOU WILL NEVER BE CONSIDERED FOR THE TITANS!
P-THOOM
WHATEVER, DORK KNIGHT-- I'M CALLING MY DAD!
LIKE HELL YOU ARE.
OOF!
JERK!
YOU'RE PUSHING IT, DAMI--
NAMES!

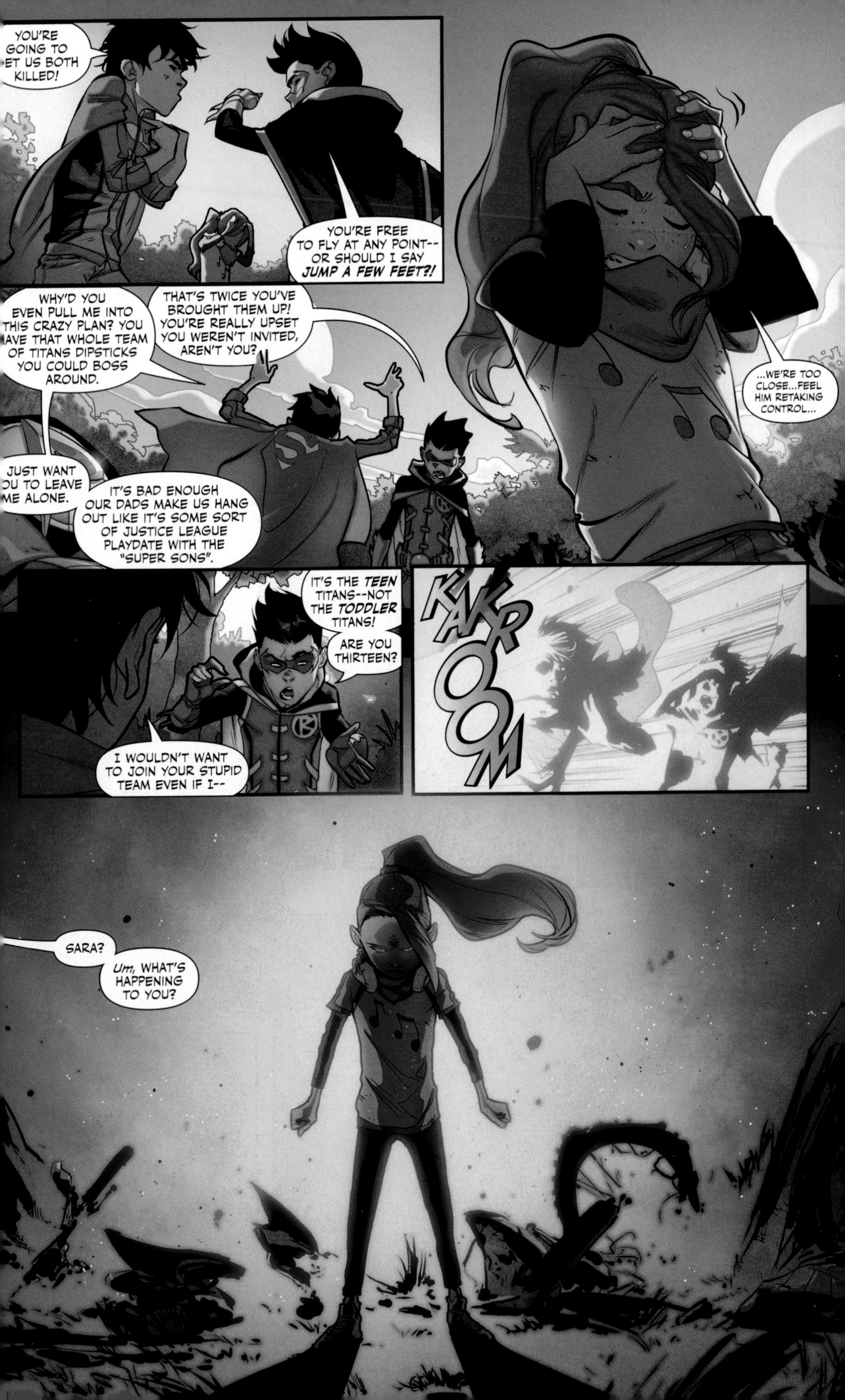
YOU'RE GOING TO ET US BOTH KILLED!
YOU'RE FREE TO FLY AT ANY POINT-- OR SHOULD I SAY *JUMP A FEW FEET?!*
WHY'D YOU EVEN PULL ME INTO THIS CRAZY PLAN? YOU AVE THAT WHOLE TEAM OF TITANS DIPSTICKS YOU COULD BOSS AROUND.
THAT'S TWICE YOU'VE BROUGHT THEM UP! YOU'RE REALLY UPSET YOU WEREN'T INVITED, AREN'T YOU?
JUST WANT OU TO LEAVE ME ALONE.
IT'S BAD ENOUGH OUR DADS MAKE US HANG OUT LIKE IT'S SOME SORT OF JUSTICE LEAGUE PLAYDATE WITH THE "SUPER SONS".
...WE'RE TOO CLOSE...FEEL HIM RETAKING CONTROL...
IT'S THE *TEEN* TITANS--NOT THE *TODDLER* TITANS!
ARE YOU THIRTEEN?
I WOULDN'T WANT TO JOIN YOUR STUPID TEAM EVEN IF I--
KAKROOOM
SARA?
Um, WHAT'S HAPPENING TO YOU?

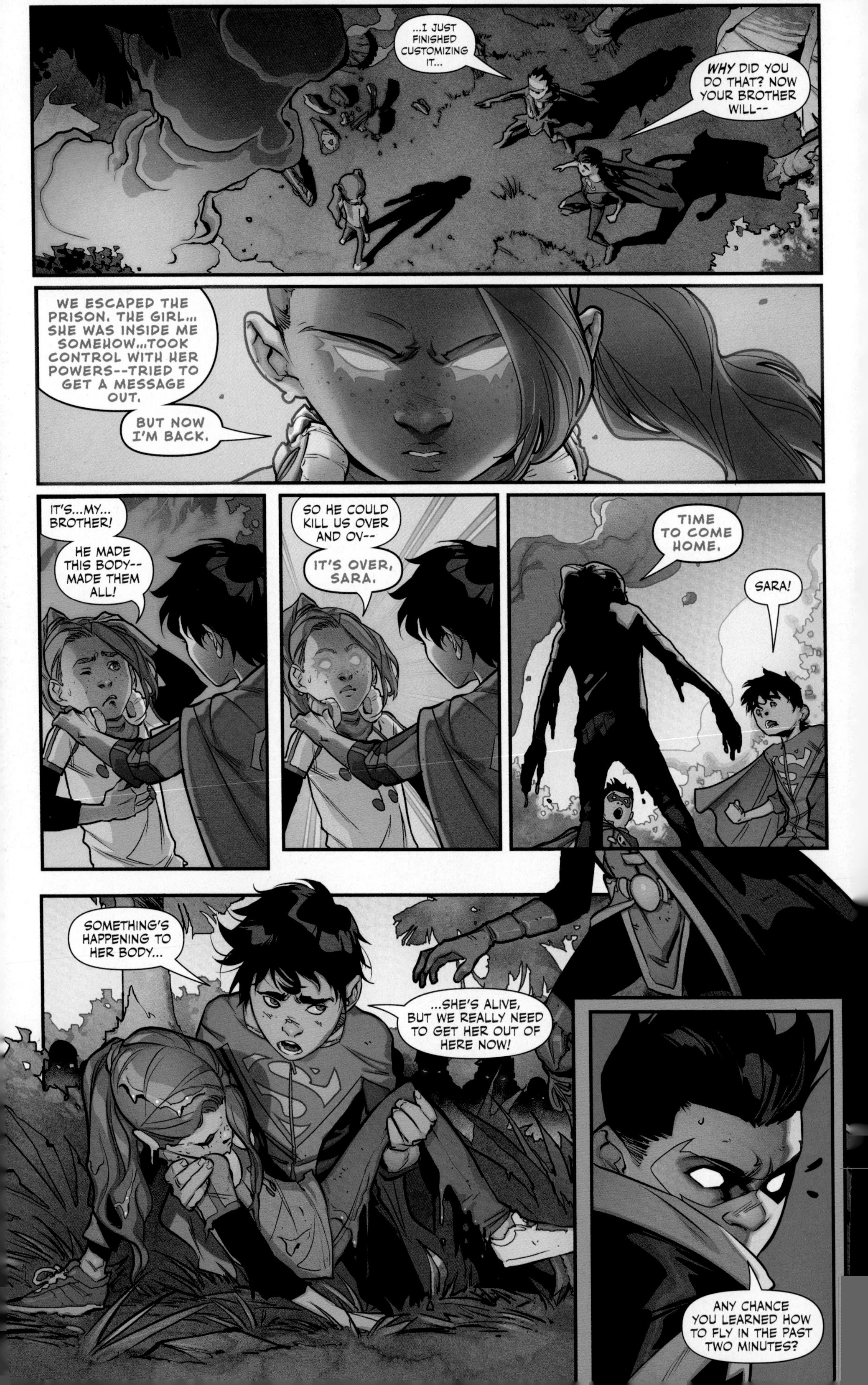
...I JUST FINISHED CUSTOMIZING IT...
WHY DID YOU DO THAT? NOW YOUR BROTHER WILL--
WE ESCAPED THE PRISON. THE GIRL... SHE WAS INSIDE ME SOMEHOW...TOOK CONTROL WITH HER POWERS--TRIED TO GET A MESSAGE OUT.
BUT NOW I'M BACK.
IT'S...MY... BROTHER!
HE MADE THIS BODY-- MADE THEM ALL!
SO HE COULD KILL US OVER AND OV--
IT'S OVER, SARA.
TIME TO COME HOME.
SARA!
SOMETHING'S HAPPENING TO HER BODY...
...SHE'S ALIVE, BUT WE REALLY NEED TO GET HER OUT OF HERE NOW!
ANY CHANCE YOU LEARNED HOW TO FLY IN THE PAST TWO MINUTES?

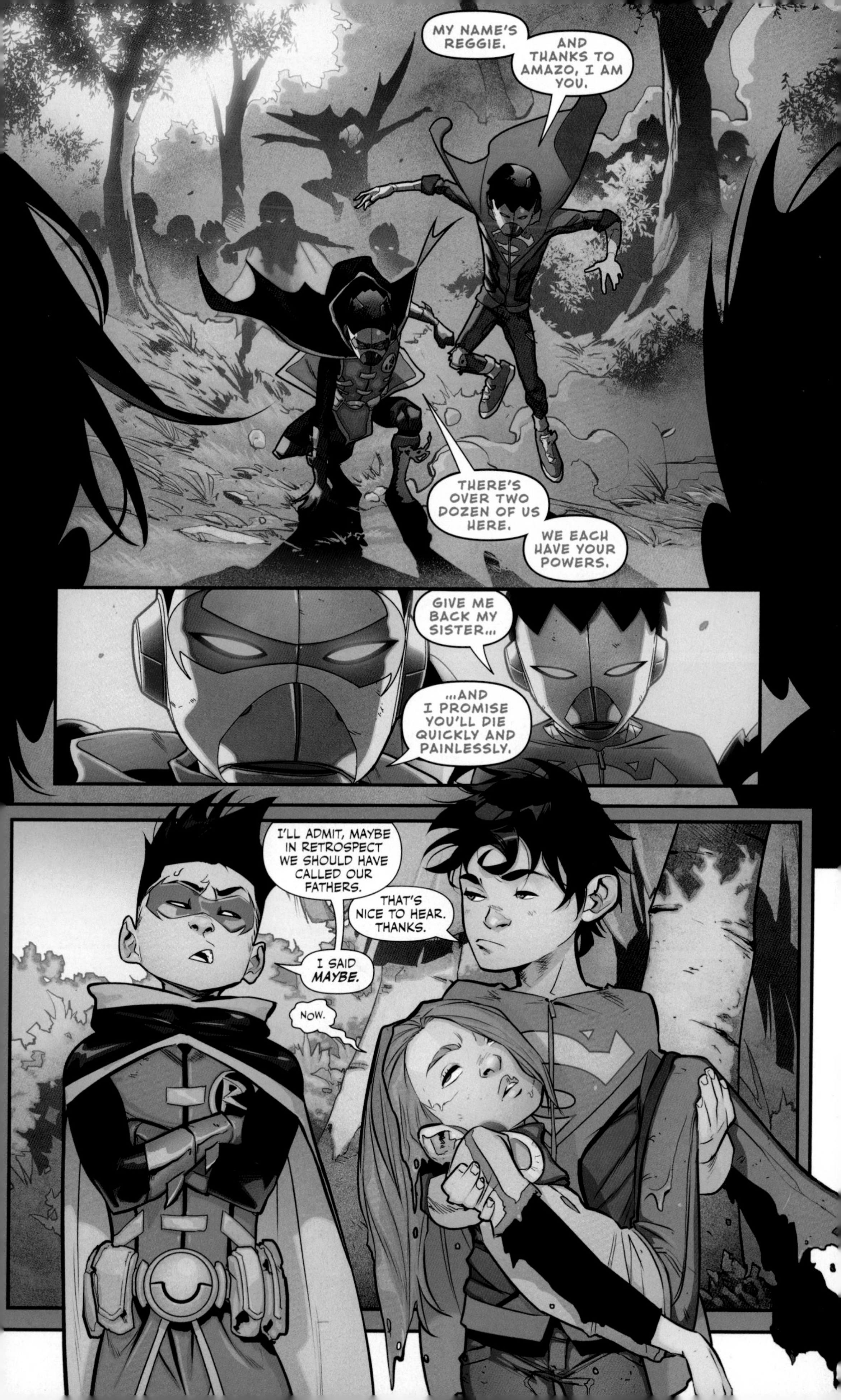

MY NAME'S REGGIE.
AND THANKS TO AMAZO, I AM YOU.
THERE'S OVER TWO DOZEN OF US HERE.
WE EACH HAVE YOUR POWERS.
GIVE ME BACK MY SISTER...
...AND I PROMISE YOU'LL DIE QUICKLY AND PAINLESSLY.
I'LL ADMIT, MAYBE IN RETROSPECT WE SHOULD HAVE CALLED OUR FATHERS.
THAT'S NICE TO HEAR. THANKS.
I SAID *MAYBE.*
NOW.

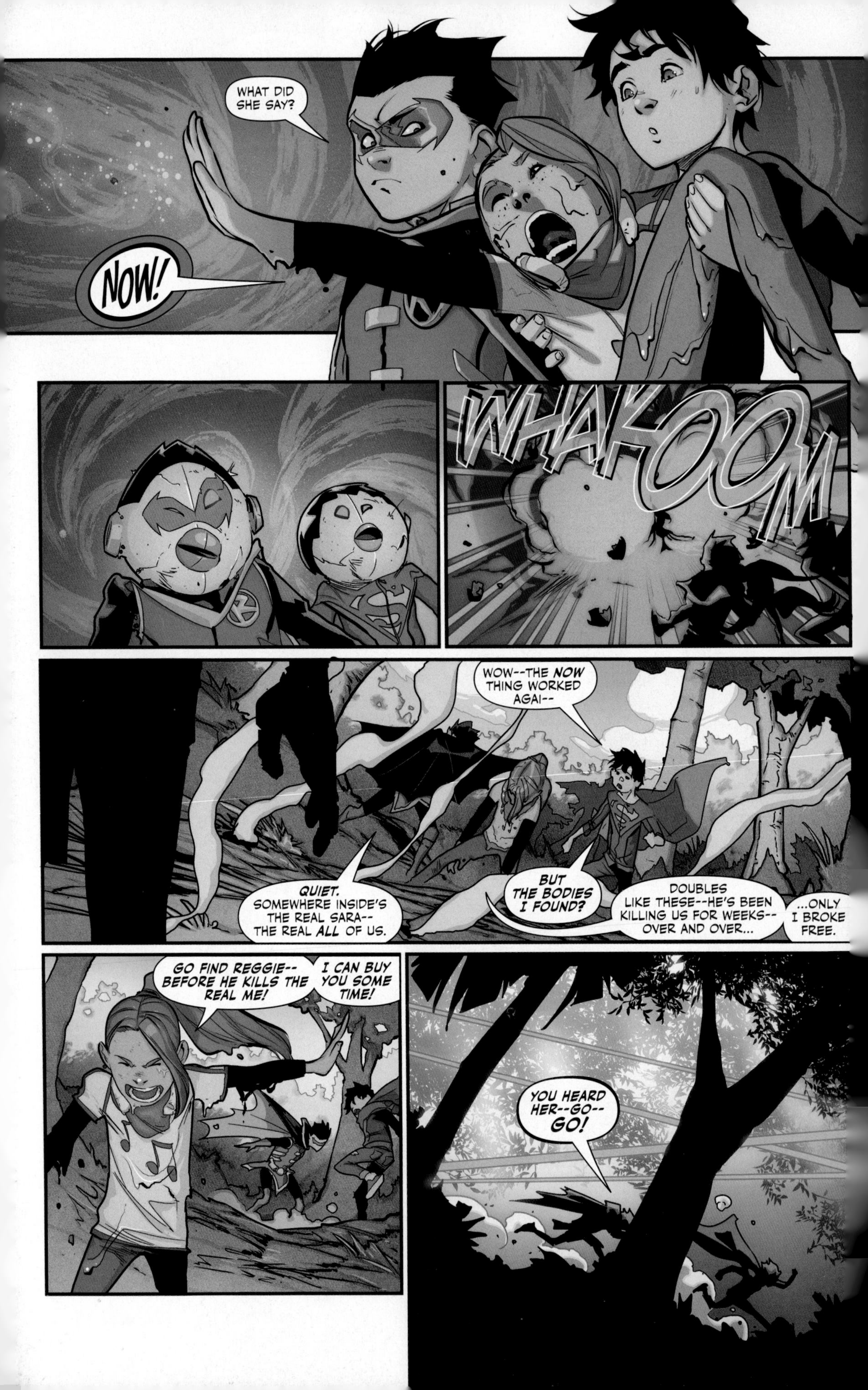
WHAT DID SHE SAY?
NOW!
WHAKOOM
WOW--THE NOW THING WORKED AGAI--
QUIET. SOMEWHERE INSIDE'S THE REAL SARA-- THE REAL ALL OF US.
BUT THE BODIES I FOUND?
DOUBLES LIKE THESE--HE'S BEEN KILLING US FOR WEEKS-- OVER AND OVER...
...ONLY I BROKE FREE.
GO FIND REGGIE-- BEFORE HE KILLS THE REAL ME!
I CAN BUY YOU SOME TIME!
YOU HEARD HER--GO-- GO!

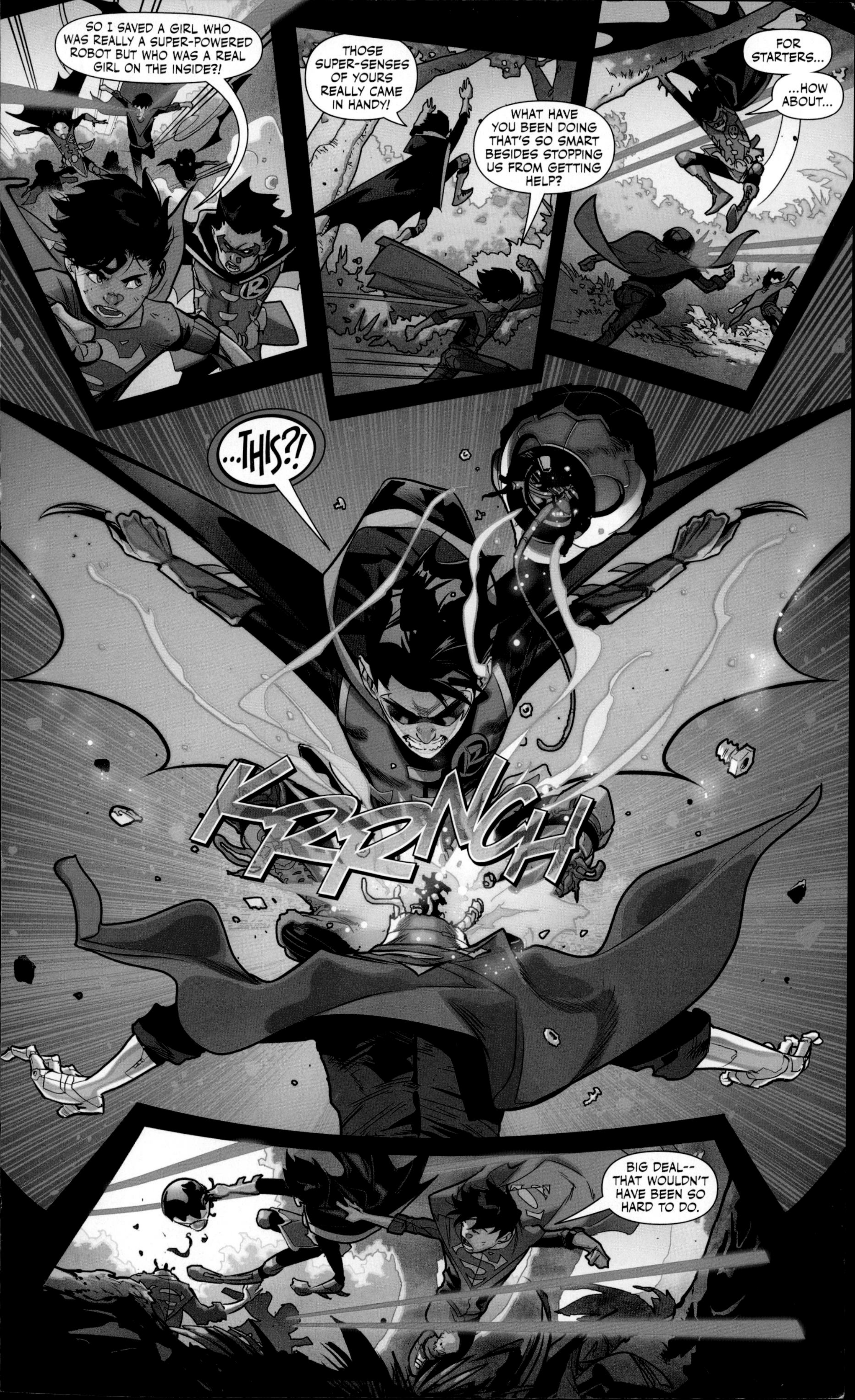
SO I SAVED A GIRL WHO WAS REALLY A SUPER-POWERED ROBOT BUT WHO WAS A REAL GIRL ON THE INSIDE?!
THOSE SUPER-SENSES OF YOURS REALLY CAME IN HANDY!
WHAT HAVE YOU BEEN DOING THAT'S SO SMART BESIDES STOPPING US FROM GETTING HELP?
FOR STARTERS...
...HOW ABOUT...
...THIS?!
KRRNCH
BIG DEAL-- THAT WOULDN'T HAVE BEEN SO HARD TO DO.

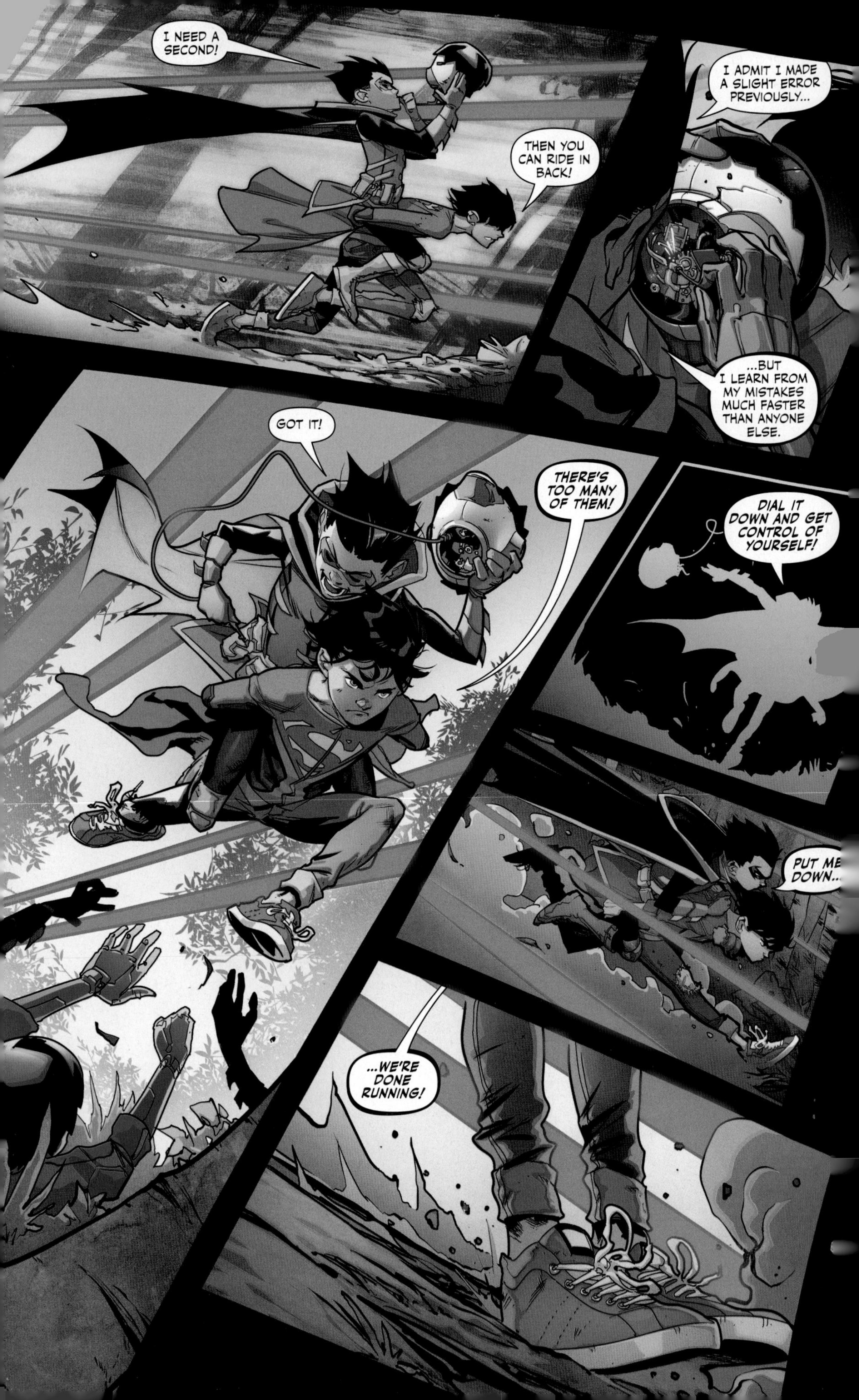
I NEED A SECOND!
THEN YOU CAN RIDE IN BACK!
I ADMIT I MADE A SLIGHT ERROR PREVIOUSLY...
...BUT I LEARN FROM MY MISTAKES MUCH FASTER THAN ANYONE ELSE.
GOT IT!
THERE'S TOO MANY OF THEM!
DIAL IT DOWN AND GET CONTROL OF YOURSELF!
PUT ME DOWN...
...WE'RE DONE RUNNING!

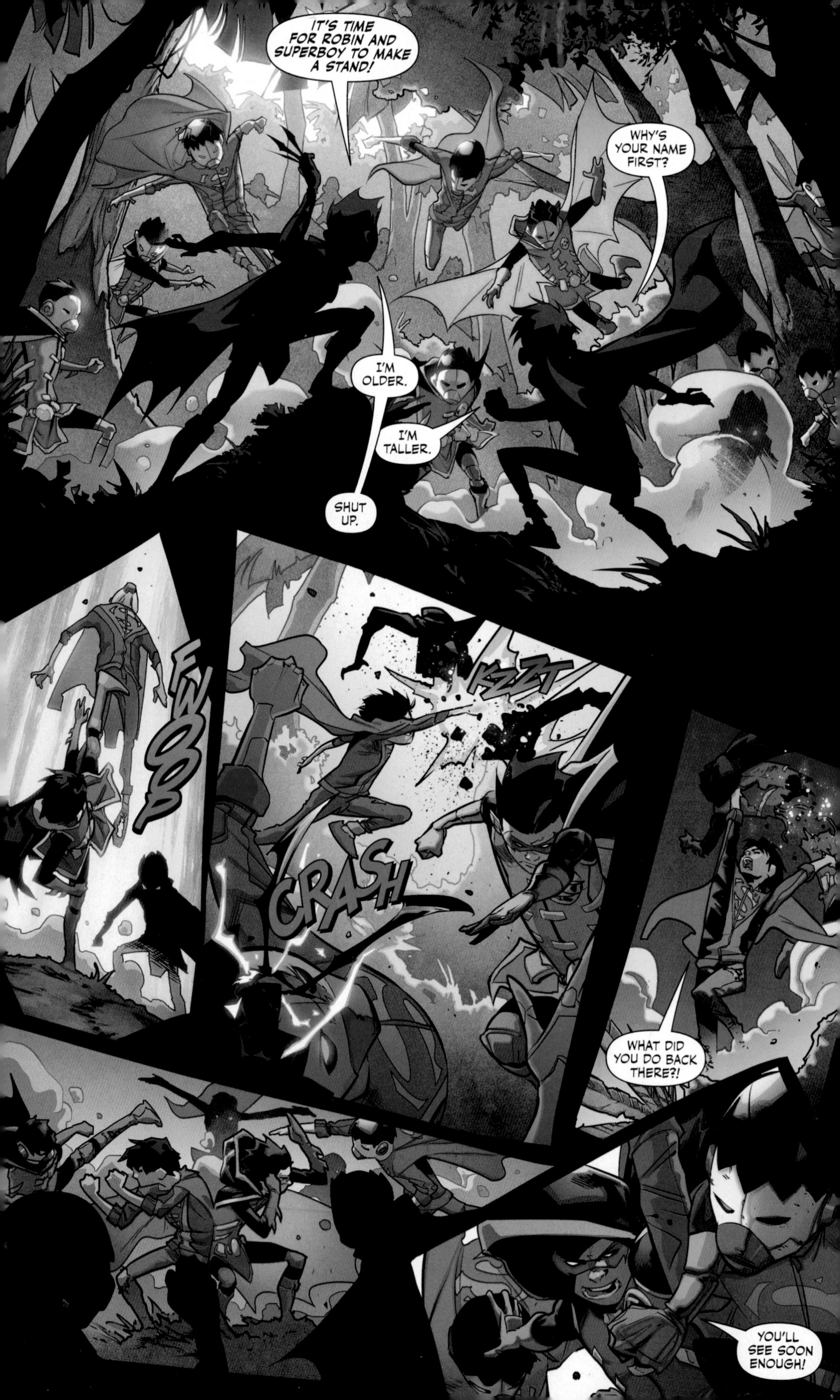
IT'S TIME FOR ROBIN AND SUPERBOY TO MAKE A STAND!
WHY'S YOUR NAME FIRST?
I'M OLDER.
I'M TALLER.
SHUT UP.
FWOOOP
KZZZT
CRASH
WHAT DID YOU DO BACK THERE?!
YOU'LL SEE SOON ENOUGH!

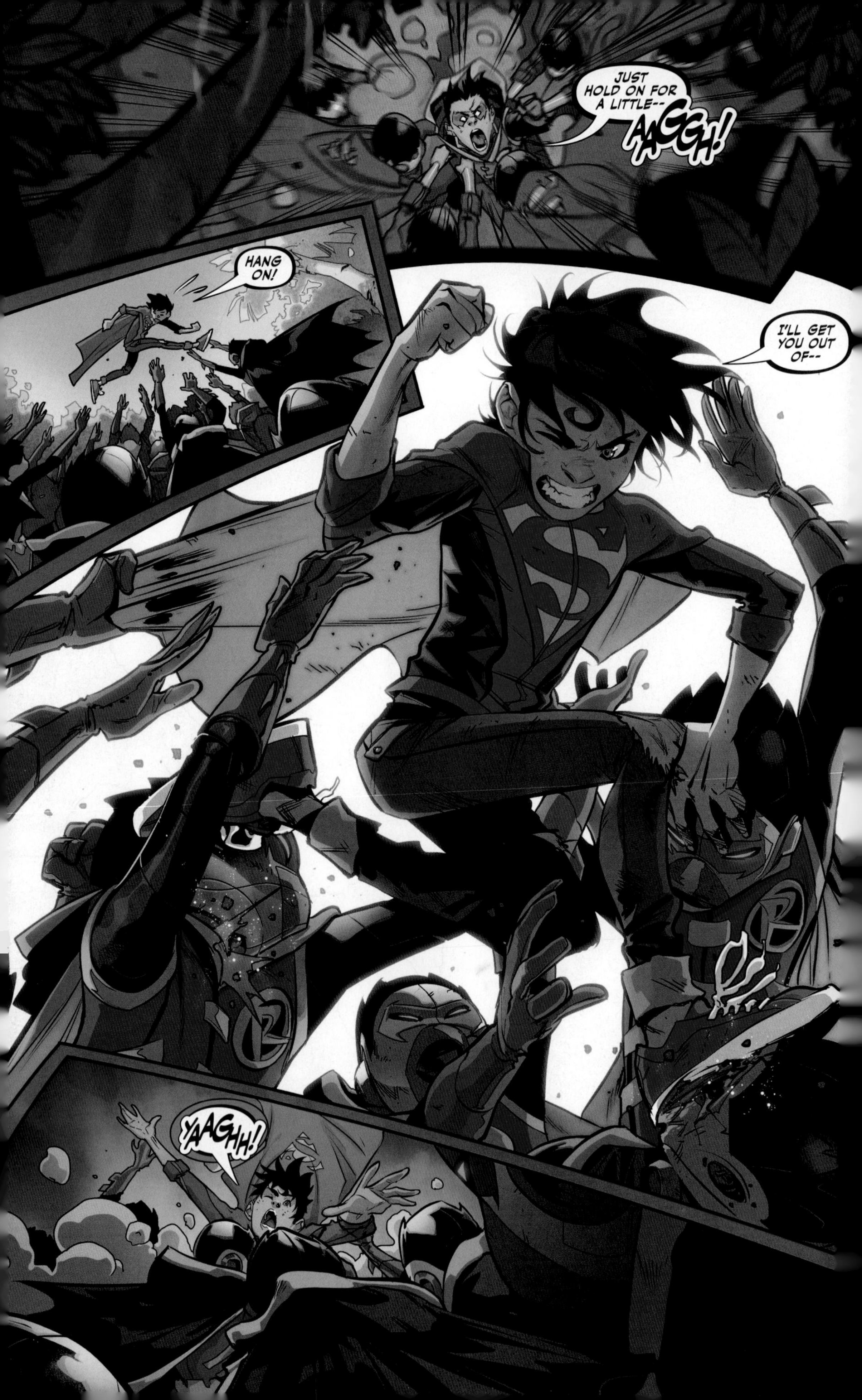
JUST HOLD ON FOR A LITTLE--
AAGGH!
HANG ON!
I'LL GET YOU OUT OF--
YAAGHH!

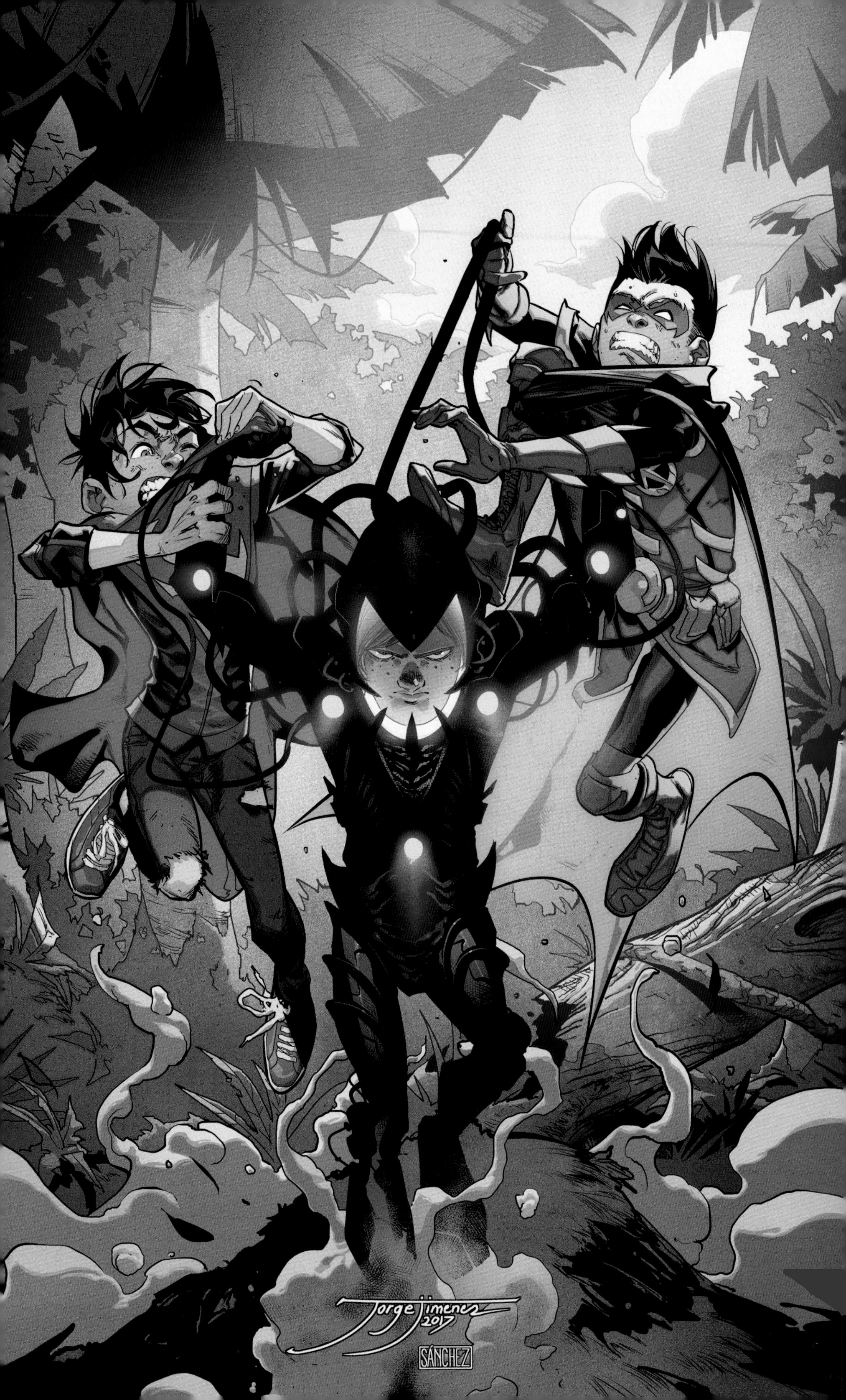
Jorge Jimenez 2017
SÁNCHEZ

WHEN I GROW UP... PART FOUR: SON DAY, BLOODY SON DAY!

JORGE JIMENEZ artist * ALEJANDRO SANCHEZ colorist

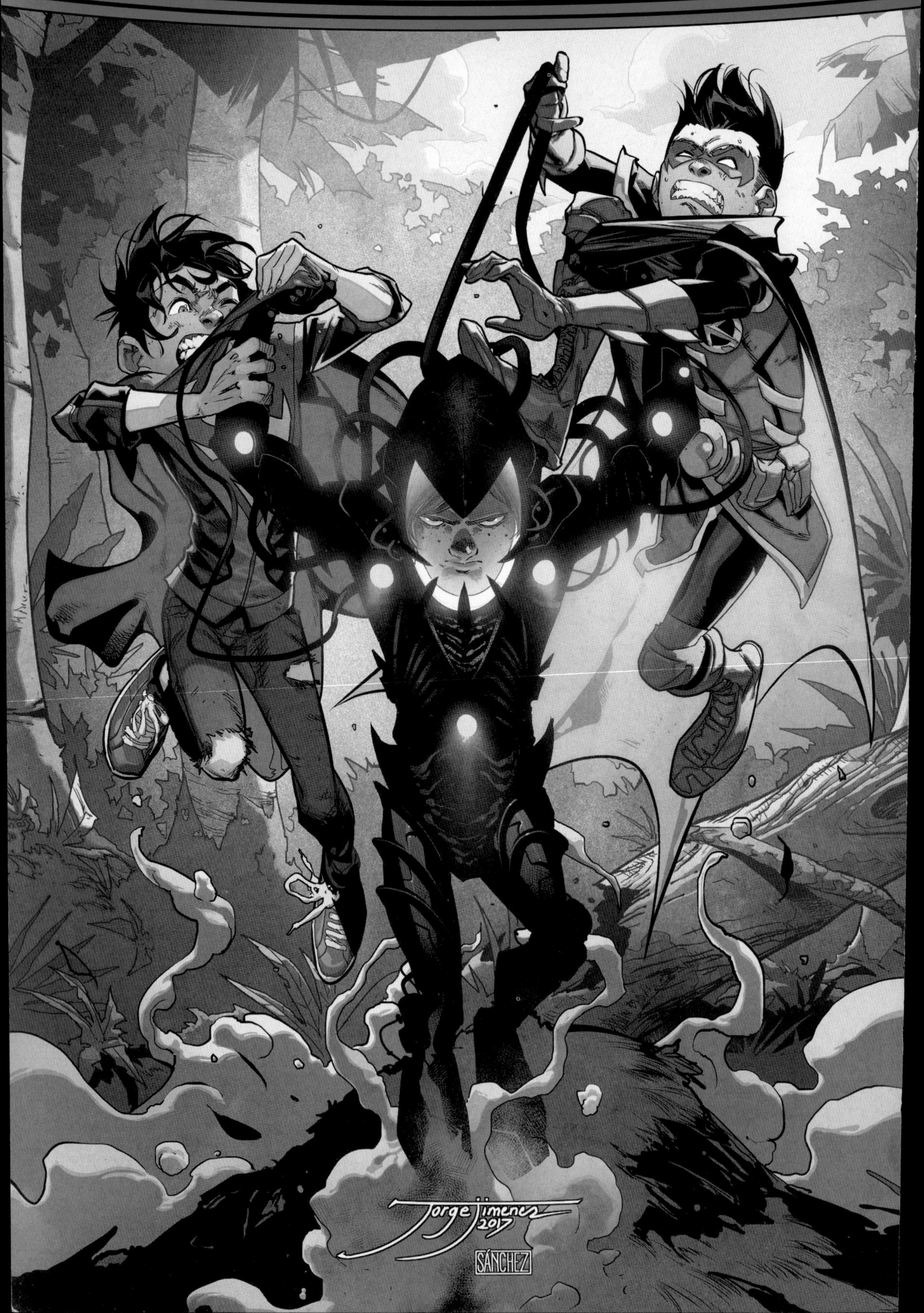
Jorge Jimenez 2017
SÁNCHEZ

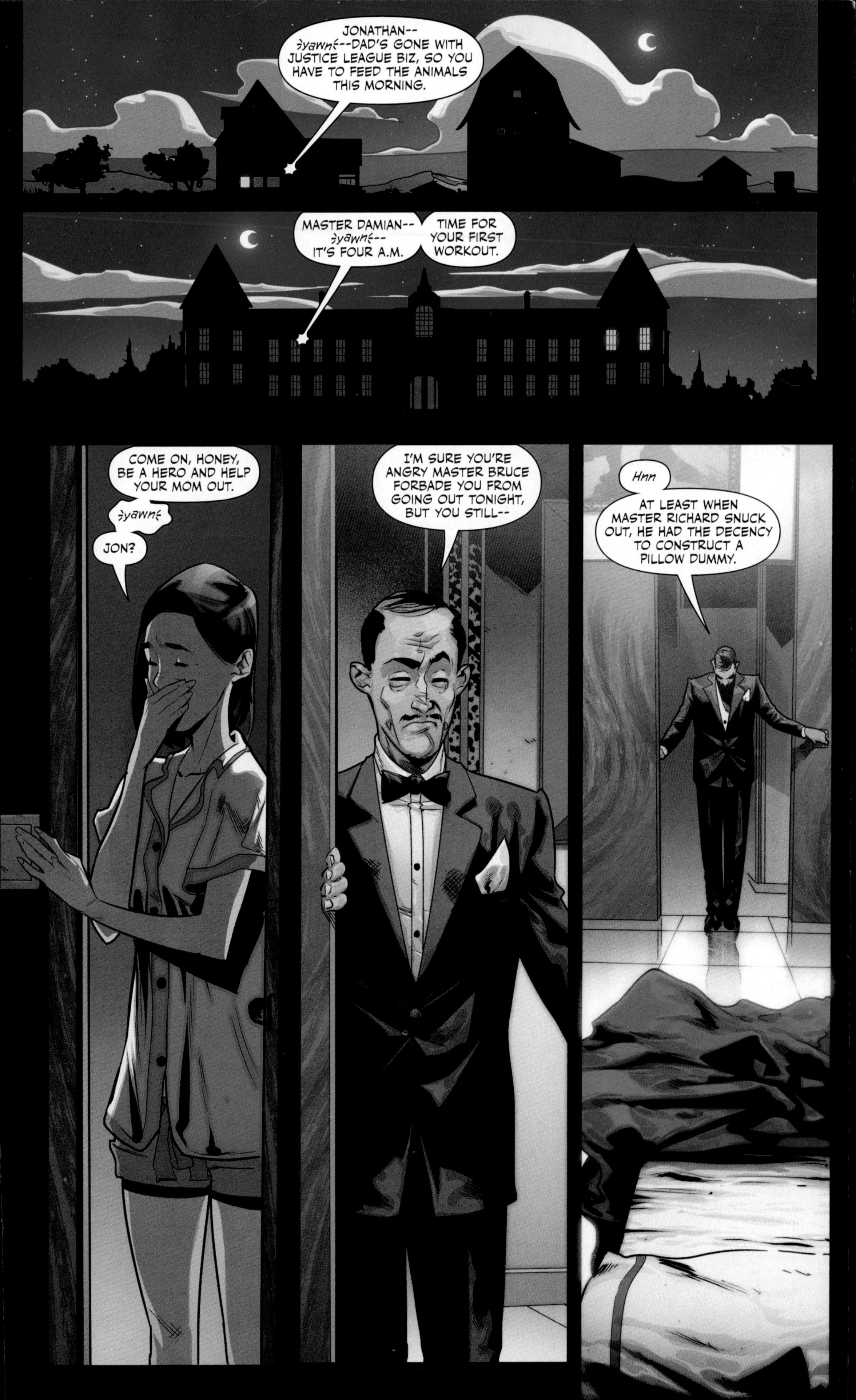
JONATHAN-- ⸗yawn⸗ --DAD'S GONE WITH JUSTICE LEAGUE BIZ, SO YOU HAVE TO FEED THE ANIMALS THIS MORNING.
MASTER DAMIAN-- ⸗yawn⸗-- IT'S FOUR A.M.
TIME FOR YOUR FIRST WORKOUT.
COME ON, HONEY, BE A HERO AND HELP YOUR MOM OUT.
⸗yawn⸗
JON?
I'M SURE YOU'RE ANGRY MASTER BRUCE FORBADE YOU FROM GOING OUT TONIGHT, BUT YOU STILL--
Hnn
AT LEAST WHEN MASTER RICHARD SNUCK OUT, HE HAD THE DECENCY TO CONSTRUCT A PILLOW DUMMY.

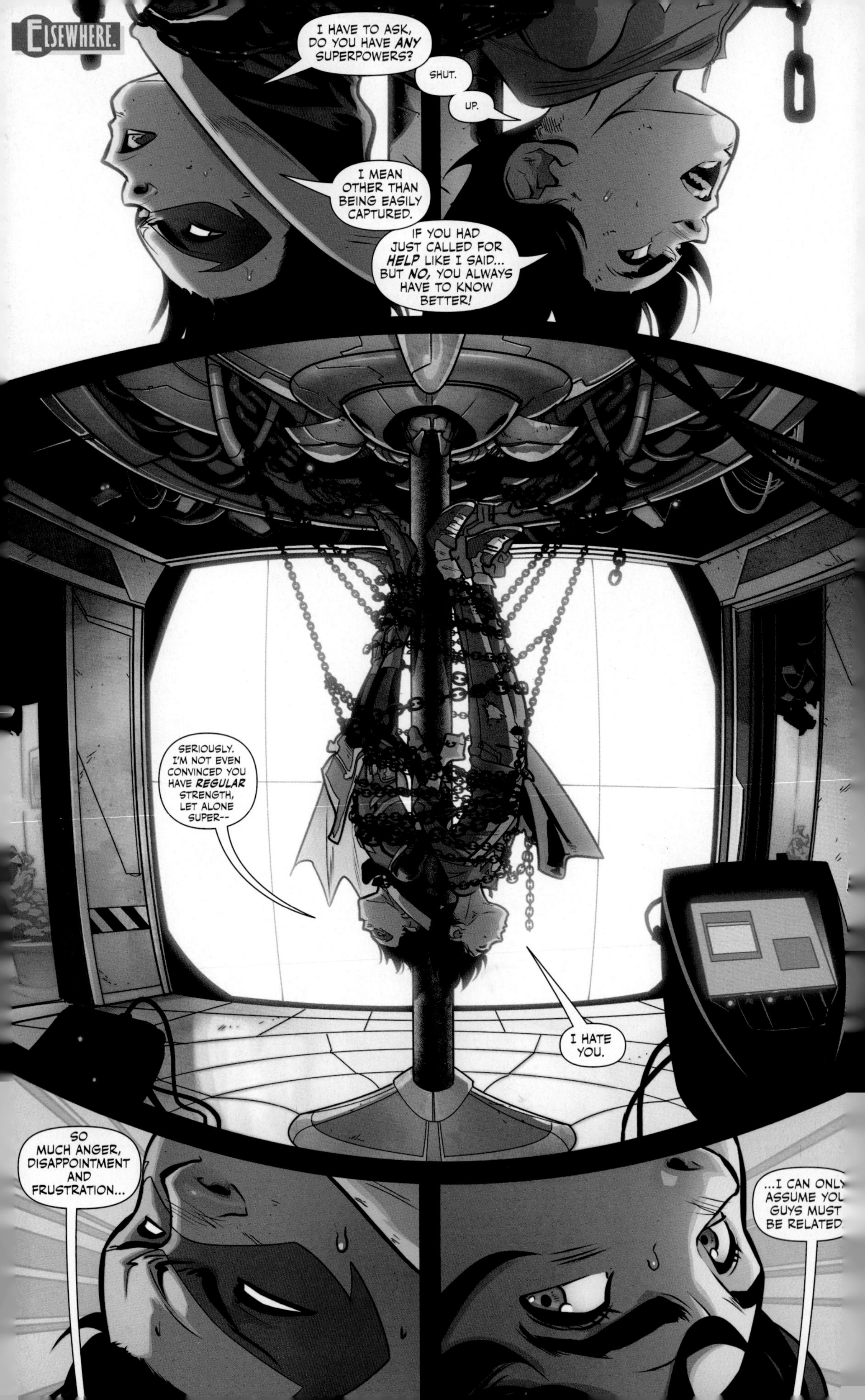
ELSEWHERE.
I HAVE TO ASK, DO YOU HAVE ANY SUPERPOWERS?
SHUT.
UP.
I MEAN OTHER THAN BEING EASILY CAPTURED.
IF YOU HAD JUST CALLED FOR HELP LIKE I SAID... BUT NO, YOU ALWAYS HAVE TO KNOW BETTER!
SERIOUSLY. I'M NOT EVEN CONVINCED YOU HAVE REGULAR STRENGTH, LET ALONE SUPER--
I HATE YOU.
SO MUCH ANGER, DISAPPOINTMENT AND FRUSTRATION...
...I CAN ONLY ASSUME YOU GUYS MUST BE RELATED.

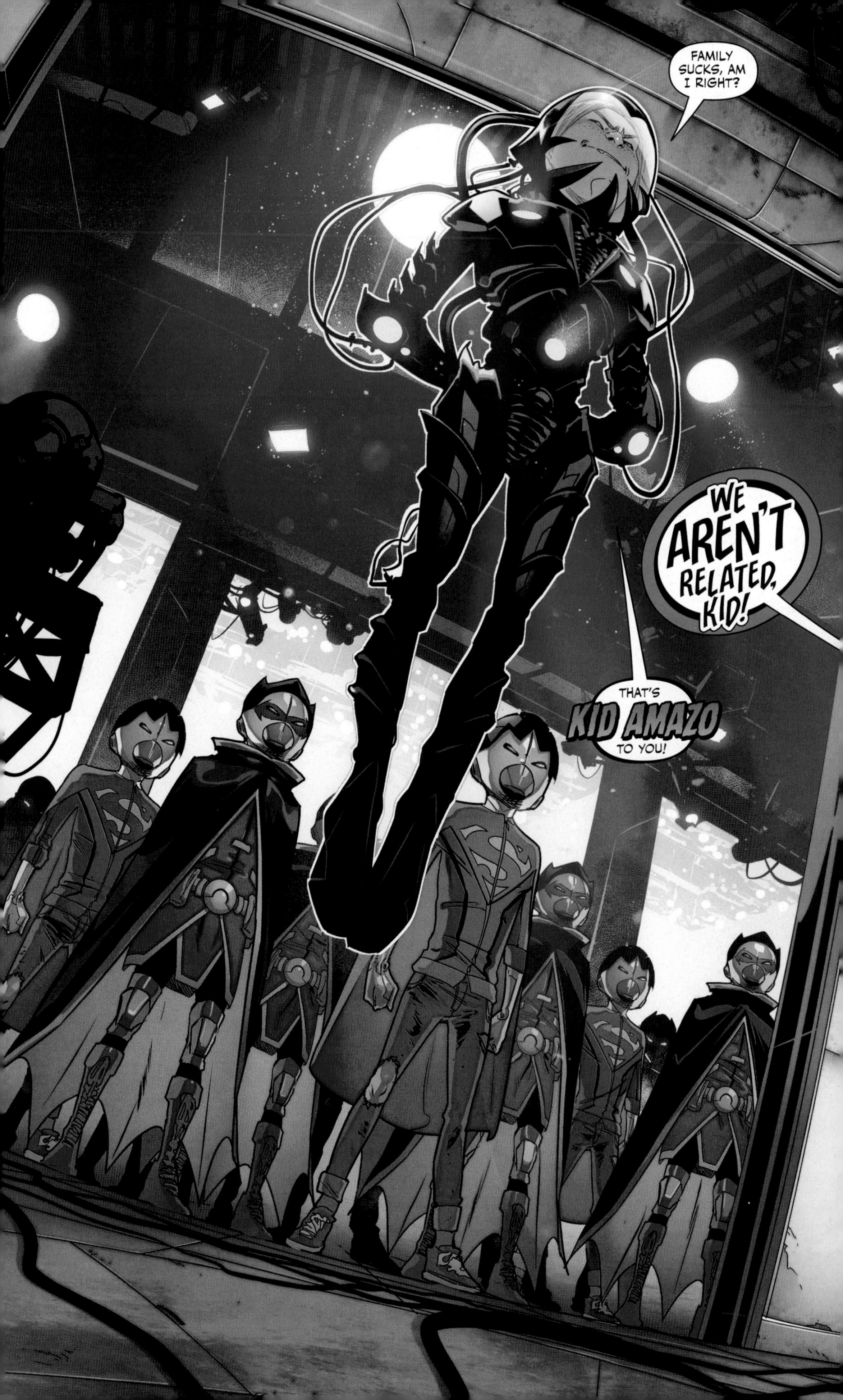
FAMILY SUCKS, AM I RIGHT?
WE AREN'T RELATED, KID!
THAT'S KID AMAZO TO YOU!

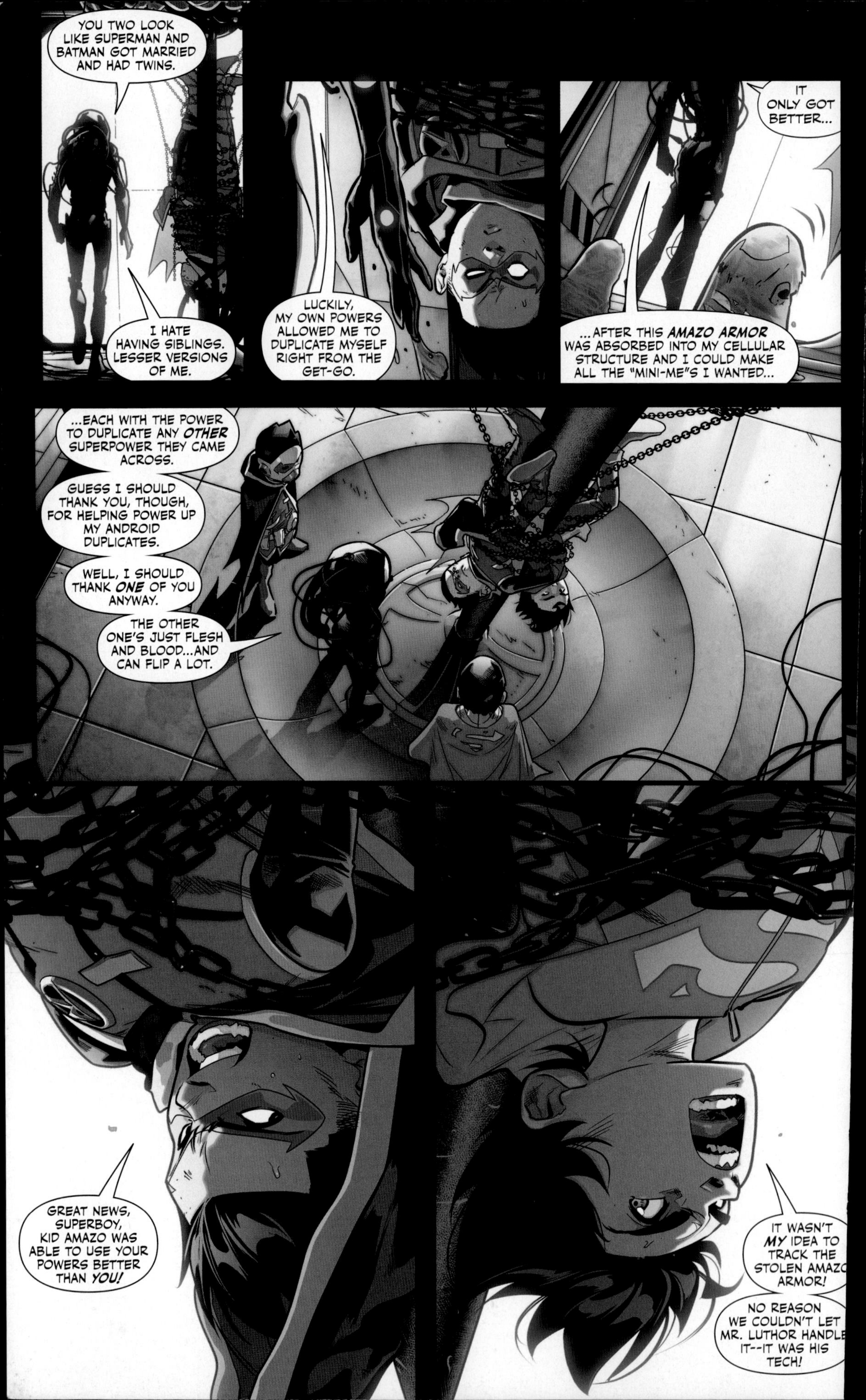
YOU TWO LOOK LIKE SUPERMAN AND BATMAN GOT MARRIED AND HAD TWINS.
I HATE HAVING SIBLINGS. LESSER VERSIONS OF ME.
LUCKILY, MY OWN POWERS ALLOWED ME TO DUPLICATE MYSELF RIGHT FROM THE GET-GO.
IT ONLY GOT BETTER...
...AFTER THIS AMAZO ARMOR WAS ABSORBED INTO MY CELLULAR STRUCTURE AND I COULD MAKE ALL THE "MINI-ME"S I WANTED...
...EACH WITH THE POWER TO DUPLICATE ANY OTHER SUPERPOWER THEY CAME ACROSS.
GUESS I SHOULD THANK YOU, THOUGH, FOR HELPING POWER UP MY ANDROID DUPLICATES.
WELL, I SHOULD THANK ONE OF YOU ANYWAY.
THE OTHER ONE'S JUST FLESH AND BLOOD...AND CAN FLIP A LOT.
GREAT NEWS, SUPERBOY, KID AMAZO WAS ABLE TO USE YOUR POWERS BETTER THAN YOU!
IT WASN'T MY IDEA TO TRACK THE STOLEN AMAZO ARMOR!
NO REASON WE COULDN'T LET MR. LUTHOR HANDLE IT--IT WAS HIS TECH!

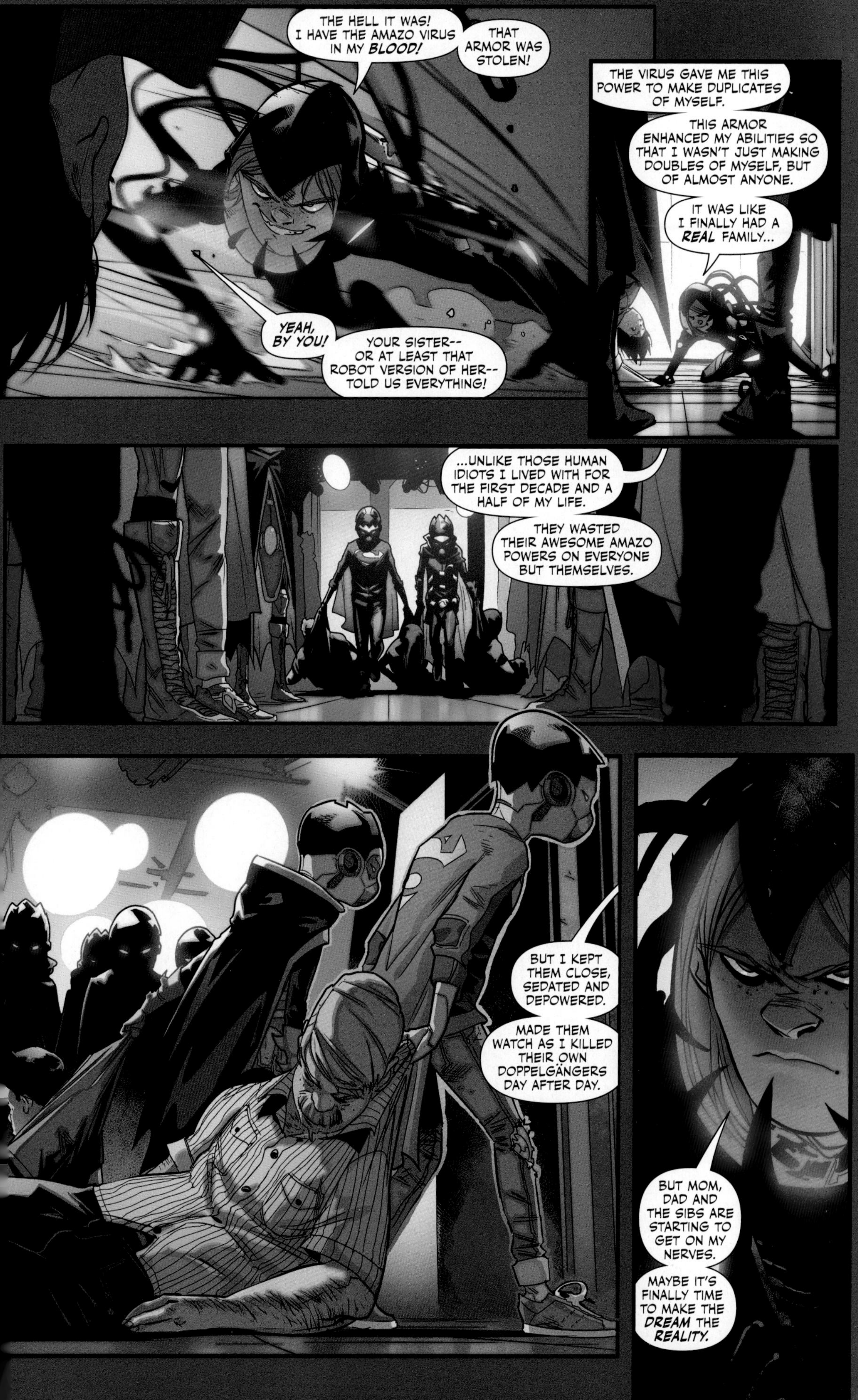
THE HELL IT WAS! I HAVE THE AMAZO VIRUS IN MY BLOOD!
THAT ARMOR WAS STOLEN!
YEAH, BY YOU!
YOUR SISTER-- OR AT LEAST THAT ROBOT VERSION OF HER-- TOLD US EVERYTHING!
THE VIRUS GAVE ME THIS POWER TO MAKE DUPLICATES OF MYSELF.
THIS ARMOR ENHANCED MY ABILITIES SO THAT I WASN'T JUST MAKING DOUBLES OF MYSELF, BUT OF ALMOST ANYONE.
IT WAS LIKE I FINALLY HAD A REAL FAMILY...
...UNLIKE THOSE HUMAN IDIOTS I LIVED WITH FOR THE FIRST DECADE AND A HALF OF MY LIFE.
THEY WASTED THEIR AWESOME AMAZO POWERS ON EVERYONE BUT THEMSELVES.
BUT I KEPT THEM CLOSE, SEDATED AND DEPOWERED.
MADE THEM WATCH AS I KILLED THEIR OWN DOPPELGÄNGERS DAY AFTER DAY.
BUT MOM, DAD AND THE SIBS ARE STARTING TO GET ON MY NERVES.
MAYBE IT'S FINALLY TIME TO MAKE THE DREAM THE REALITY.

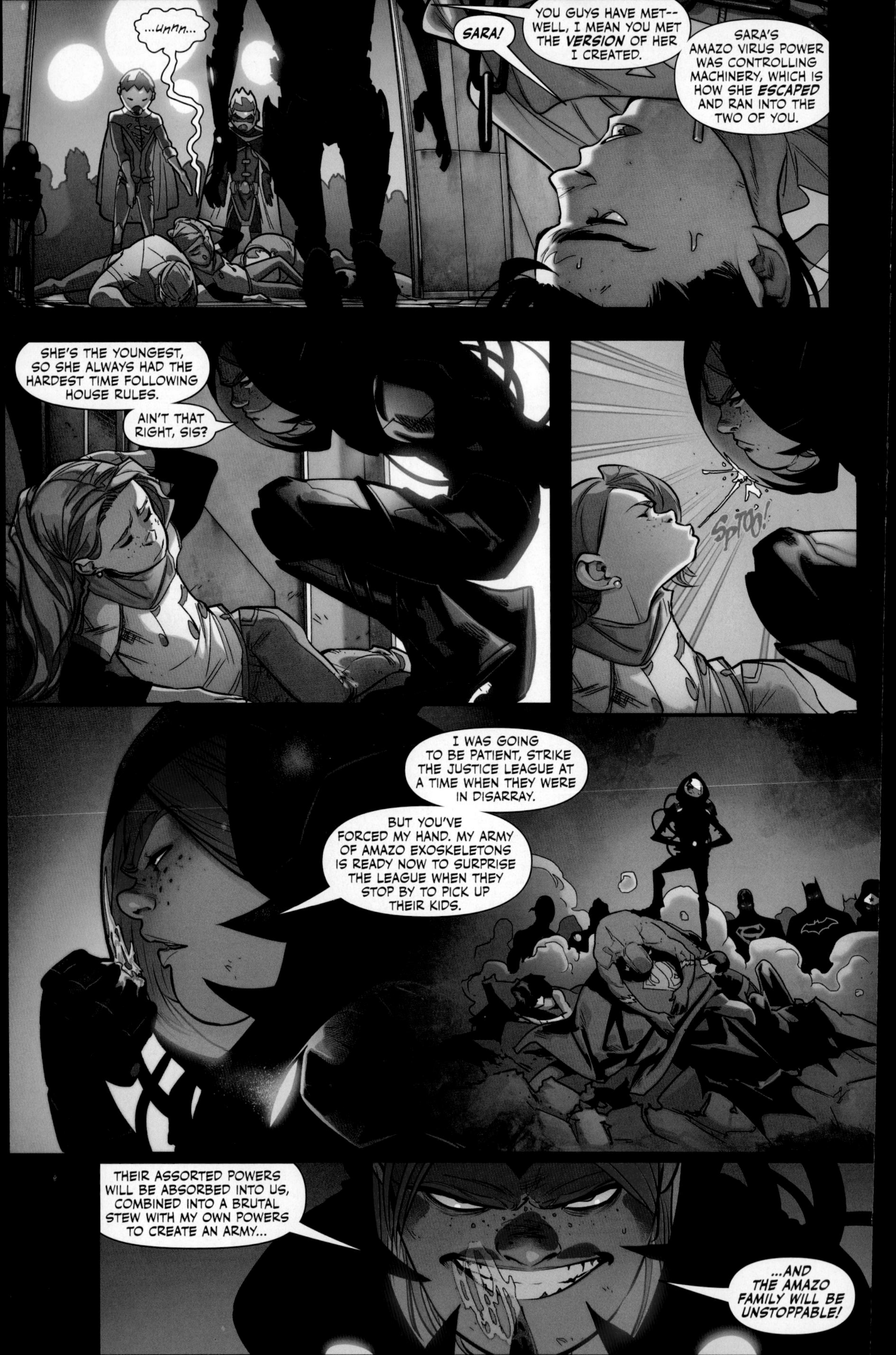
...unnn...
SARA!
YOU GUYS HAVE MET--WELL, I MEAN YOU MET THE VERSION OF HER I CREATED.
SARA'S AMAZO VIRUS POWER WAS CONTROLLING MACHINERY, WHICH IS HOW SHE ESCAPED AND RAN INTO THE TWO OF YOU.
SHE'S THE YOUNGEST, SO SHE ALWAYS HAD THE HARDEST TIME FOLLOWING HOUSE RULES.
AIN'T THAT RIGHT, SIS?
SPTOO!
I WAS GOING TO BE PATIENT, STRIKE THE JUSTICE LEAGUE AT A TIME WHEN THEY WERE IN DISARRAY.
BUT YOU'VE FORCED MY HAND. MY ARMY OF AMAZO EXOSKELETONS IS READY NOW TO SURPRISE THE LEAGUE WHEN THEY STOP BY TO PICK UP THEIR KIDS.
THEIR ASSORTED POWERS WILL BE ABSORBED INTO US, COMBINED INTO A BRUTAL STEW WITH MY OWN POWERS TO CREATE AN ARMY...
...AND THE AMAZO FAMILY WILL BE UNSTOPPABLE!

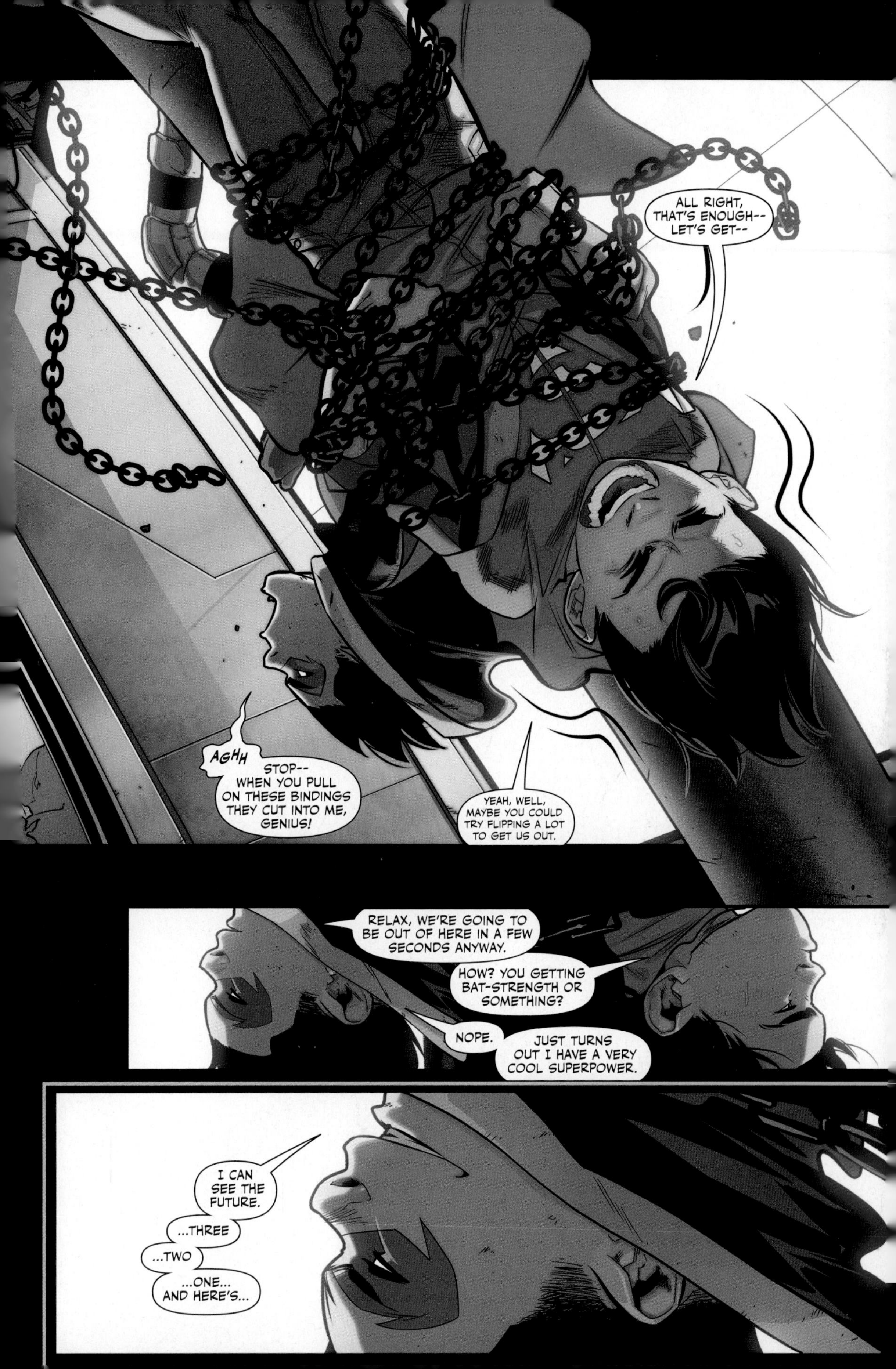
ALL RIGHT, THAT'S ENOUGH-- LET'S GET--
AGHH
STOP-- WHEN YOU PULL ON THESE BINDINGS THEY CUT INTO ME, GENIUS!
YEAH, WELL, MAYBE YOU COULD TRY FLIPPING A LOT TO GET US OUT.
RELAX, WE'RE GOING TO BE OUT OF HERE IN A FEW SECONDS ANYWAY.
HOW? YOU GETTING BAT-STRENGTH OR SOMETHING?
NOPE.
JUST TURNS OUT I HAVE A VERY COOL SUPERPOWER.
I CAN SEE THE FUTURE.
...THREE
...TWO
...ONE... AND HERE'S...

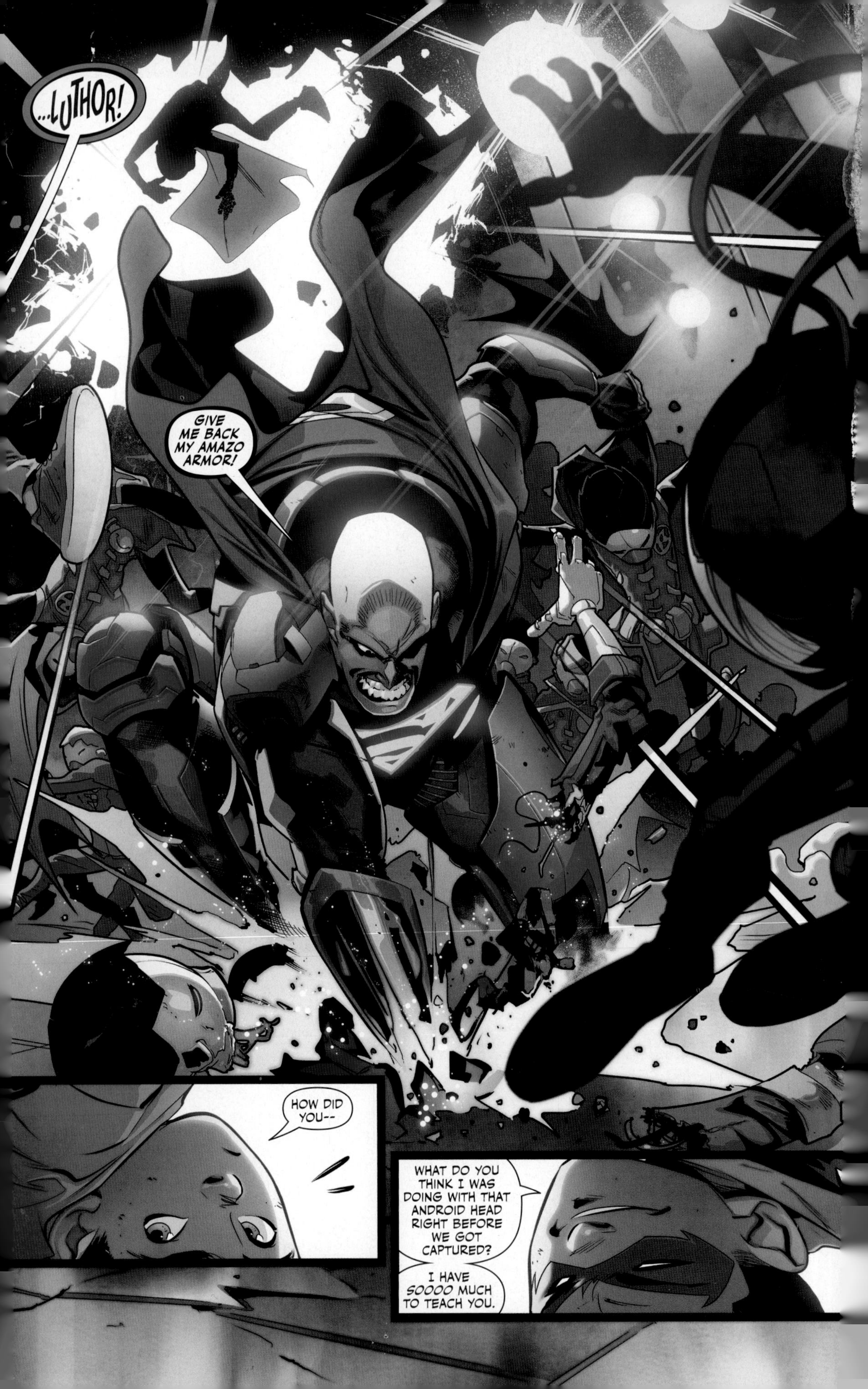
...LUTHOR!
GIVE ME BACK MY AMAZO ARMOR!
HOW DID YOU--
WHAT DO YOU THINK I WAS DOING WITH THAT ANDROID HEAD RIGHT BEFORE WE GOT CAPTURED?
I HAVE SOOOO MUCH TO TEACH YOU.

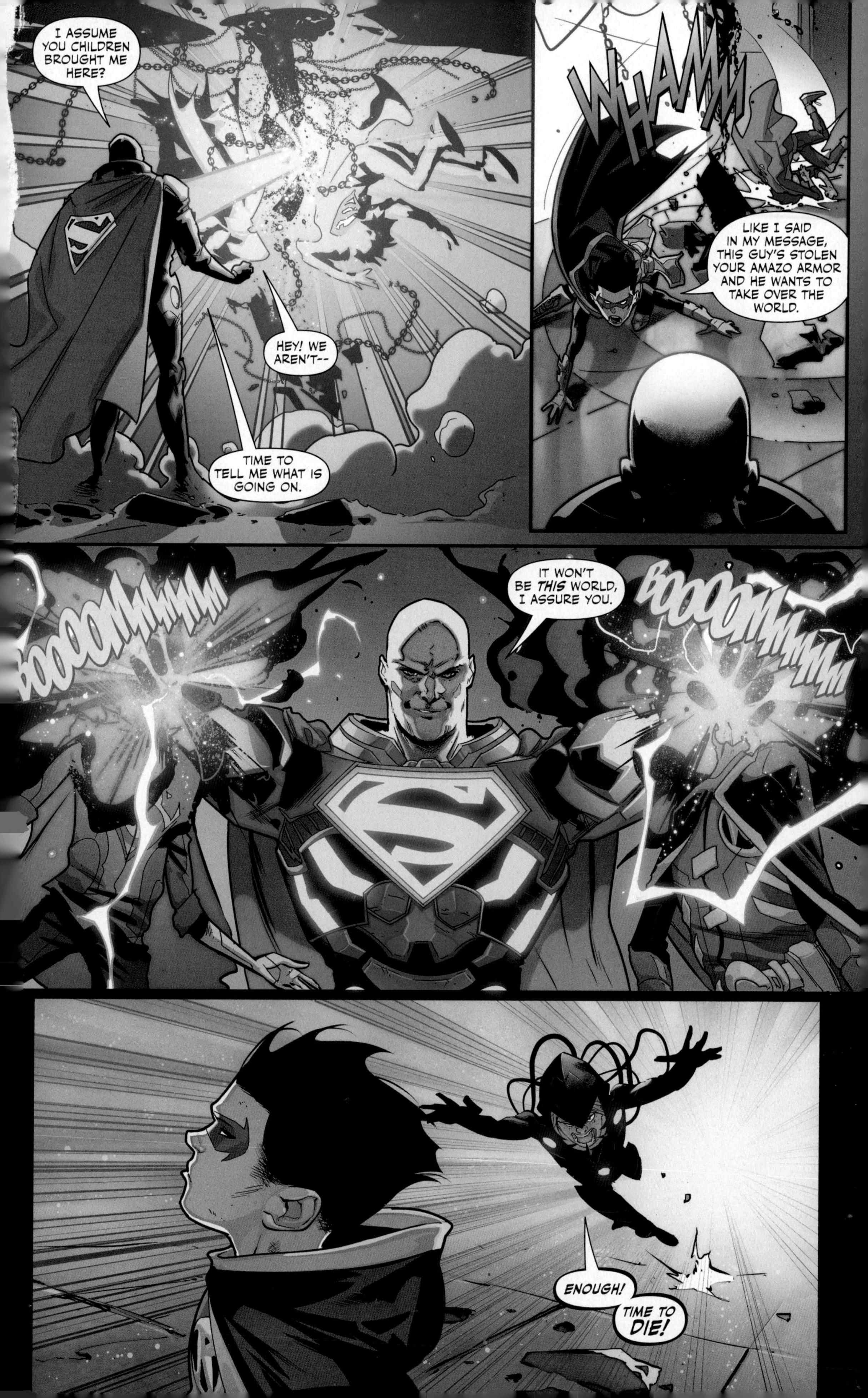
I ASSUME YOU CHILDREN BROUGHT ME HERE?
HEY! WE AREN'T--
TIME TO TELL ME WHAT IS GOING ON.
WHAMM
LIKE I SAID IN MY MESSAGE, THIS GUY'S STOLEN YOUR AMAZO ARMOR AND HE WANTS TO TAKE OVER THE WORLD.
BOOOOMMMMMM
IT WON'T BE THIS WORLD, I ASSURE YOU.
BOOOOMMMMMM
ENOUGH!
TIME TO DIE!

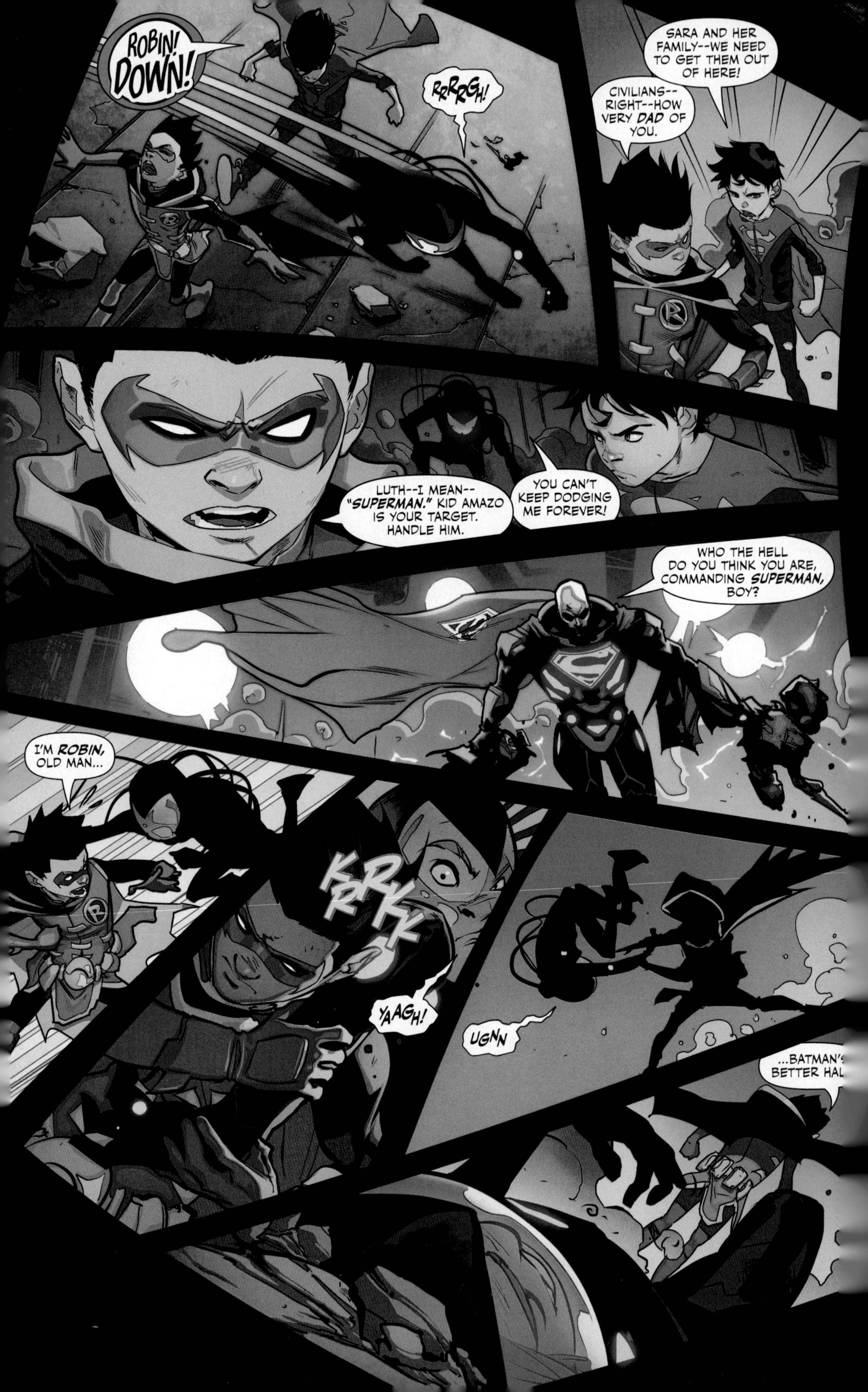
ROBIN! DOWN!
RRRRGH!
SARA AND HER FAMILY--WE NEED TO GET THEM OUT OF HERE!
CIVILIANS--RIGHT--HOW VERY DAD OF YOU.
LUTH--I MEAN--"SUPERMAN." KID AMAZO IS YOUR TARGET. HANDLE HIM.
YOU CAN'T KEEP DODGING ME FOREVER!
WHO THE HELL DO YOU THINK YOU ARE, COMMANDING SUPERMAN, BOY?
I'M ROBIN, OLD MAN...
KRRKK
YAAGH!
UGNN
...BATMAN'S BETTER HAL

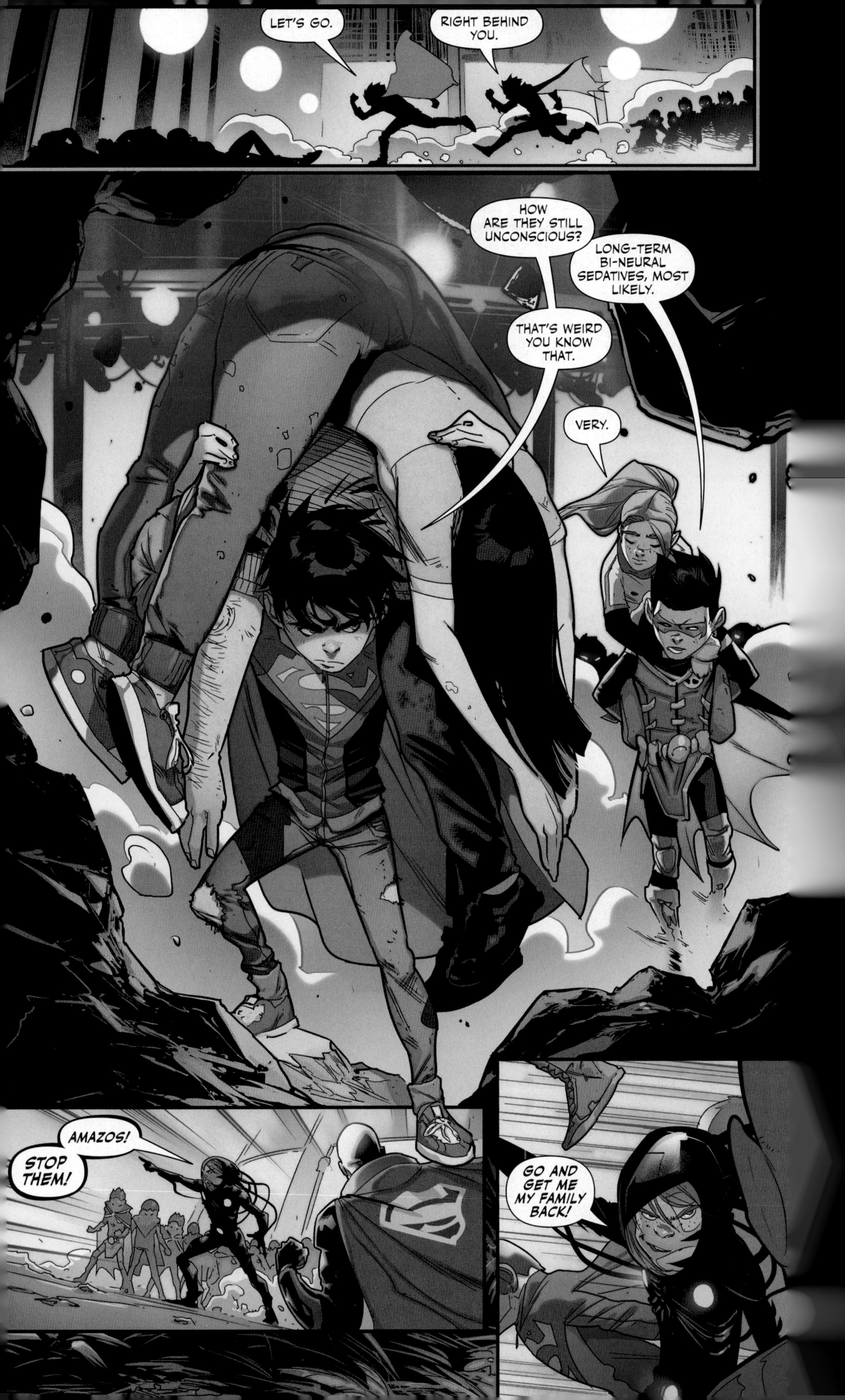
LET'S GO.
RIGHT BEHIND YOU.
HOW ARE THEY STILL UNCONSCIOUS?
LONG-TERM BI-NEURAL SEDATIVES, MOST LIKELY.
THAT'S WEIRD YOU KNOW THAT.
VERY.
AMAZOS!
STOP THEM!
GO AND GET ME MY FAMILY BACK!

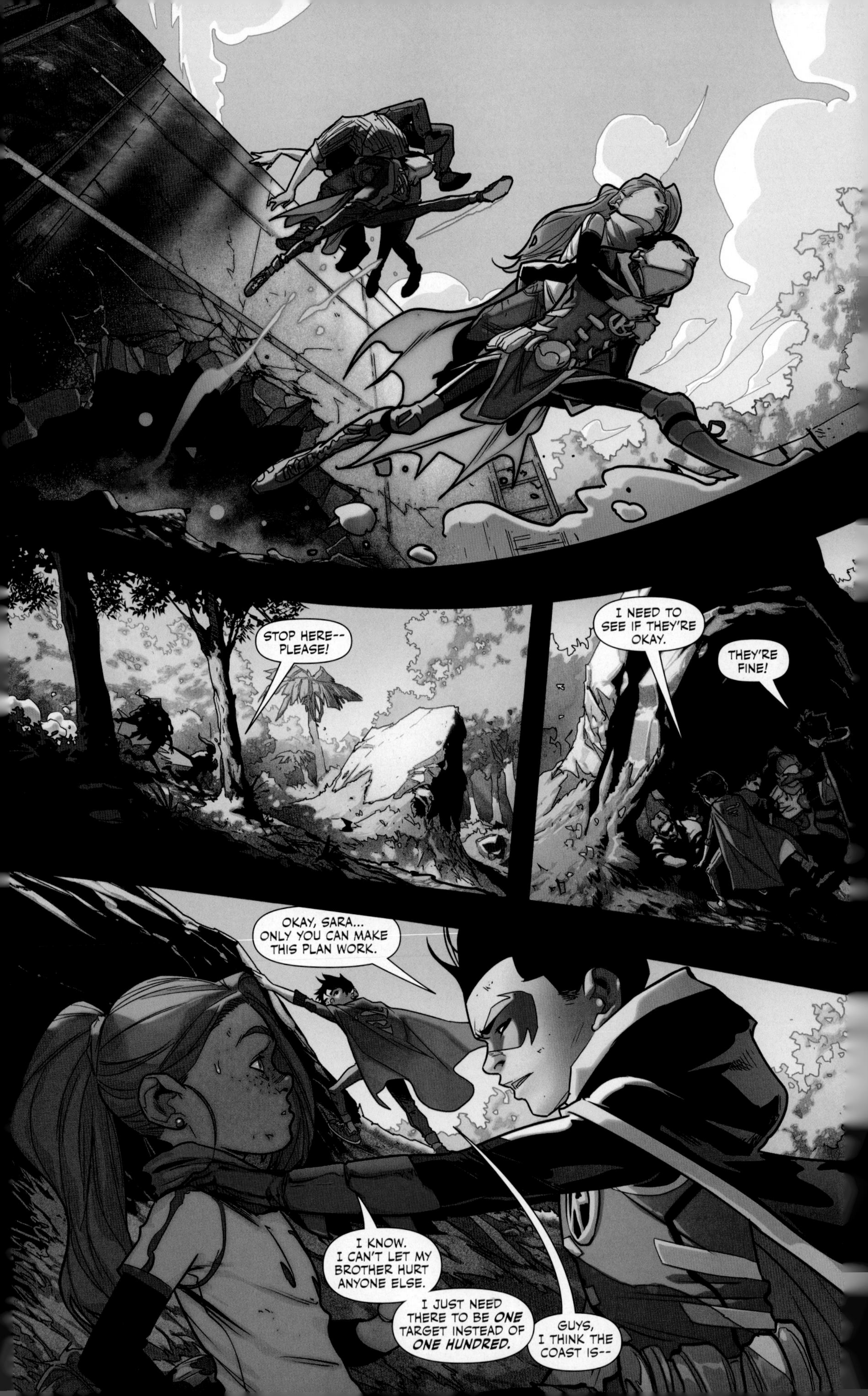
STOP HERE-- PLEASE!
I NEED TO SEE IF THEY'RE OKAY.
THEY'RE FINE!
OKAY, SARA... ONLY YOU CAN MAKE THIS PLAN WORK.
I KNOW. I CAN'T LET MY BROTHER HURT ANYONE ELSE.
I JUST NEED THERE TO BE *ONE* TARGET INSTEAD OF *ONE HUNDRED.*
GUYS, I THINK THE COAST IS--

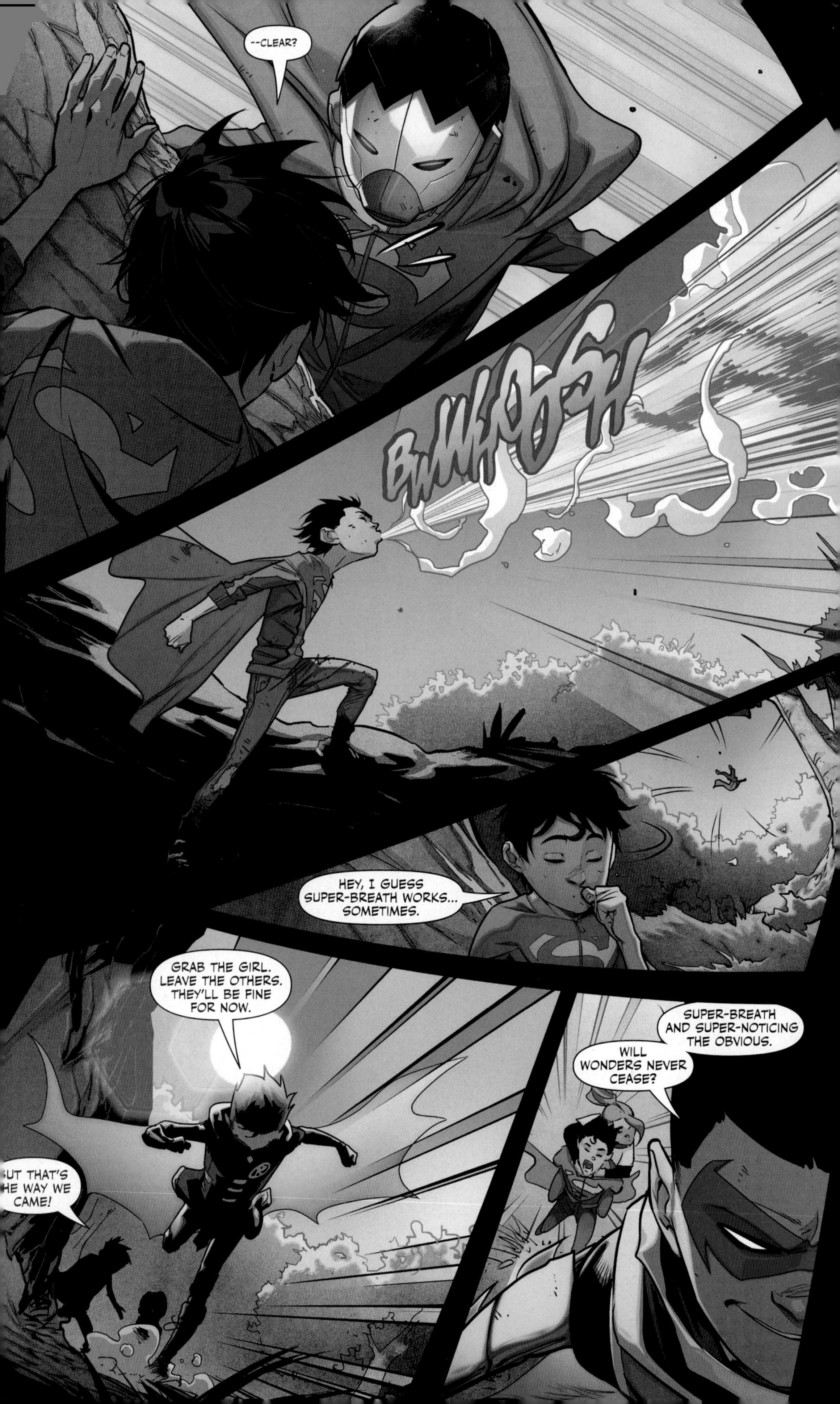
--CLEAR?
BWHOOSH
HEY, I GUESS SUPER-BREATH WORKS... SOMETIMES.
GRAB THE GIRL. LEAVE THE OTHERS. THEY'LL BE FINE FOR NOW.
UT THAT'S HE WAY WE CAME!
SUPER-BREATH AND SUPER-NOTICING THE OBVIOUS.
WILL WONDERS NEVER CEASE?

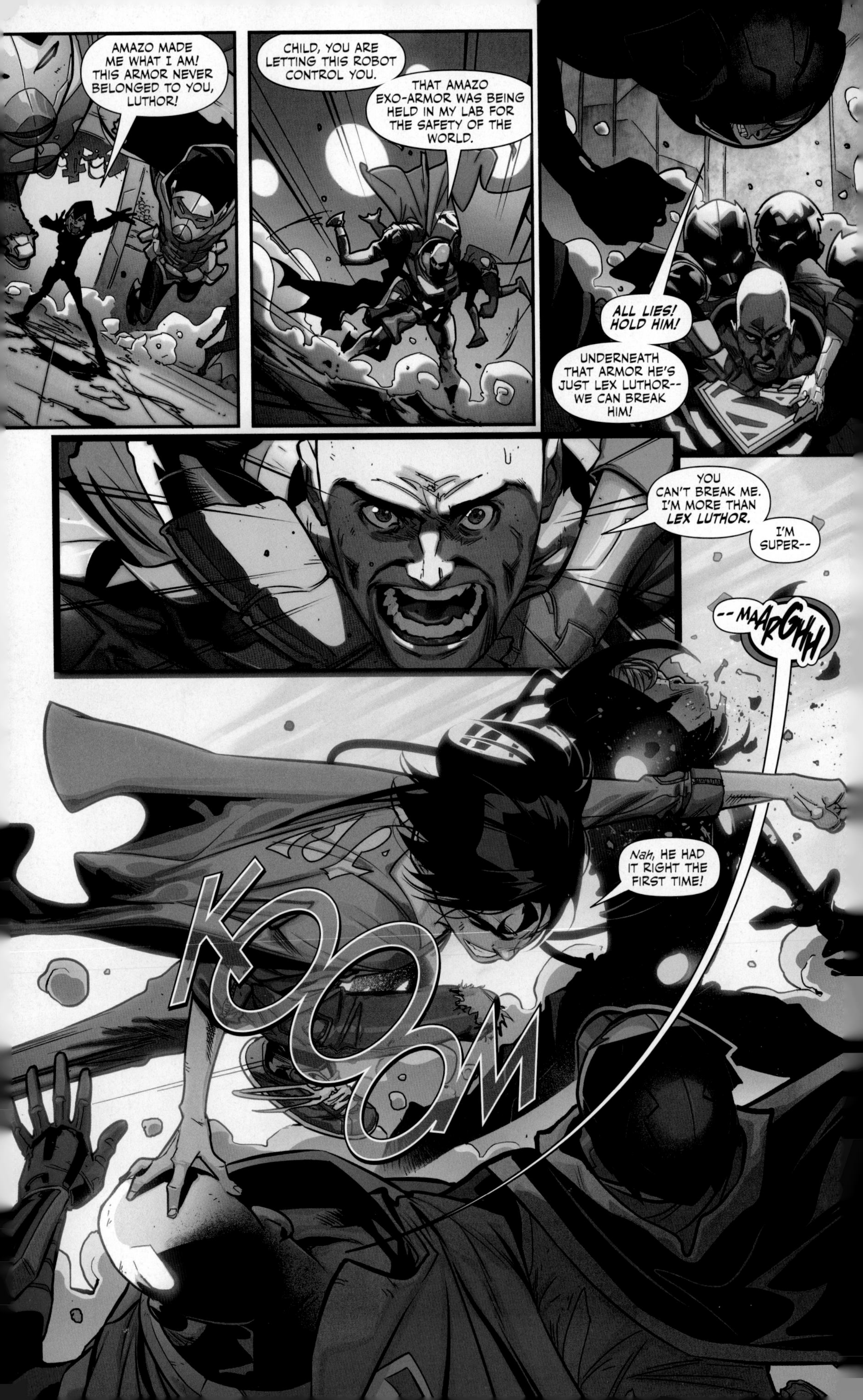
AMAZO MADE ME WHAT I AM! THIS ARMOR NEVER BELONGED TO YOU, LUTHOR!
CHILD, YOU ARE LETTING THIS ROBOT CONTROL YOU.
THAT AMAZO EXO-ARMOR WAS BEING HELD IN MY LAB FOR THE SAFETY OF THE WORLD.
ALL LIES! HOLD HIM!
UNDERNEATH THAT ARMOR HE'S JUST LEX LUTHOR-- WE CAN BREAK HIM!
YOU CAN'T BREAK ME. I'M MORE THAN LEX LUTHOR.
I'M SUPER--
--MAARGHH
Nah, HE HAD IT RIGHT THE FIRST TIME!
KOOOOM

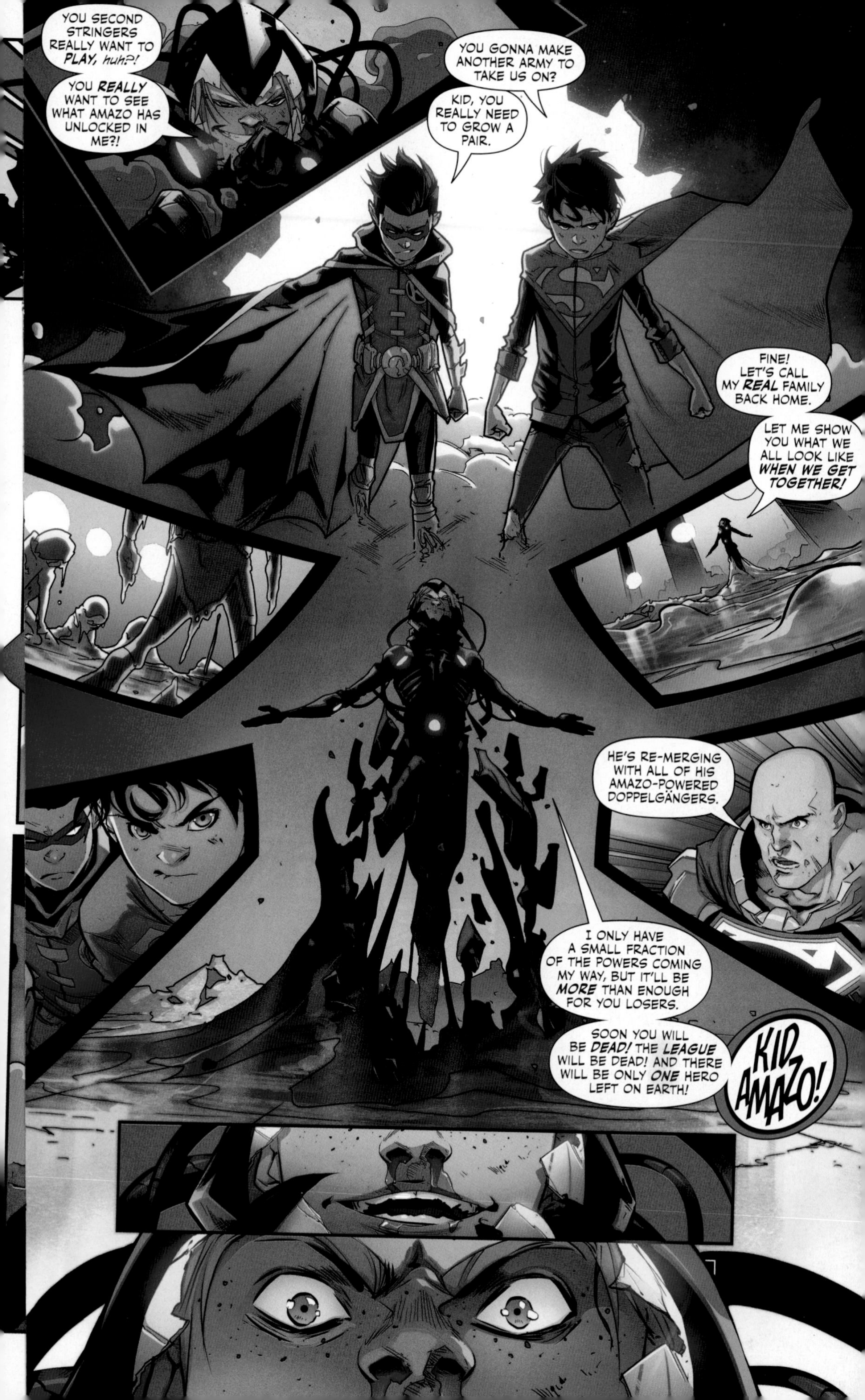
YOU SECOND STRINGERS REALLY WANT TO PLAY, huh?!
YOU REALLY WANT TO SEE WHAT AMAZO HAS UNLOCKED IN ME?!
YOU GONNA MAKE ANOTHER ARMY TO TAKE US ON?
KID, YOU REALLY NEED TO GROW A PAIR.
FINE! LET'S CALL MY REAL FAMILY BACK HOME.
LET ME SHOW YOU WHAT WE ALL LOOK LIKE WHEN WE GET TOGETHER!
HE'S RE-MERGING WITH ALL OF HIS AMAZO-POWERED DOPPELGÄNGERS.
I ONLY HAVE A SMALL FRACTION OF THE POWERS COMING MY WAY, BUT IT'LL BE MORE THAN ENOUGH FOR YOU LOSERS.
SOON YOU WILL BE DEAD! THE LEAGUE WILL BE DEAD! AND THERE WILL BE ONLY ONE HERO LEFT ON EARTH!
KID AMAZO!

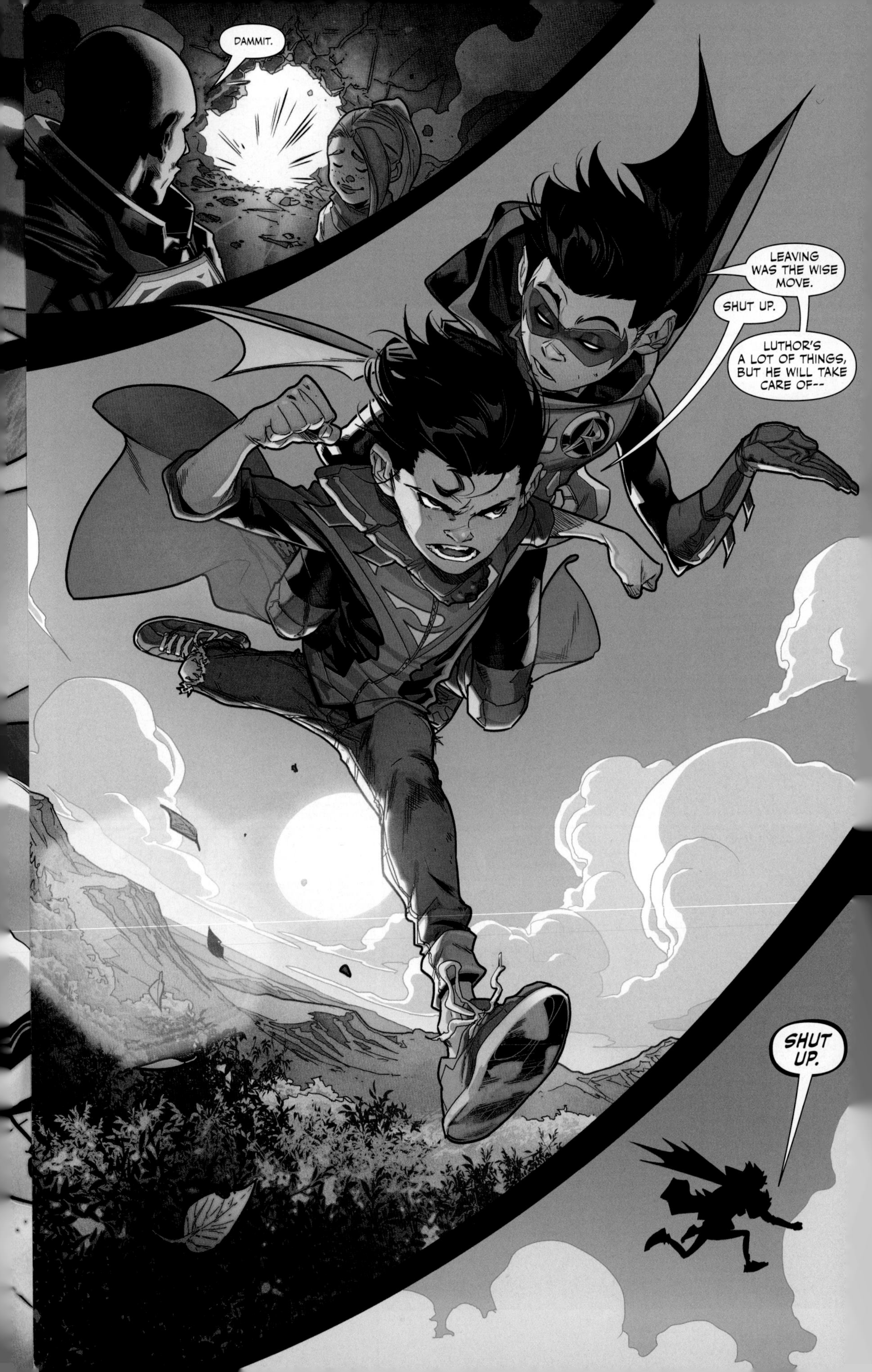
DAMMIT.
LEAVING WAS THE WISE MOVE.
SHUT UP.
LUTHOR'S A LOT OF THINGS, BUT HE WILL TAKE CARE OF--
SHUT UP.

WHAT ABOUT TAKING ME TO GOTHAM?

FIND YOUR OWN WAY HOME.

MY CYCLE WAS DESTROYED IN THE BATTLE.

YOU KNOW, THE ONE WHERE WE SAVED A *FAMILY*.

NONE OF THAT HAD TO HAPPEN-- WE COULD HAVE JUST TOLD OUR DADS AND THEY COULD HAVE HANDLED IT!

WHATEVER, I'LL JUST SEND FOR A NEW ONE REMOTELY. BE HERE IN A MINUTE.

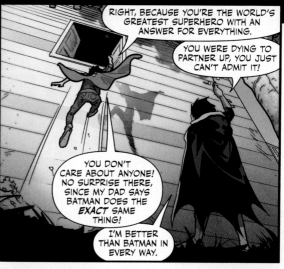

RIGHT, BECAUSE YOU'RE THE WORLD'S GREATEST SUPERHERO WITH AN ANSWER FOR EVERYTHING.

YOU WERE DYING TO PARTNER UP, YOU JUST CAN'T ADMIT IT!

YOU DON'T CARE ABOUT ANYONE! NO SURPRISE THERE, SINCE MY DAD SAYS BATMAN DOES THE *EXACT* SAME THING!

I'M BETTER THAN BATMAN IN EVERY WAY.

NO, YOU'RE NOT. YOU'RE ROBIN, A THIRTEEN-YEAR-OLD KID LIVING IN *HIS* HOUSE AND WORKING OUT OF *HIS* CAVE AND USING ALL *HIS* STUFF.

YOU'RE NOT THE ONE THE BAD GUYS ARE SCARED OF.

IT'S BATMAN.

NOT ROBIN.

NEXT TIME YOU'RE LOOKING FOR A PARTNER, CALL SOMEONE ELSE, 'CAUSE I QUI--

AHEM...

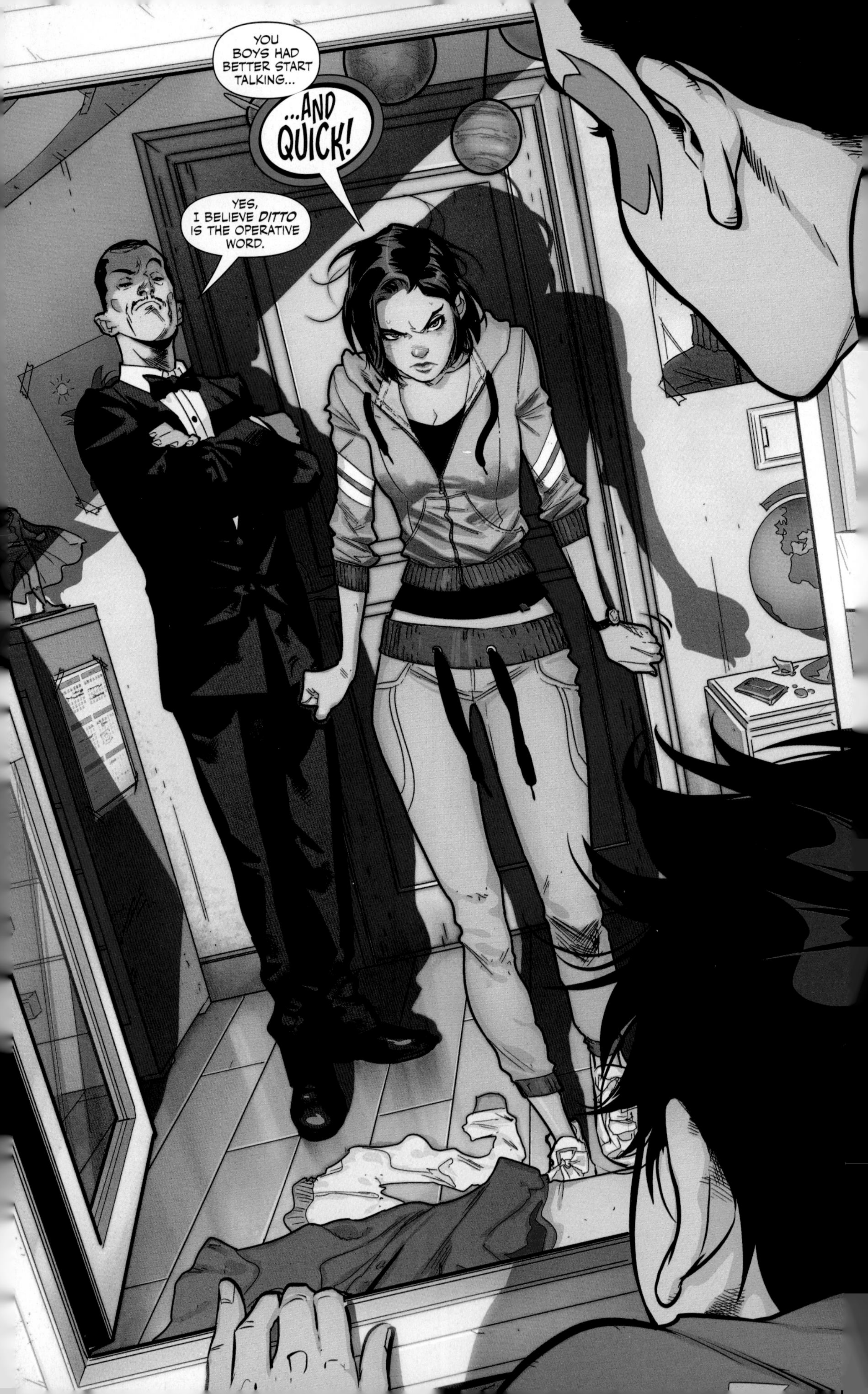
YOU BOYS HAD BETTER START TALKING...
...AND QUICK!
YES, I BELIEVE *DITTO* IS THE OPERATIVE WORD.

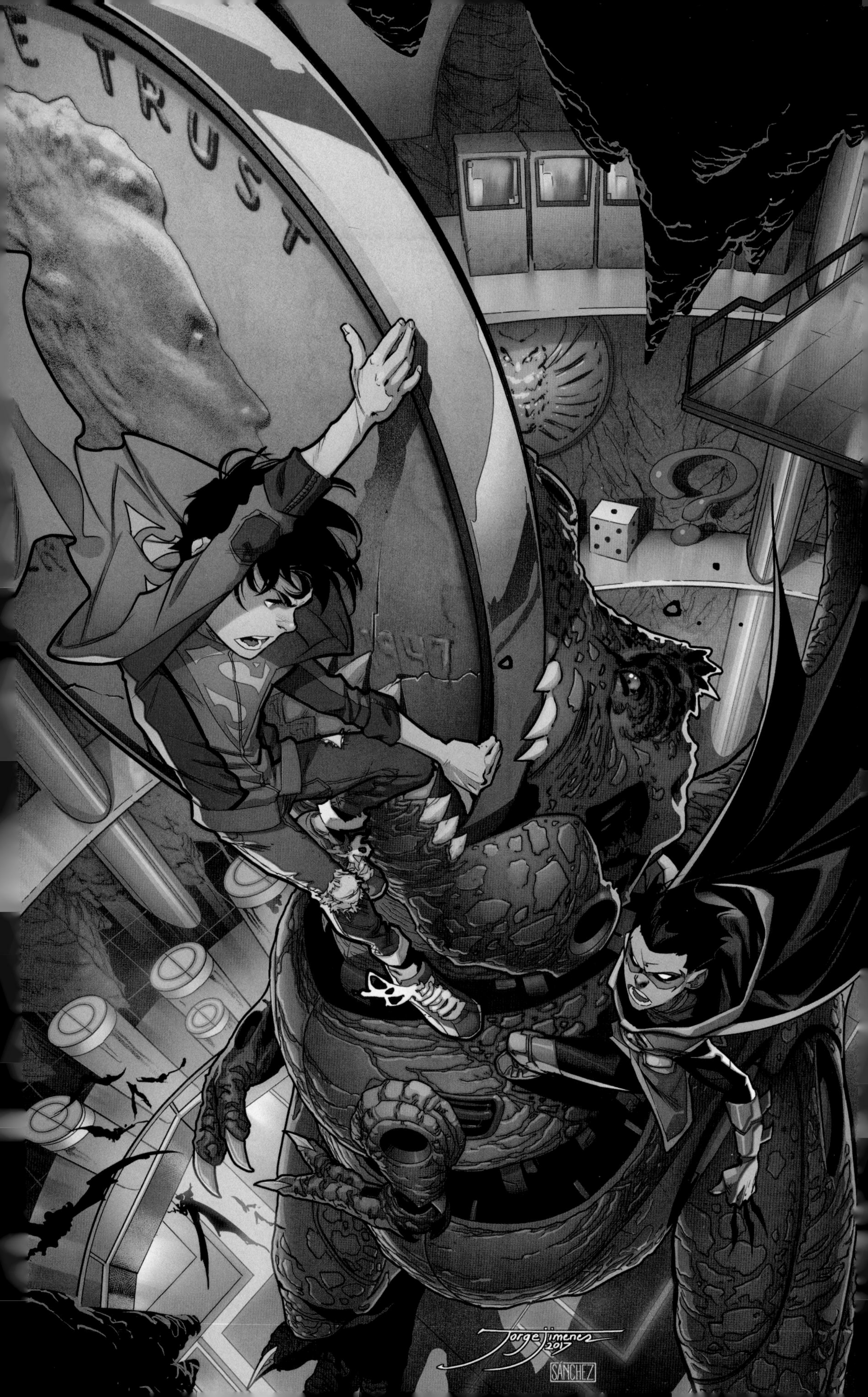
TRUST
Jorge Jimenez 2017
SÁNCHEZ

BATTLE IN THE BATCAVE

ALISSON BORGES artist * HI-FI colorist

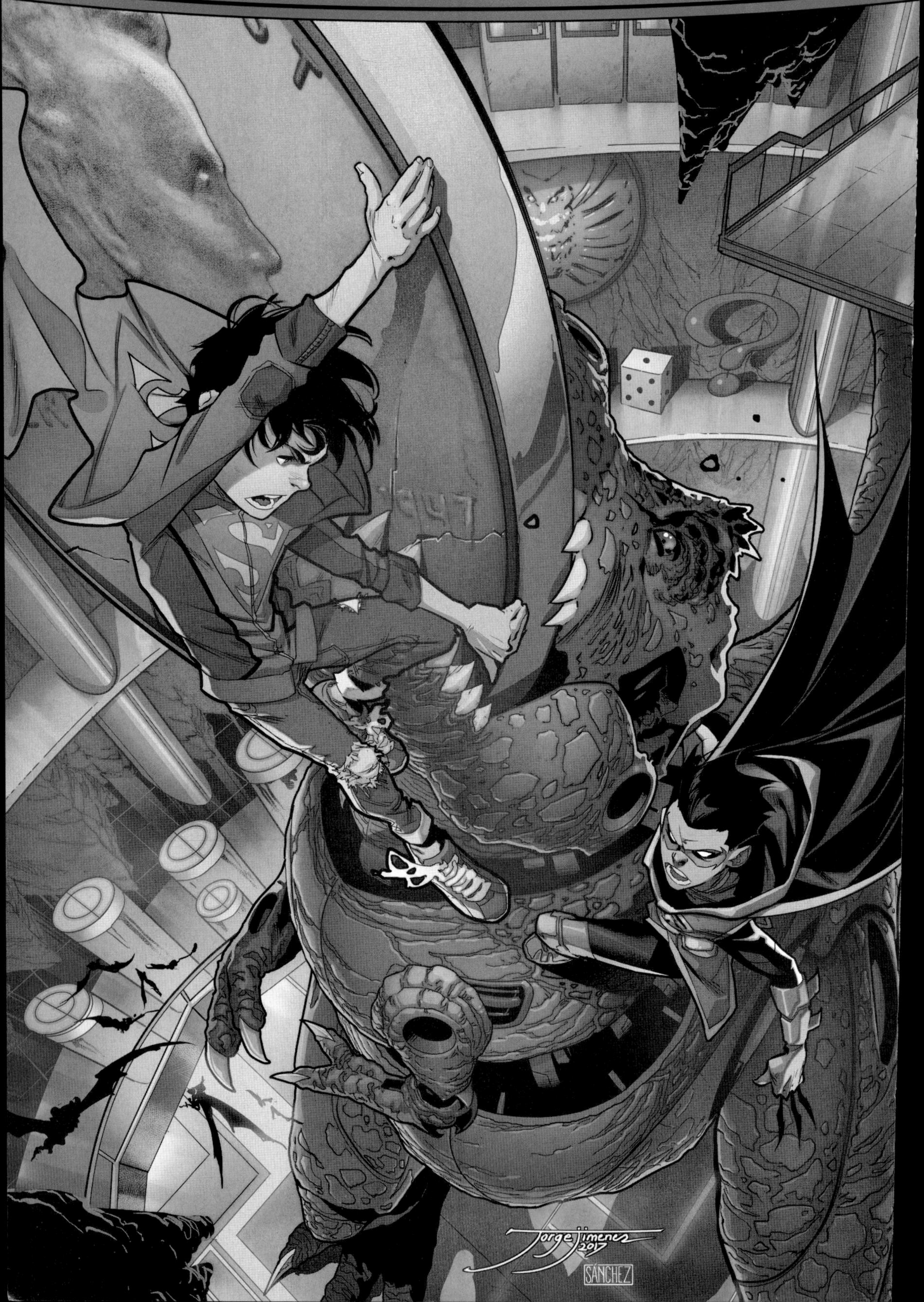
Jorge Jimenez 2017
SÁNCHEZ

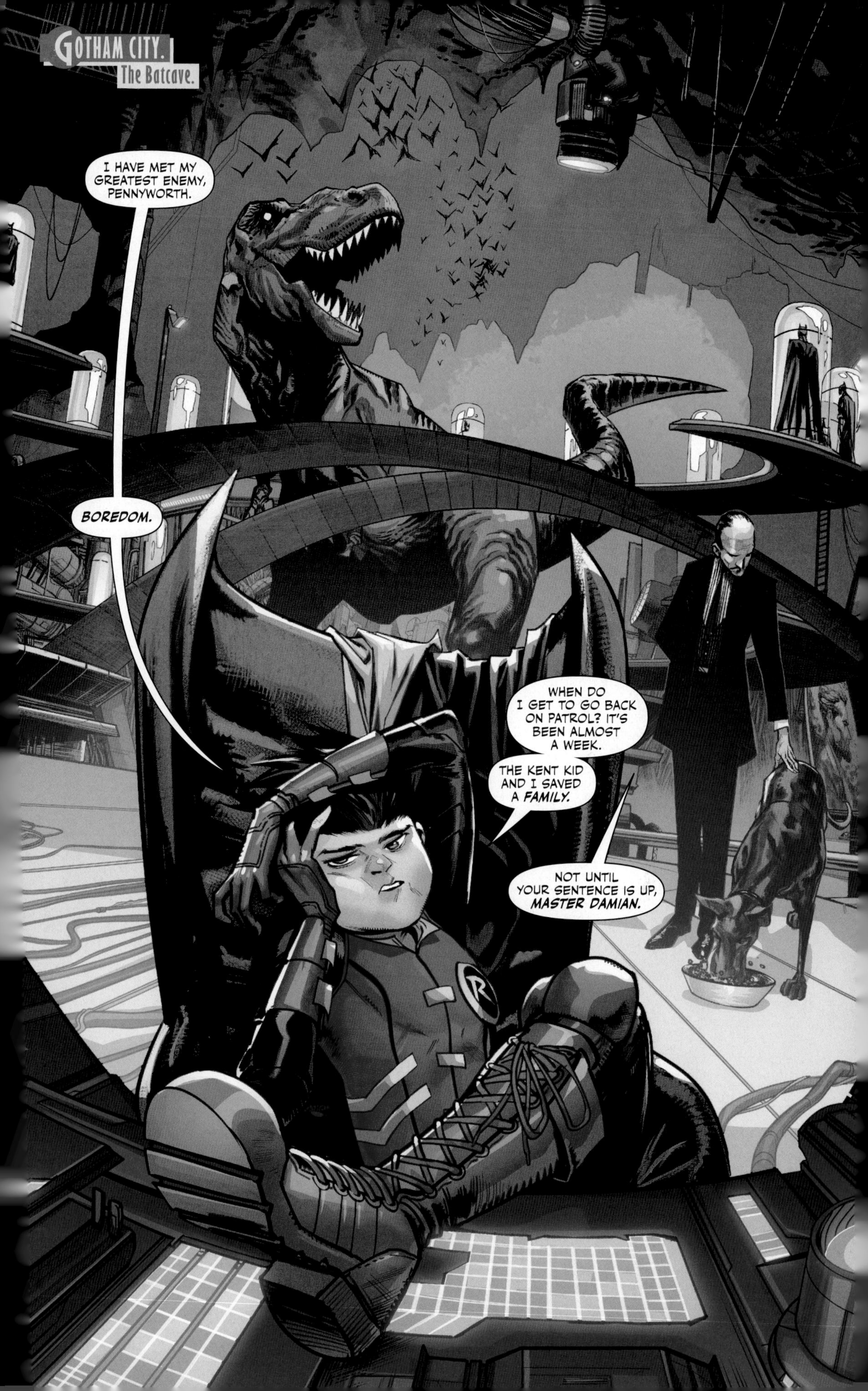
GOTHAM CITY.
The Batcave.
I HAVE MET MY GREATEST ENEMY, PENNYWORTH.
BOREDOM.
WHEN DO I GET TO GO BACK ON PATROL? IT'S BEEN ALMOST A WEEK.
THE KENT KID AND I SAVED A FAMILY.
NOT UNTIL YOUR SENTENCE IS UP, MASTER DAMIAN.

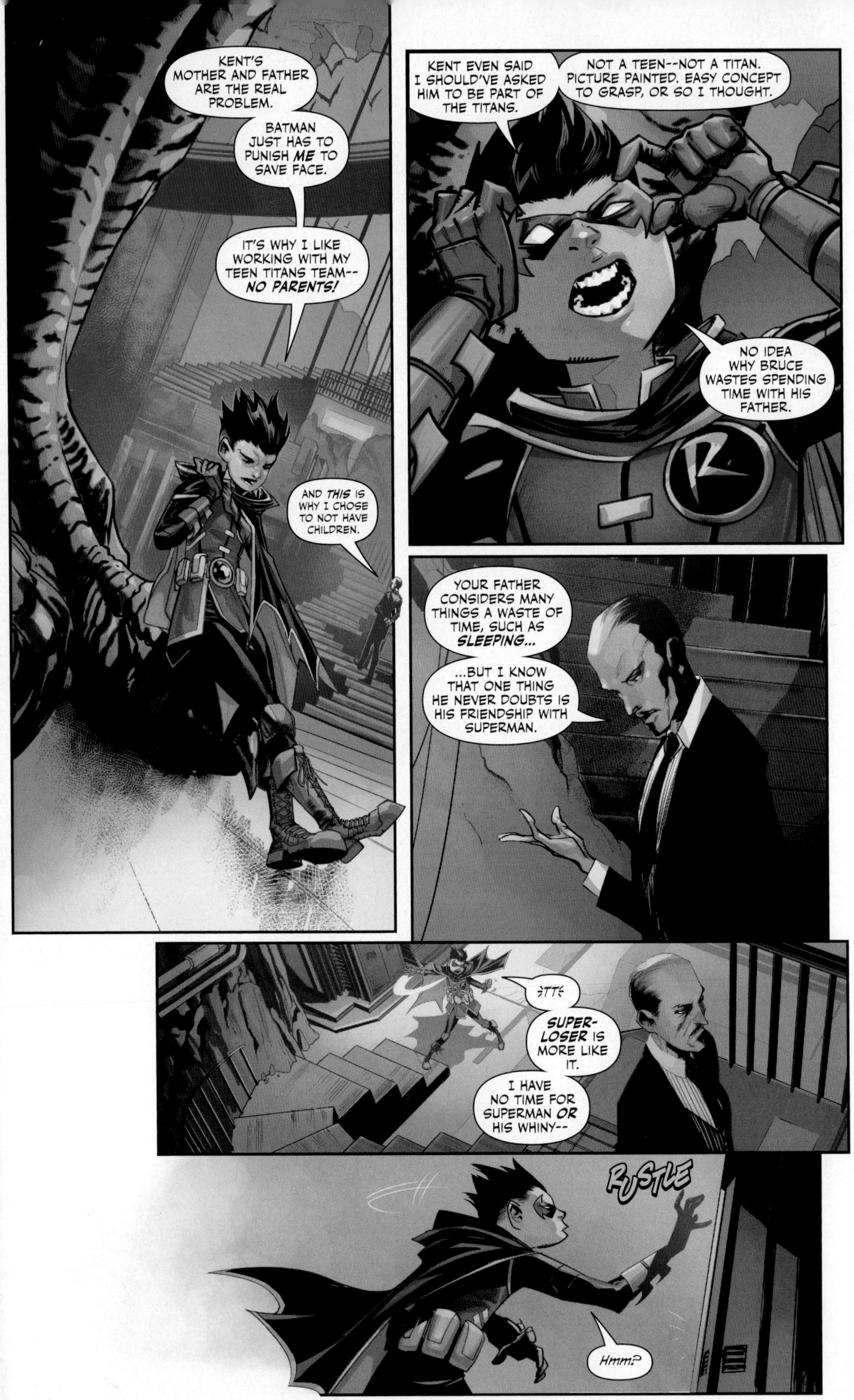
KENT'S MOTHER AND FATHER ARE THE REAL PROBLEM.
BATMAN JUST HAS TO PUNISH ME TO SAVE FACE.
IT'S WHY I LIKE WORKING WITH MY TEEN TITANS TEAM-- NO PARENTS!
AND THIS IS WHY I CHOSE TO NOT HAVE CHILDREN.
KENT EVEN SAID I SHOULD'VE ASKED HIM TO BE PART OF THE TITANS.
NOT A TEEN--NOT A TITAN. PICTURE PAINTED. EASY CONCEPT TO GRASP, OR SO I THOUGHT.
NO IDEA WHY BRUCE WASTES SPENDING TIME WITH HIS FATHER.
YOUR FATHER CONSIDERS MANY THINGS A WASTE OF TIME, SUCH AS SLEEPING...
...BUT I KNOW THAT ONE THING HE NEVER DOUBTS IS HIS FRIENDSHIP WITH SUPERMAN.
TT
SUPER-LOSER IS MORE LIKE IT.
I HAVE NO TIME FOR SUPERMAN OR HIS WHINY--
RUSTLE
Hmm?

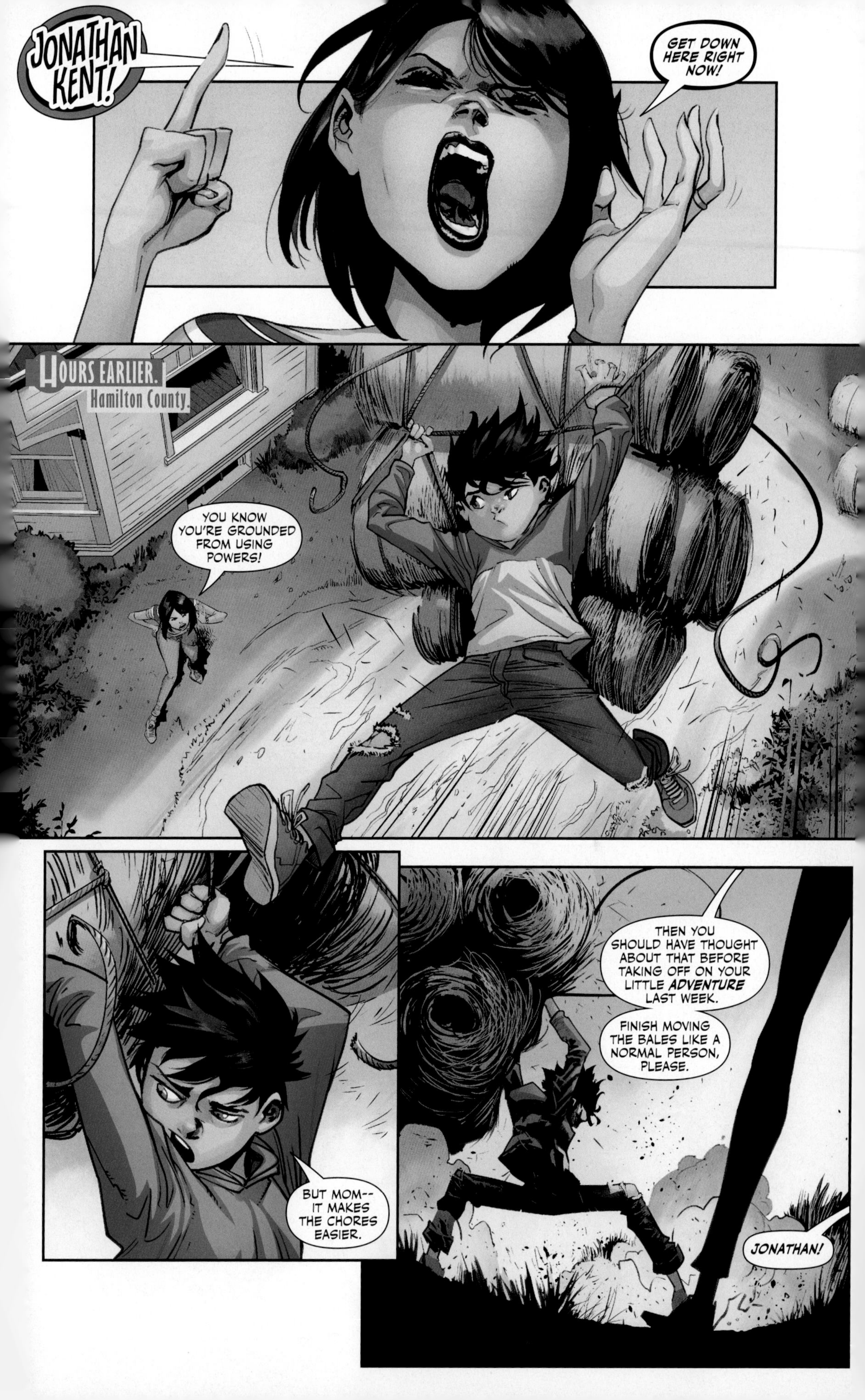
JONATHAN KENT!
GET DOWN HERE RIGHT NOW!
HOURS EARLIER.
Hamilton County.
YOU KNOW YOU'RE GROUNDED FROM USING POWERS!
BUT MOM-- IT MAKES THE CHORES EASIER.
THEN YOU SHOULD HAVE THOUGHT ABOUT THAT BEFORE TAKING OFF ON YOUR LITTLE ADVENTURE LAST WEEK.
FINISH MOVING THE BALES LIKE A NORMAL PERSON, PLEASE.
JONATHAN!

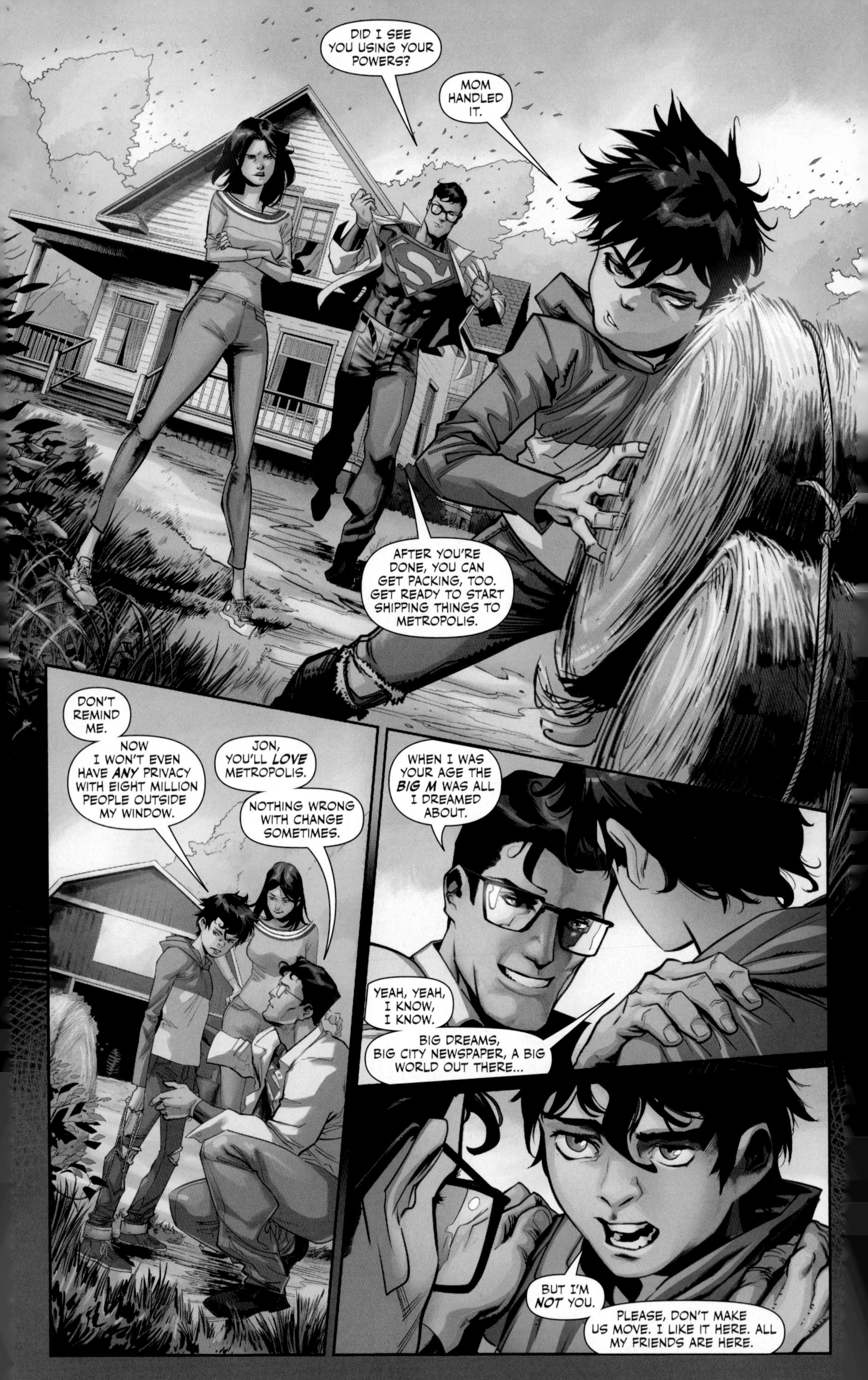
DID I SEE YOU USING YOUR POWERS?
MOM HANDLED IT.
AFTER YOU'RE DONE, YOU CAN GET PACKING, TOO. GET READY TO START SHIPPING THINGS TO METROPOLIS.
DON'T REMIND ME.
NOW I WON'T EVEN HAVE ANY PRIVACY WITH EIGHT MILLION PEOPLE OUTSIDE MY WINDOW.
JON, YOU'LL LOVE METROPOLIS.
NOTHING WRONG WITH CHANGE SOMETIMES.
WHEN I WAS YOUR AGE THE BIG M WAS ALL I DREAMED ABOUT.
YEAH, YEAH, I KNOW, I KNOW.
BIG DREAMS, BIG CITY NEWSPAPER, A BIG WORLD OUT THERE...
BUT I'M NOT YOU.
PLEASE, DON'T MAKE US MOVE. I LIKE IT HERE. ALL MY FRIENDS ARE HERE.

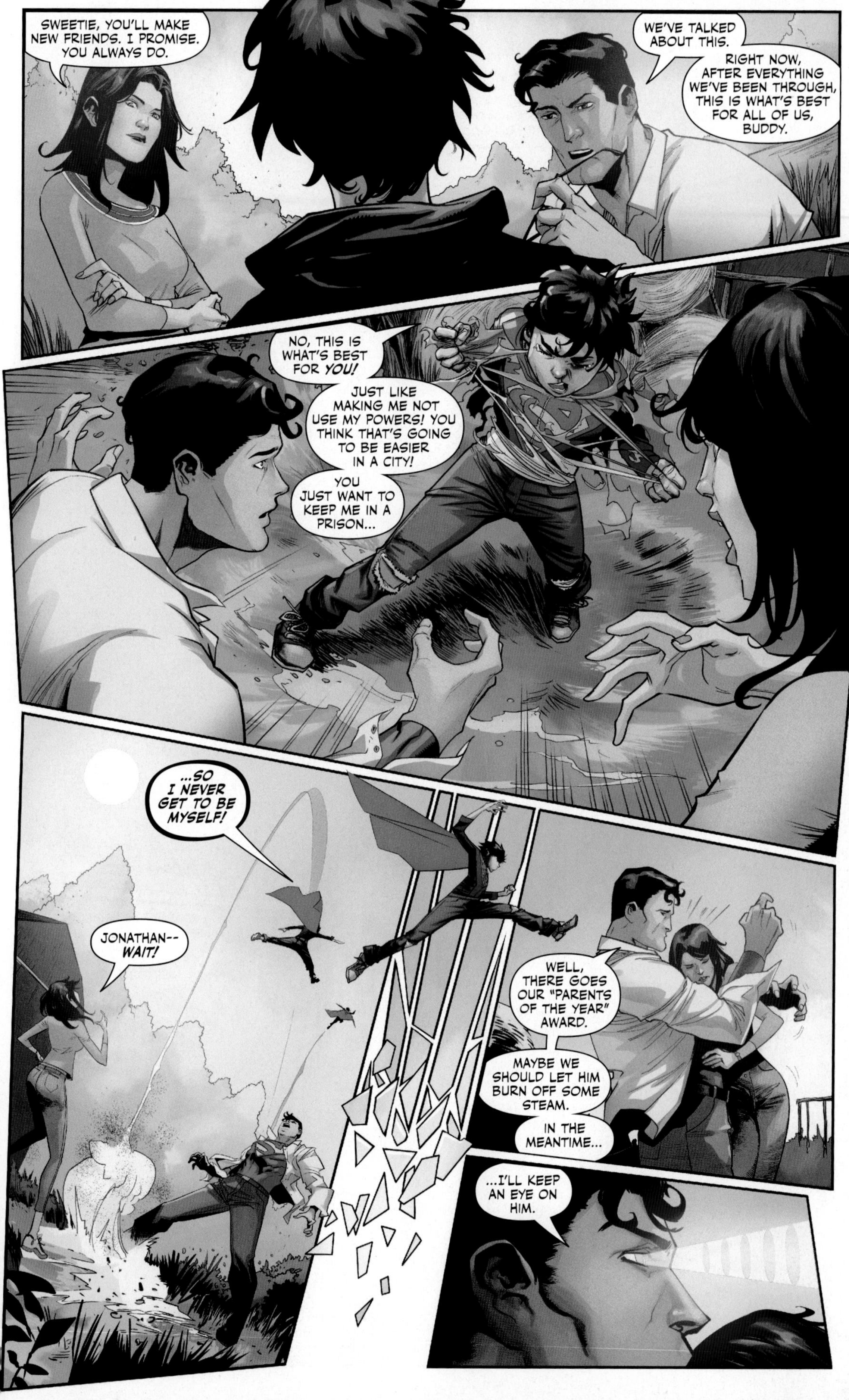
SWEETIE, YOU'LL MAKE NEW FRIENDS. I PROMISE. YOU ALWAYS DO.
WE'VE TALKED ABOUT THIS.
RIGHT NOW, AFTER EVERYTHING WE'VE BEEN THROUGH, THIS IS WHAT'S BEST FOR ALL OF US, BUDDY.
NO, THIS IS WHAT'S BEST FOR *YOU!*
JUST LIKE MAKING ME NOT USE MY POWERS! YOU THINK THAT'S GOING TO BE EASIER IN A CITY!
YOU JUST WANT TO KEEP ME IN A PRISON...
...SO I NEVER GET TO BE MYSELF!
JONATHAN-- *WAIT!*
WELL, THERE GOES OUR "PARENTS OF THE YEAR" AWARD.
MAYBE WE SHOULD LET HIM BURN OFF SOME STEAM.
IN THE MEANTIME...
...I'LL KEEP AN EYE ON HIM.

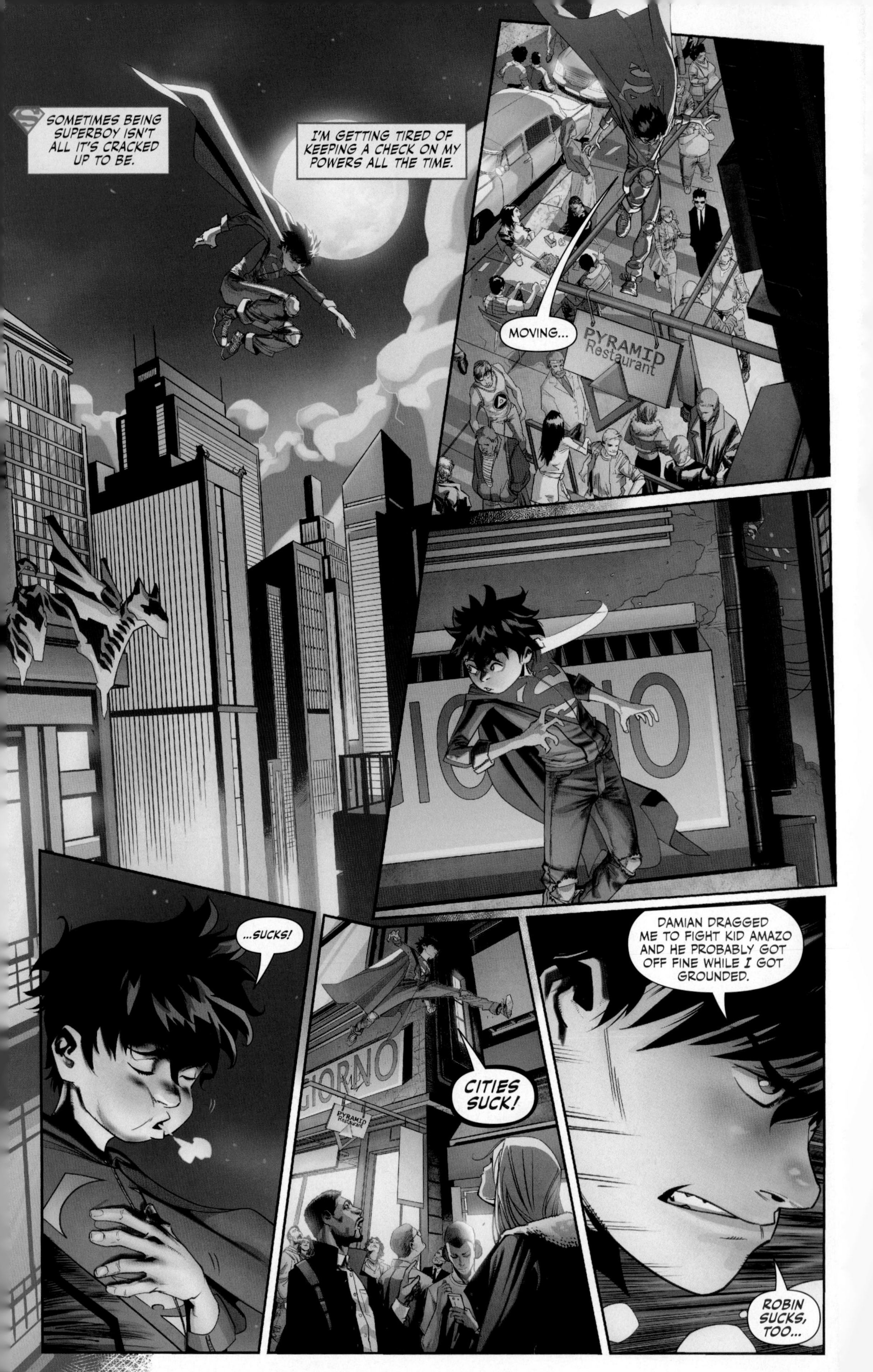
SOMETIMES BEING SUPERBOY ISN'T ALL IT'S CRACKED UP TO BE.
I'M GETTING TIRED OF KEEPING A CHECK ON MY POWERS ALL THE TIME.
MOVING...
PYRAMID Restaurant
...SUCKS!
CITIES SUCK!
DAMIAN DRAGGED ME TO FIGHT KID AMAZO AND HE PROBABLY GOT OFF FINE WHILE I GOT GROUNDED.
ROBIN SUCKS, TOO...

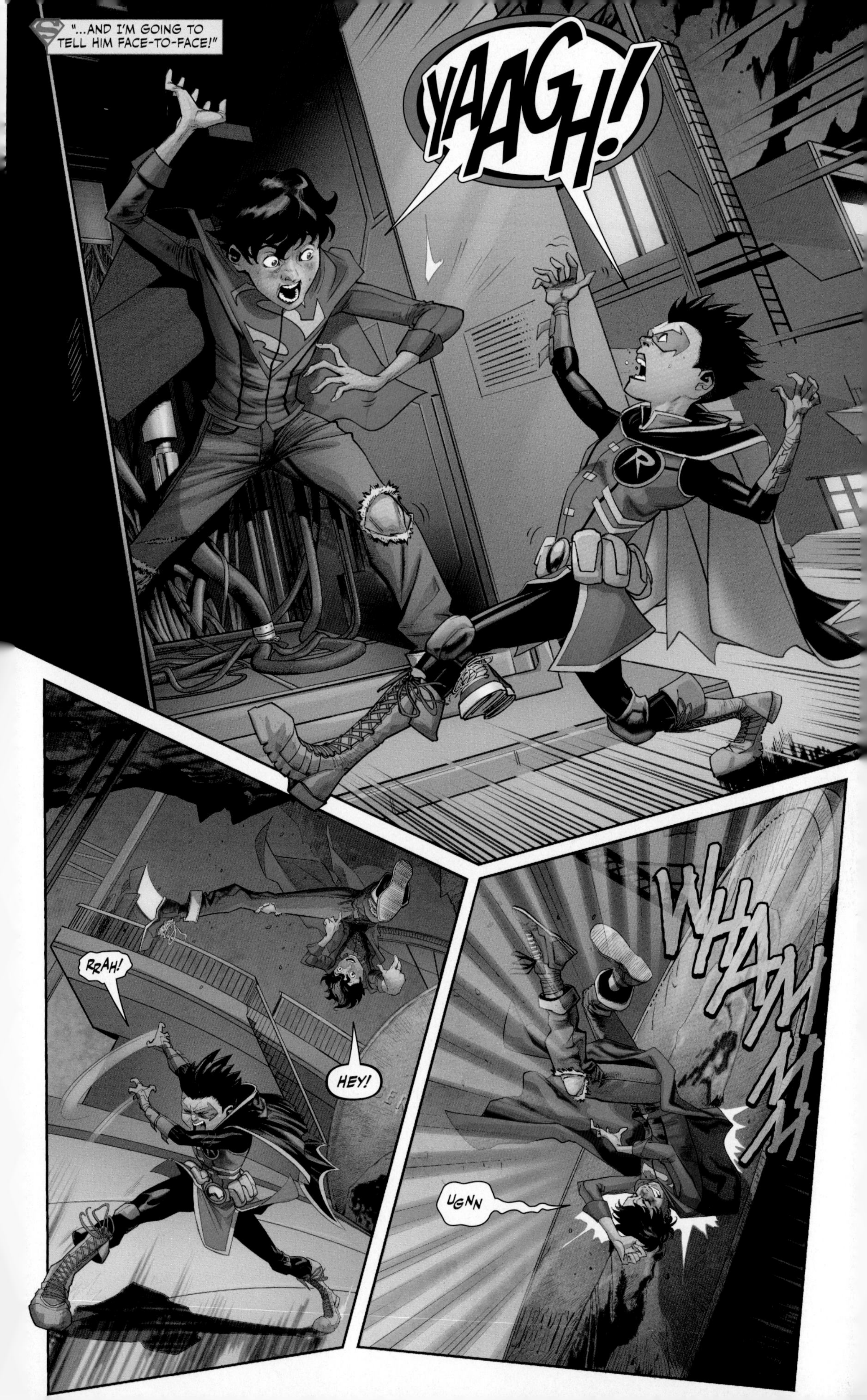
"...AND I'M GOING TO TELL HIM FACE-TO-FACE!"
YAAGH!
RRAH!
HEY!
WHAMM
UGNN

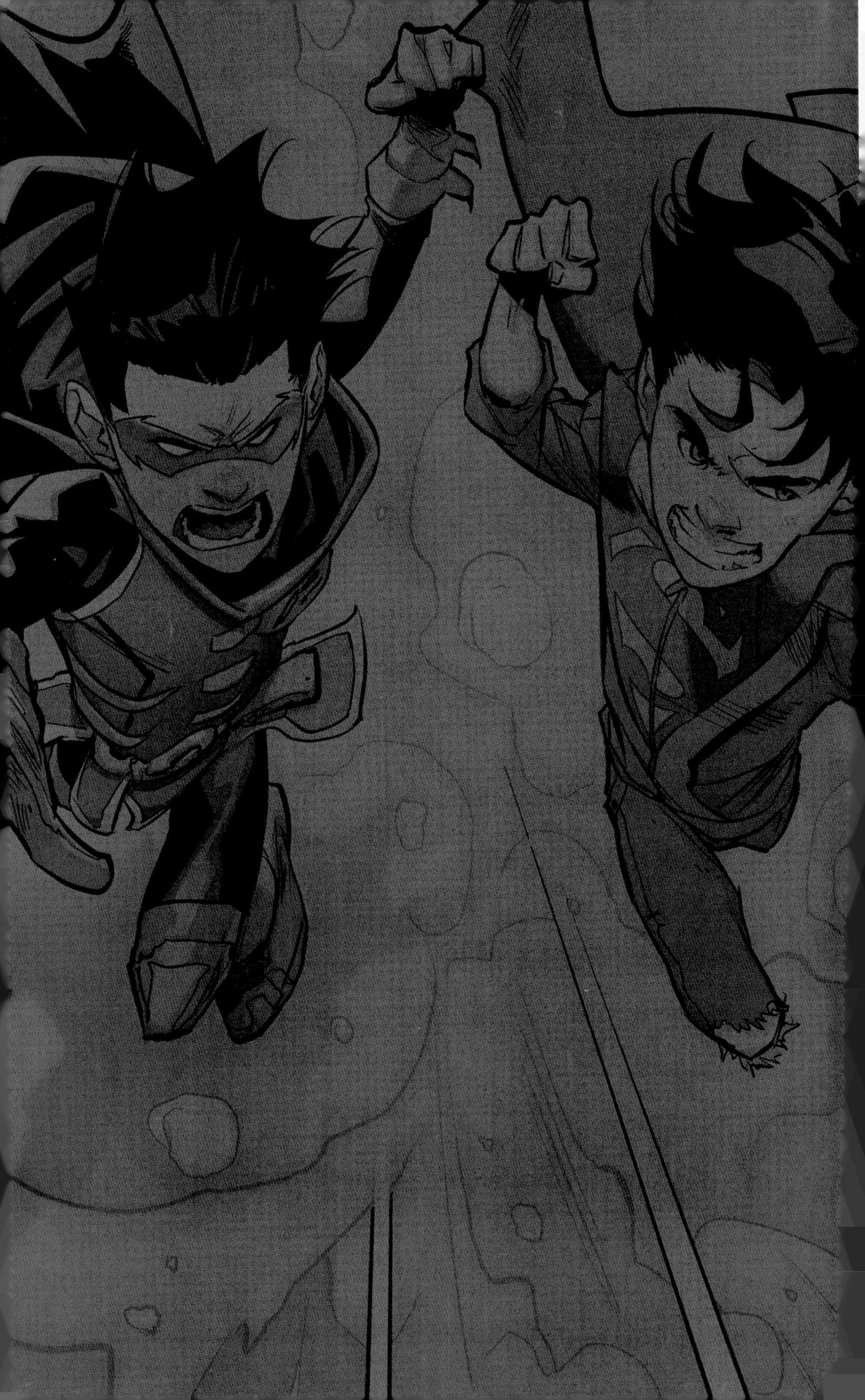

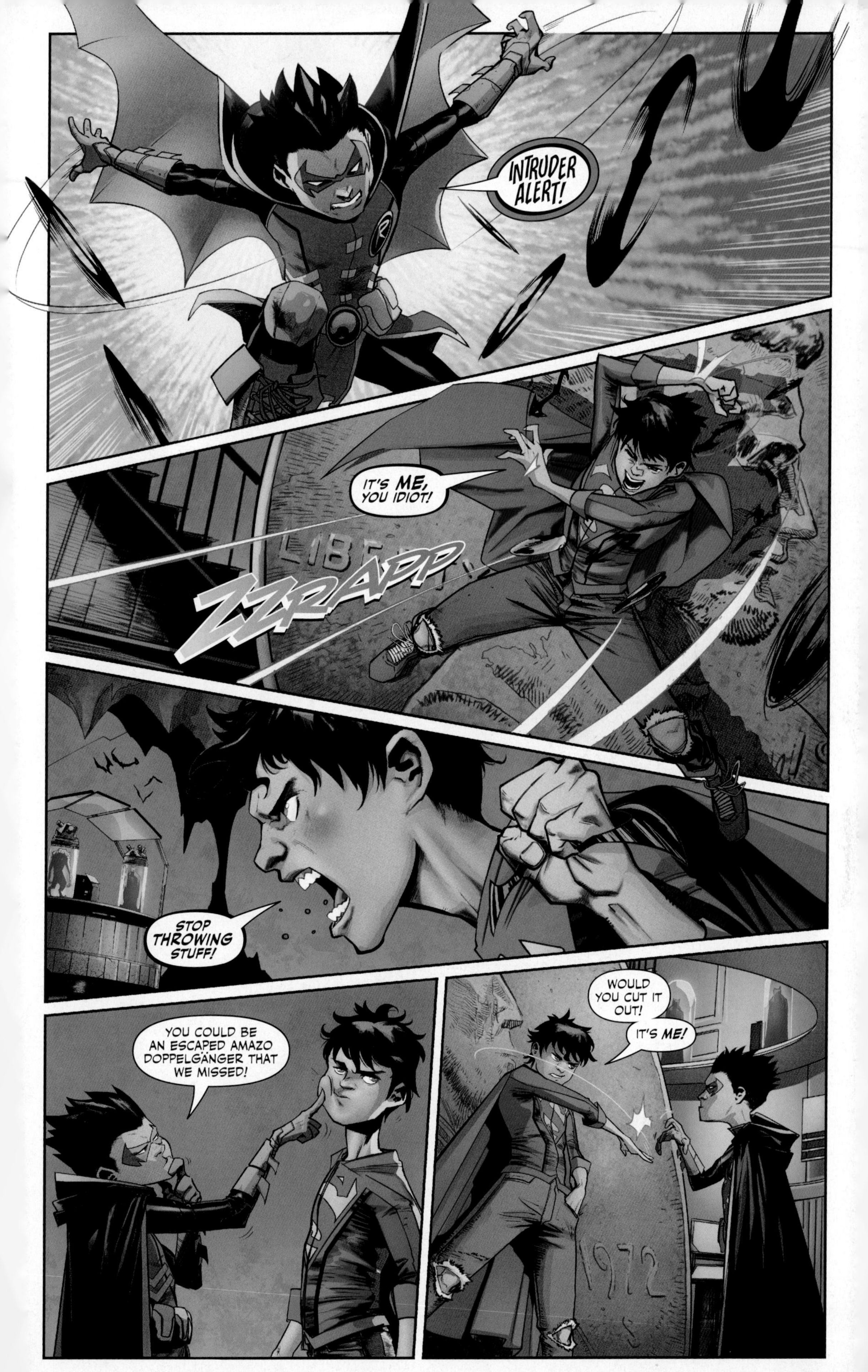
INTRUDER ALERT!
IT'S ME, YOU IDIOT!
ZZRAPP
STOP THROWING STUFF!
YOU COULD BE AN ESCAPED AMAZO DOPPELGÄNGER THAT WE MISSED!
WOULD YOU CUT IT OUT!
IT'S ME!

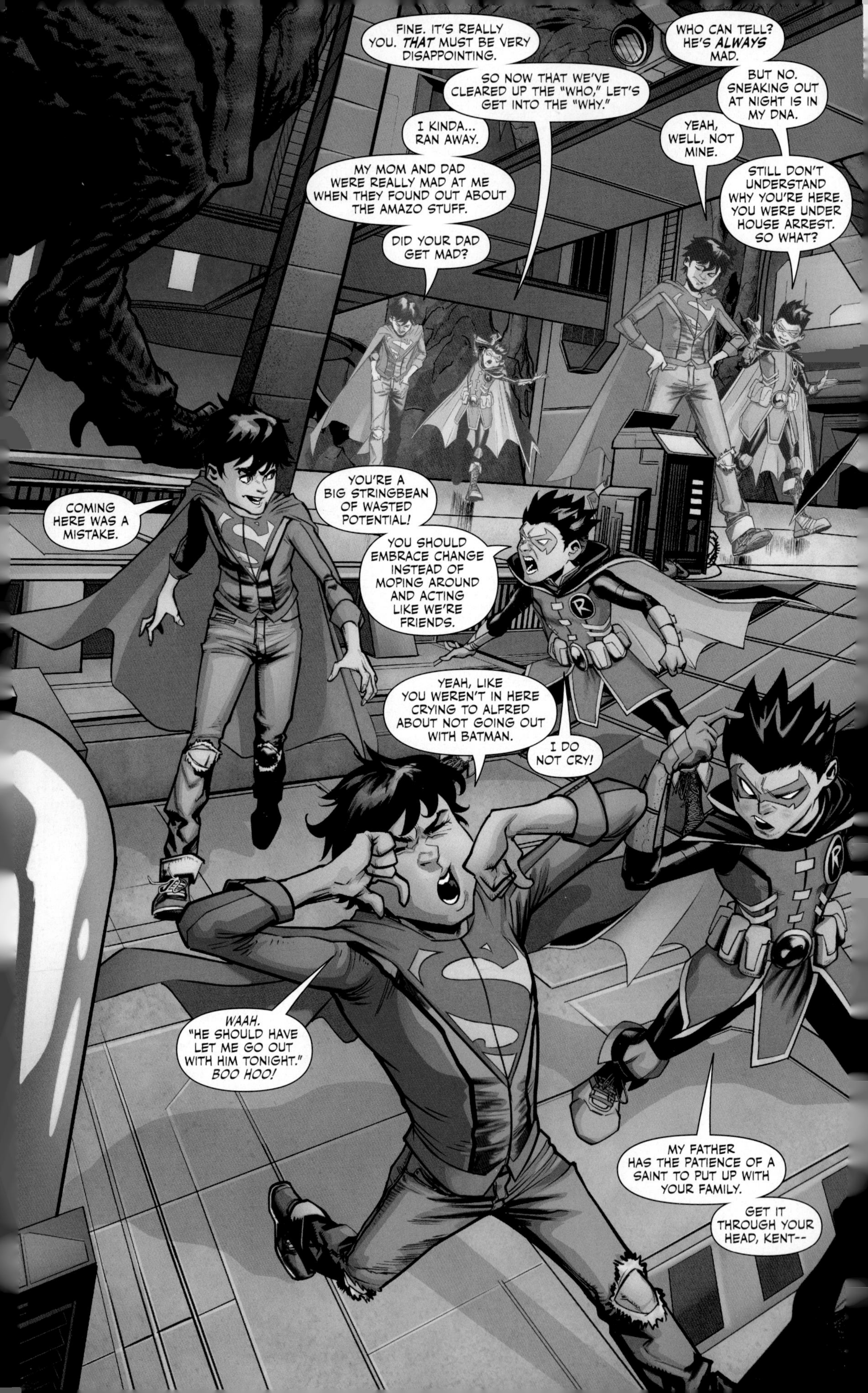
FINE. IT'S REALLY YOU. *THAT* MUST BE VERY DISAPPOINTING.
WHO CAN TELL? HE'S *ALWAYS* MAD.
SO NOW THAT WE'VE CLEARED UP THE "WHO," LET'S GET INTO THE "WHY."
I KINDA... RAN AWAY.
MY MOM AND DAD WERE REALLY MAD AT ME WHEN THEY FOUND OUT ABOUT THE AMAZO STUFF.
DID YOUR DAD GET MAD?
BUT NO. SNEAKING OUT AT NIGHT IS IN MY DNA.
YEAH, WELL, NOT MINE.
STILL DON'T UNDERSTAND WHY YOU'RE HERE. YOU WERE UNDER HOUSE ARREST. SO WHAT?
COMING HERE WAS A MISTAKE.
YOU'RE A BIG STRINGBEAN OF WASTED POTENTIAL!
YOU SHOULD EMBRACE CHANGE INSTEAD OF MOPING AROUND AND ACTING LIKE WE'RE FRIENDS.
YEAH, LIKE YOU WEREN'T IN HERE CRYING TO ALFRED ABOUT NOT GOING OUT WITH BATMAN.
I DO NOT CRY!
WAAH. "HE SHOULD HAVE LET ME GO OUT WITH HIM TONIGHT." *BOO HOO!*
MY FATHER HAS THE PATIENCE OF A SAINT TO PUT UP WITH YOUR FAMILY.
GET IT THROUGH YOUR HEAD, KENT--

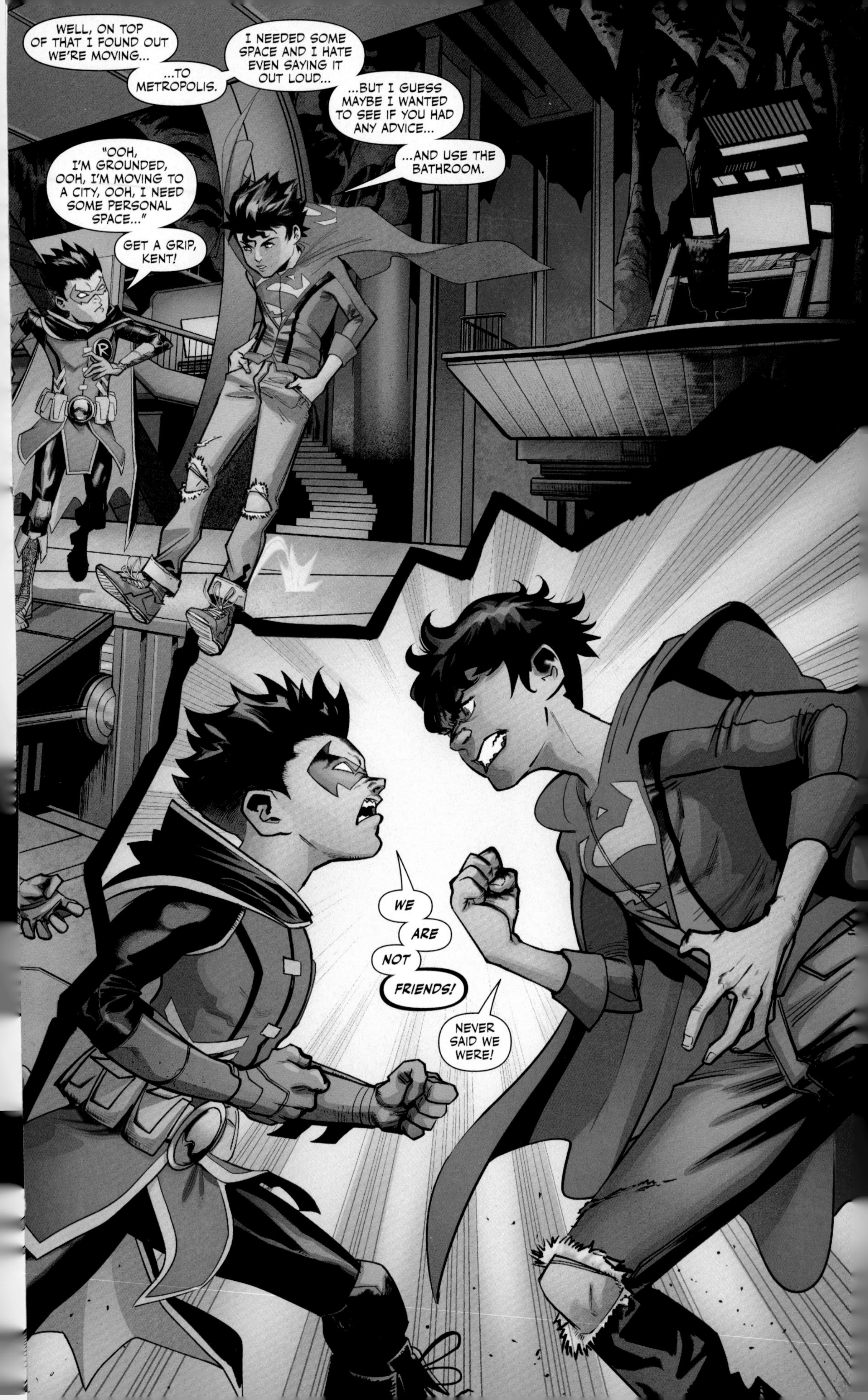
WELL, ON TOP OF THAT I FOUND OUT WE'RE MOVING...
...TO METROPOLIS.
I NEEDED SOME SPACE AND I HATE EVEN SAYING IT OUT LOUD...
...BUT I GUESS MAYBE I WANTED TO SEE IF YOU HAD ANY ADVICE...
...AND USE THE BATHROOM.
"OOH, I'M GROUNDED, OOH, I'M MOVING TO A CITY, OOH, I NEED SOME PERSONAL SPACE..."
GET A GRIP, KENT!
WE ARE NOT FRIENDS!
NEVER SAID WE WERE!

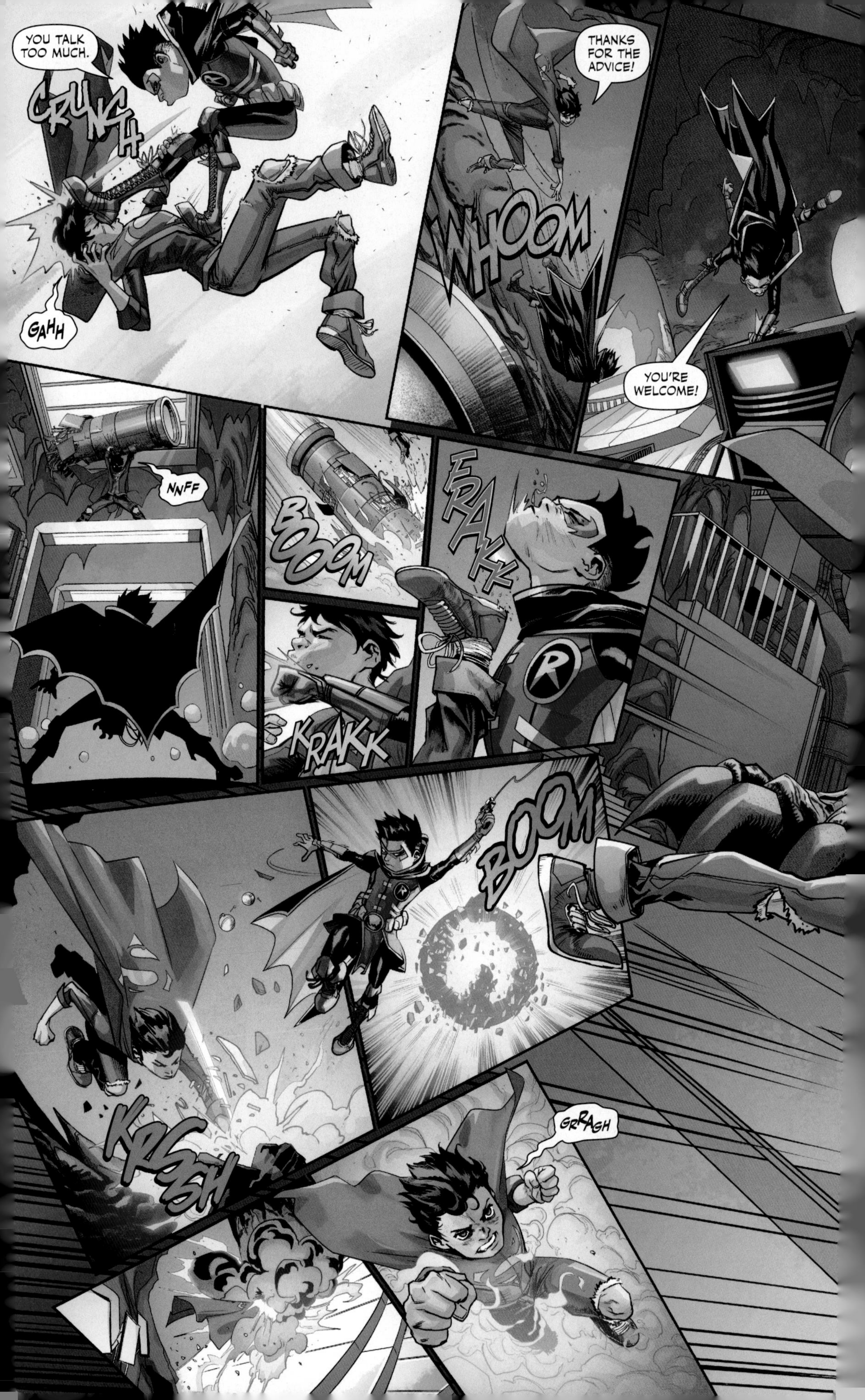
YOU TALK TOO MUCH.
CRUNCH
GAHH
THANKS FOR THE ADVICE!
WHOOM
YOU'RE WELCOME!
NNFF
BOOOOM
FRAKK
KRAKK
BOOM
KRSSH
GRRAGH

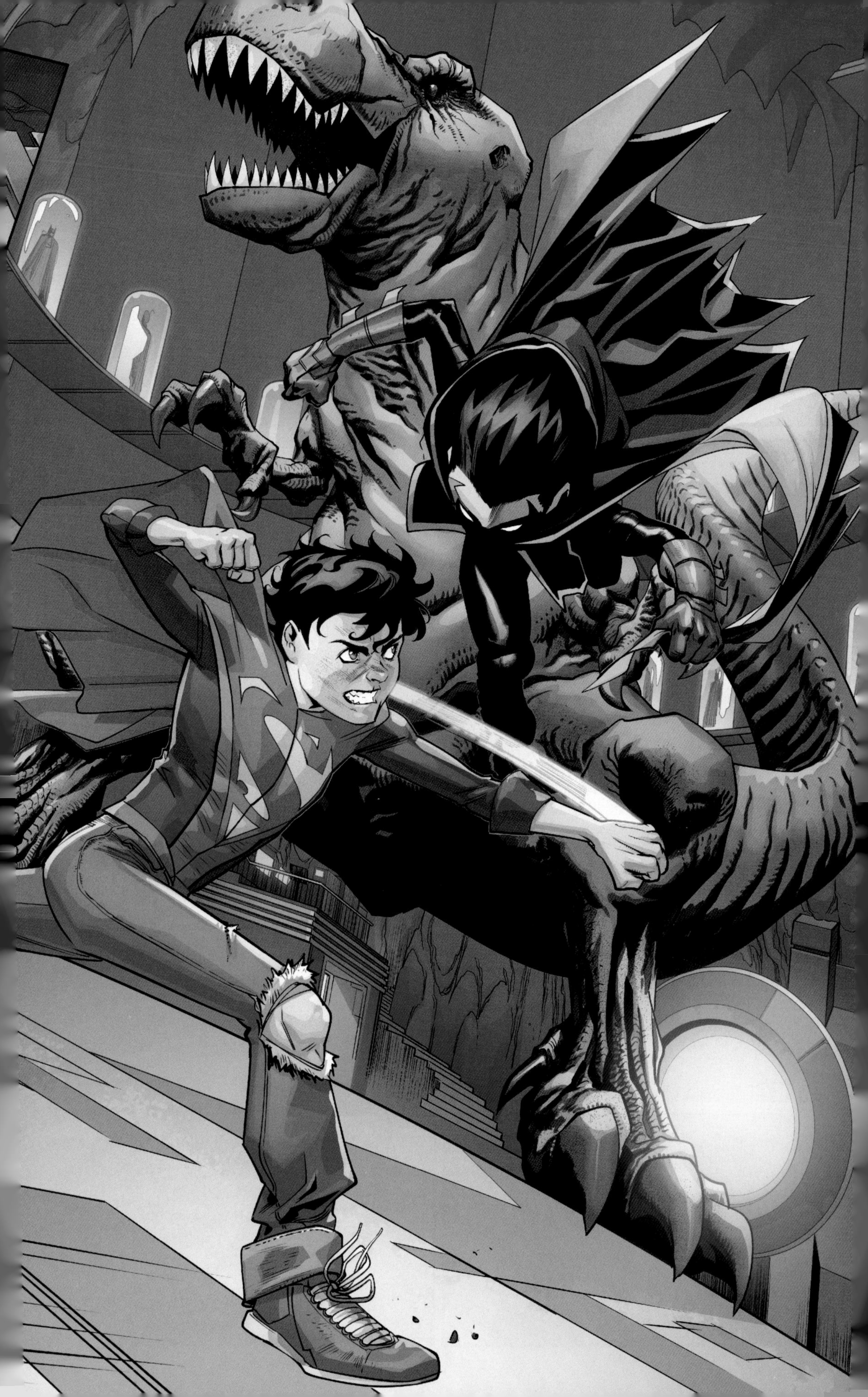

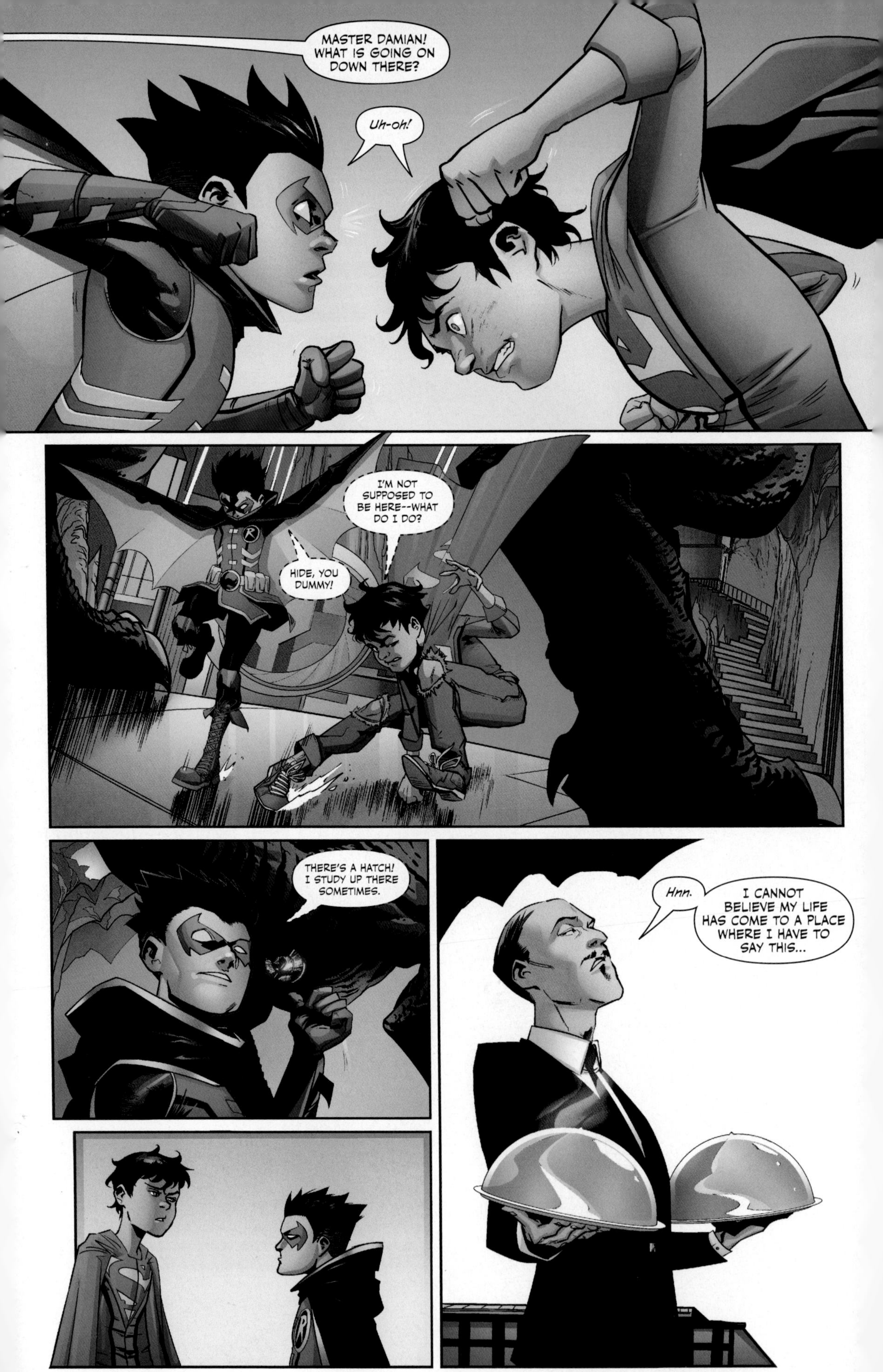
MASTER DAMIAN! WHAT IS GOING ON DOWN THERE?
Uh-oh!
I'M NOT SUPPOSED TO BE HERE--WHAT DO I DO?
HIDE, YOU DUMMY!
THERE'S A HATCH! I STUDY UP THERE SOMETIMES.
Hnn.
I CANNOT BELIEVE MY LIFE HAS COME TO A PLACE WHERE I HAVE TO SAY THIS...

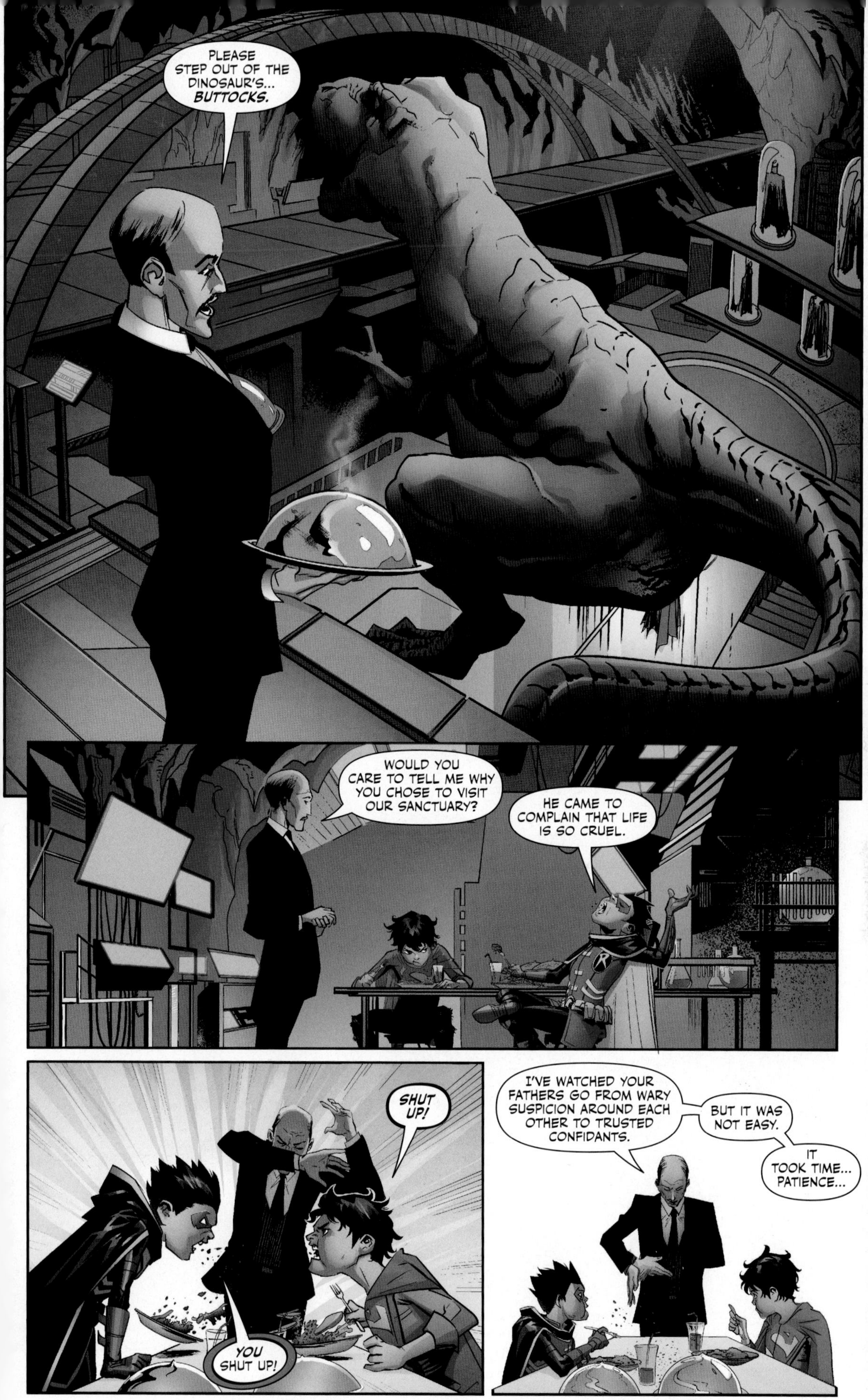
PLEASE STEP OUT OF THE DINOSAUR'S... BUTTOCKS.
WOULD YOU CARE TO TELL ME WHY YOU CHOSE TO VISIT OUR SANCTUARY?
HE CAME TO COMPLAIN THAT LIFE IS SO CRUEL.
SHUT UP!
YOU SHUT UP!
I'VE WATCHED YOUR FATHERS GO FROM WARY SUSPICION AROUND EACH OTHER TO TRUSTED CONFIDANTS.
BUT IT WAS NOT EASY.
IT TOOK TIME... PATIENCE...

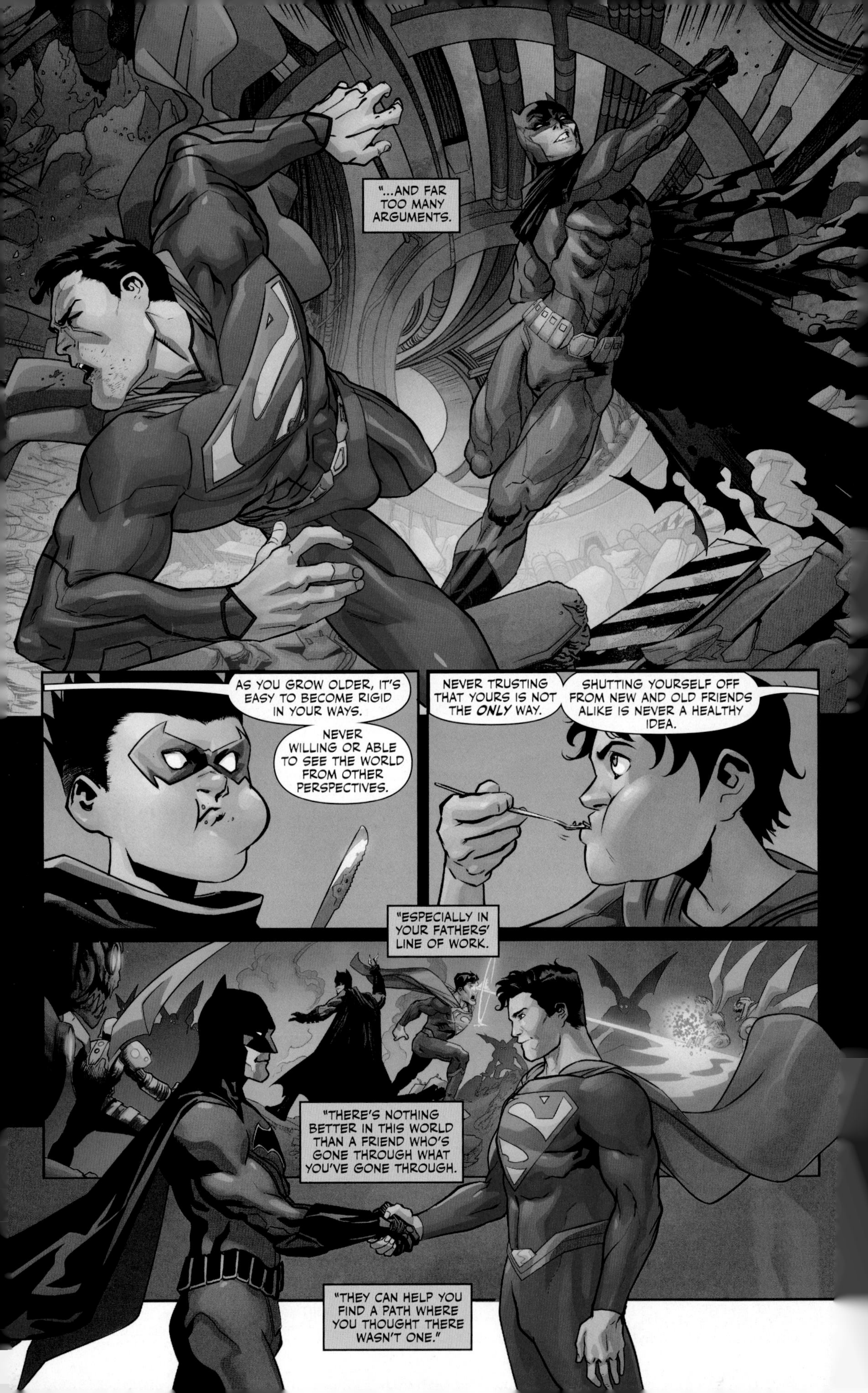
"...AND FAR TOO MANY ARGUMENTS.
AS YOU GROW OLDER, IT'S EASY TO BECOME RIGID IN YOUR WAYS.
NEVER WILLING OR ABLE TO SEE THE WORLD FROM OTHER PERSPECTIVES.
NEVER TRUSTING THAT YOURS IS NOT THE *ONLY* WAY.
SHUTTING YOURSELF OFF FROM NEW AND OLD FRIENDS ALIKE IS NEVER A HEALTHY IDEA.
"ESPECIALLY IN YOUR FATHERS' LINE OF WORK.
"THERE'S NOTHING BETTER IN THIS WORLD THAN A FRIEND WHO'S GONE THROUGH WHAT YOU'VE GONE THROUGH.
"THEY CAN HELP YOU FIND A PATH WHERE YOU THOUGHT THERE WASN'T ONE."

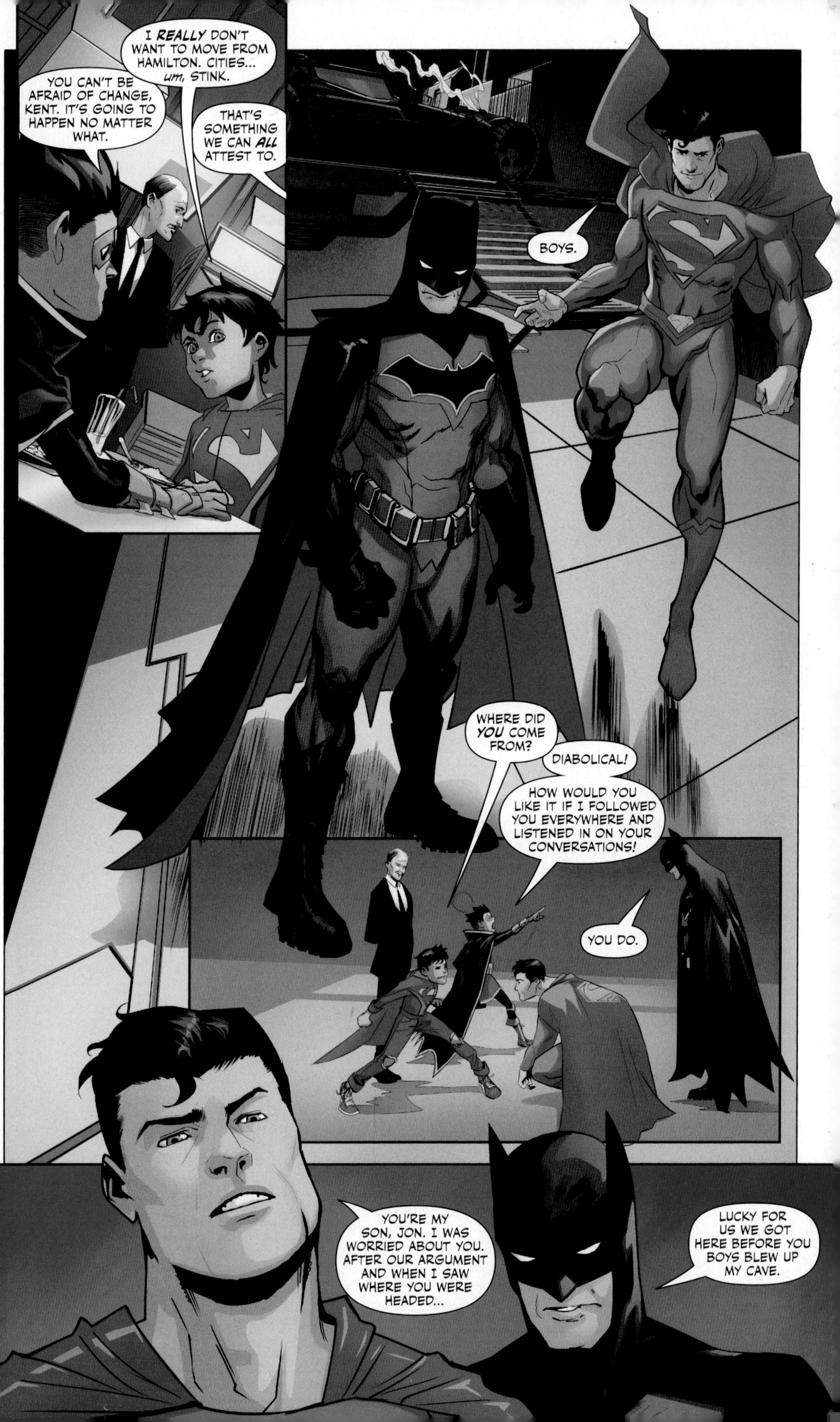
I REALLY DON'T WANT TO MOVE FROM HAMILTON. CITIES... UM, STINK.
YOU CAN'T BE AFRAID OF CHANGE, KENT. IT'S GOING TO HAPPEN NO MATTER WHAT.
THAT'S SOMETHING WE CAN ALL ATTEST TO.
BOYS.
WHERE DID YOU COME FROM?
DIABOLICAL!
HOW WOULD YOU LIKE IT IF I FOLLOWED YOU EVERYWHERE AND LISTENED IN ON YOUR CONVERSATIONS!
YOU DO.
YOU'RE MY SON, JON. I WAS WORRIED ABOUT YOU. AFTER OUR ARGUMENT AND WHEN I SAW WHERE YOU WERE HEADED...
LUCKY FOR US WE GOT HERE BEFORE YOU BOYS BLEW UP MY CAVE.

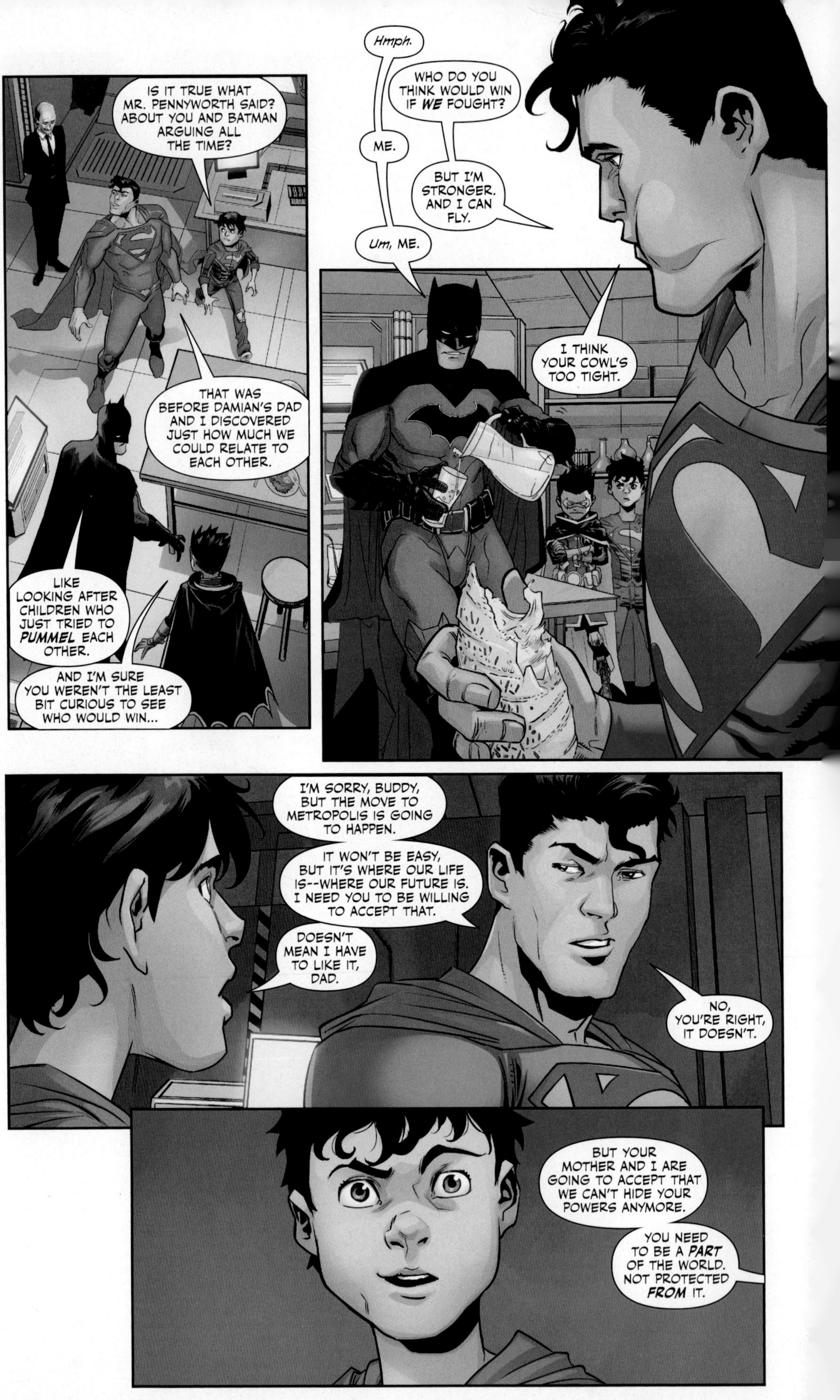
IS IT TRUE WHAT MR. PENNYWORTH SAID? ABOUT YOU AND BATMAN ARGUING ALL THE TIME?
THAT WAS BEFORE DAMIAN'S DAD AND I DISCOVERED JUST HOW MUCH WE COULD RELATE TO EACH OTHER.
LIKE LOOKING AFTER CHILDREN WHO JUST TRIED TO PUMMEL EACH OTHER.
AND I'M SURE YOU WEREN'T THE LEAST BIT CURIOUS TO SEE WHO WOULD WIN...
Hmph.
WHO DO YOU THINK WOULD WIN IF WE FOUGHT?
ME.
BUT I'M STRONGER. AND I CAN FLY.
Um, ME.
I THINK YOUR COWL'S TOO TIGHT.
I'M SORRY, BUDDY, BUT THE MOVE TO METROPOLIS IS GOING TO HAPPEN.
IT WON'T BE EASY, BUT IT'S WHERE OUR LIFE IS--WHERE OUR FUTURE IS. I NEED YOU TO BE WILLING TO ACCEPT THAT.
DOESN'T MEAN I HAVE TO LIKE IT, DAD.
NO, YOU'RE RIGHT, IT DOESN'T.
BUT YOUR MOTHER AND I ARE GOING TO ACCEPT THAT WE CAN'T HIDE YOUR POWERS ANYMORE.
YOU NEED TO BE A PART OF THE WORLD. NOT PROTECTED FROM IT.

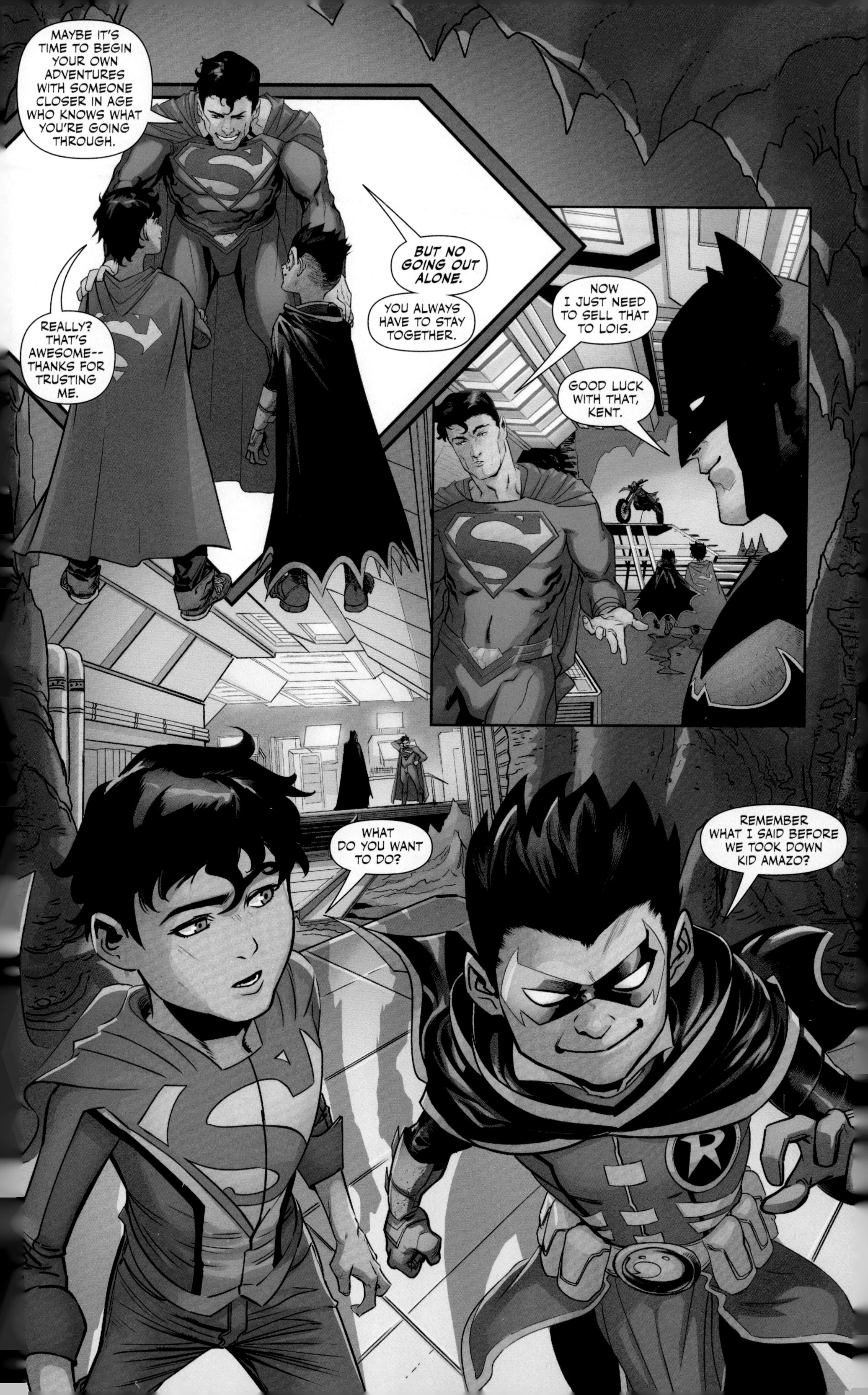
MAYBE IT'S TIME TO BEGIN YOUR OWN ADVENTURES WITH SOMEONE CLOSER IN AGE WHO KNOWS WHAT YOU'RE GOING THROUGH.
REALLY? THAT'S AWESOME-- THANKS FOR TRUSTING ME.
BUT NO GOING OUT ALONE.
YOU ALWAYS HAVE TO STAY TOGETHER.
NOW I JUST NEED TO SELL THAT TO LOIS.
GOOD LUCK WITH THAT, KENT.
WHAT DO YOU WANT TO DO?
REMEMBER WHAT I SAID BEFORE WE TOOK DOWN KID AMAZO?

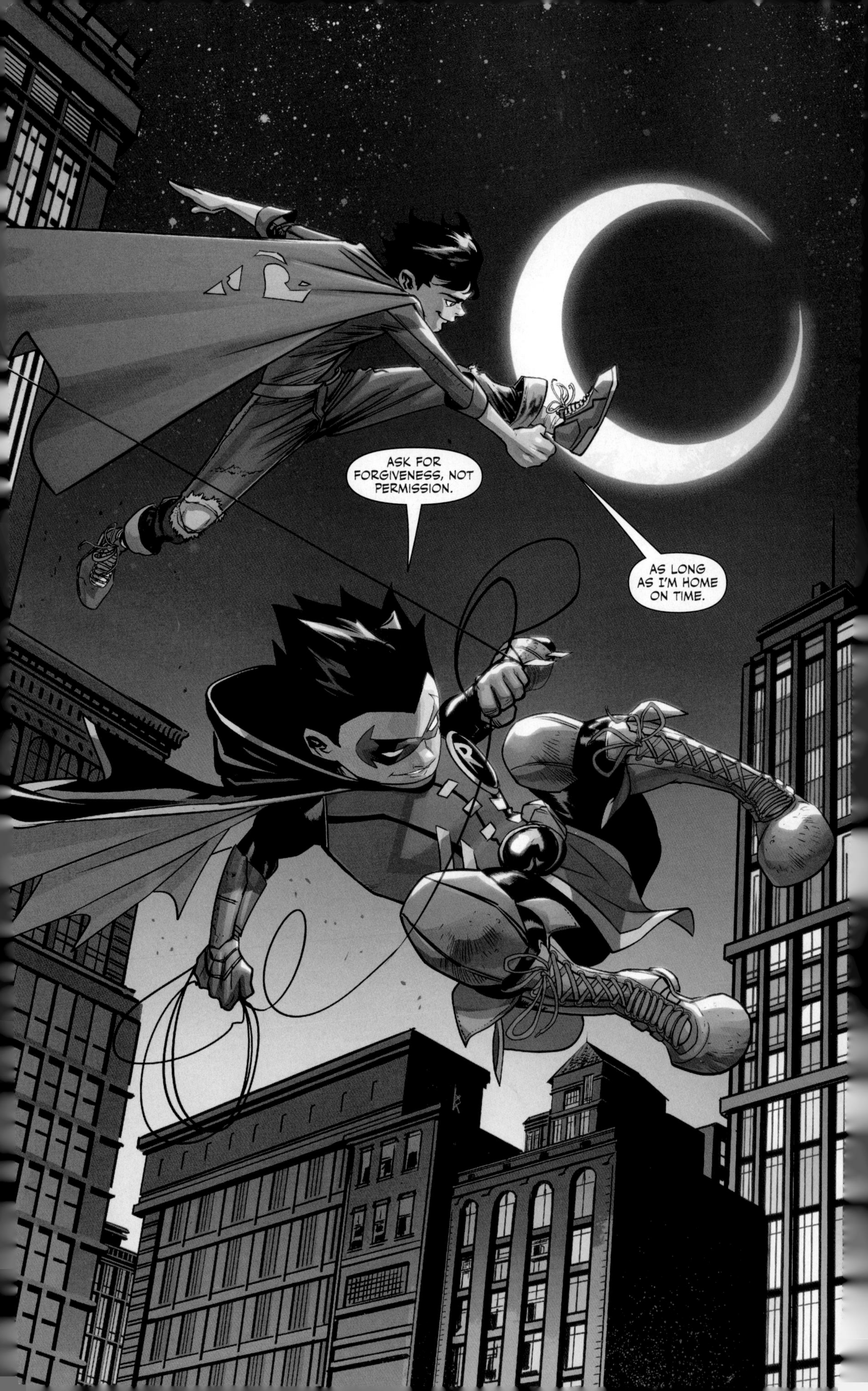
ASK FOR FORGIVENESS, NOT PERMISSION.
AS LONG AS I'M HOME ON TIME.

SUPER SONS

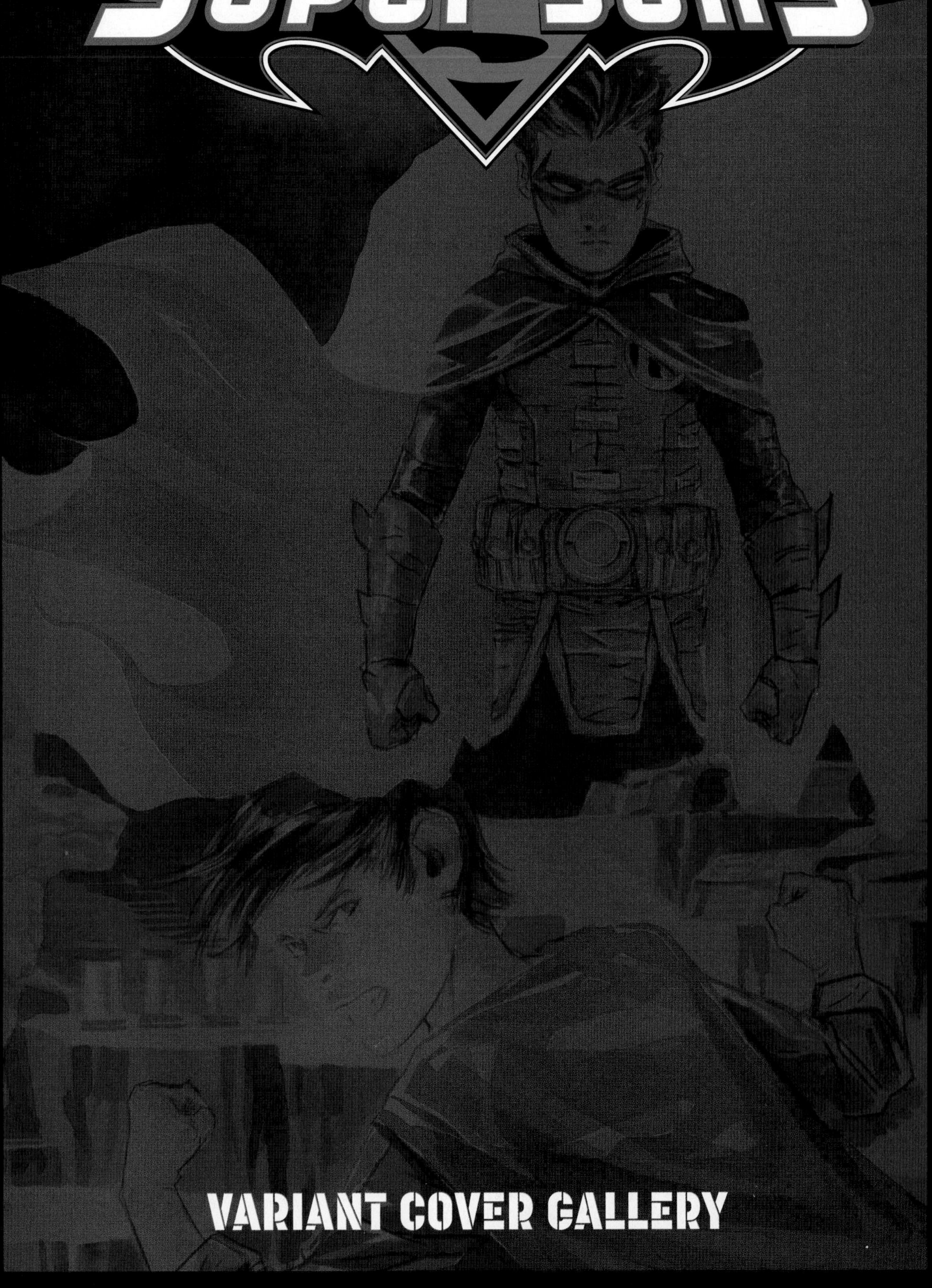

VARIANT COVER GALLERY

Variant cover art for SUPER SONS #1
by DUSTIN NGUYEN

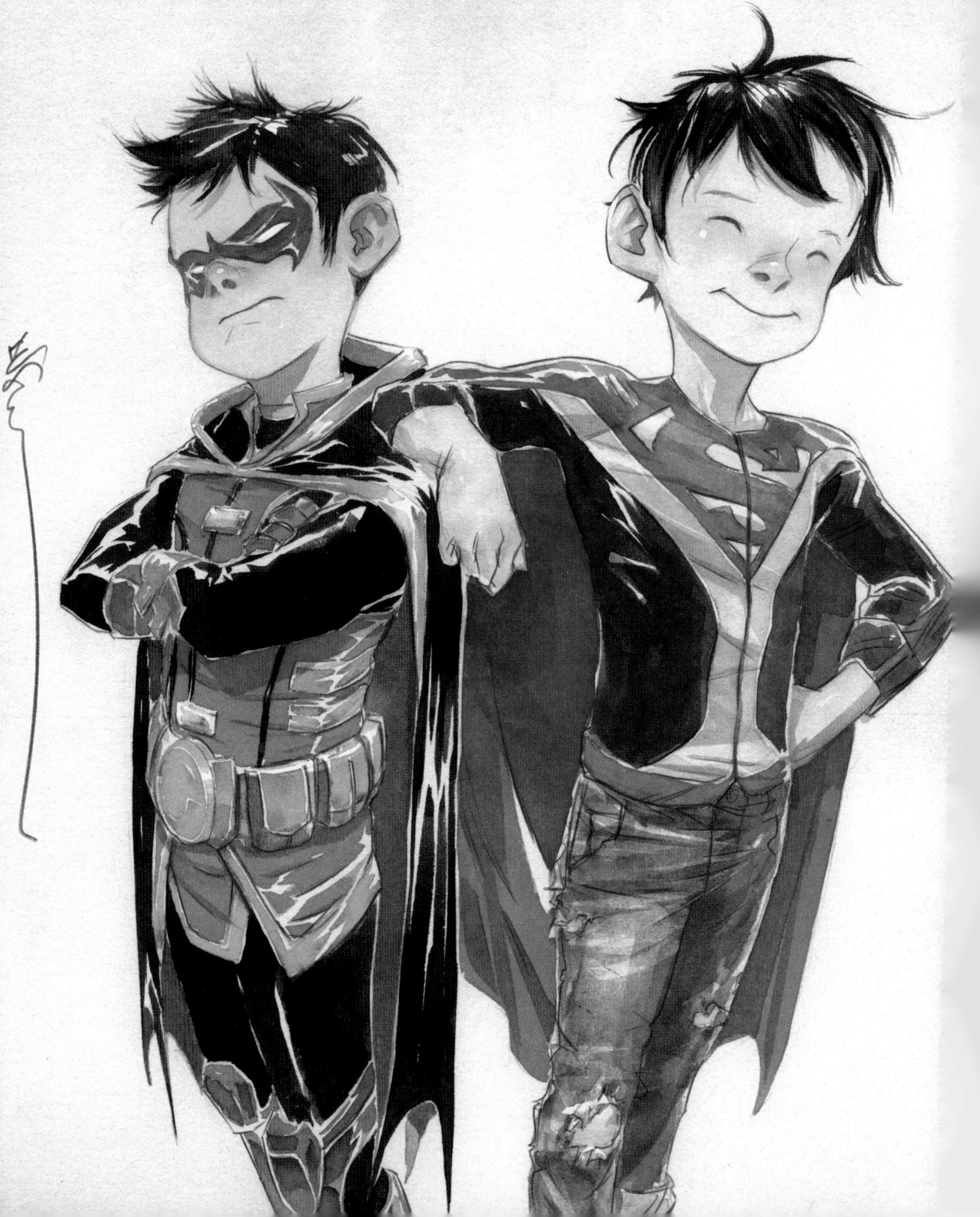

Variant cover art for SUPER SONS #2
by DUSTIN NGUYEN

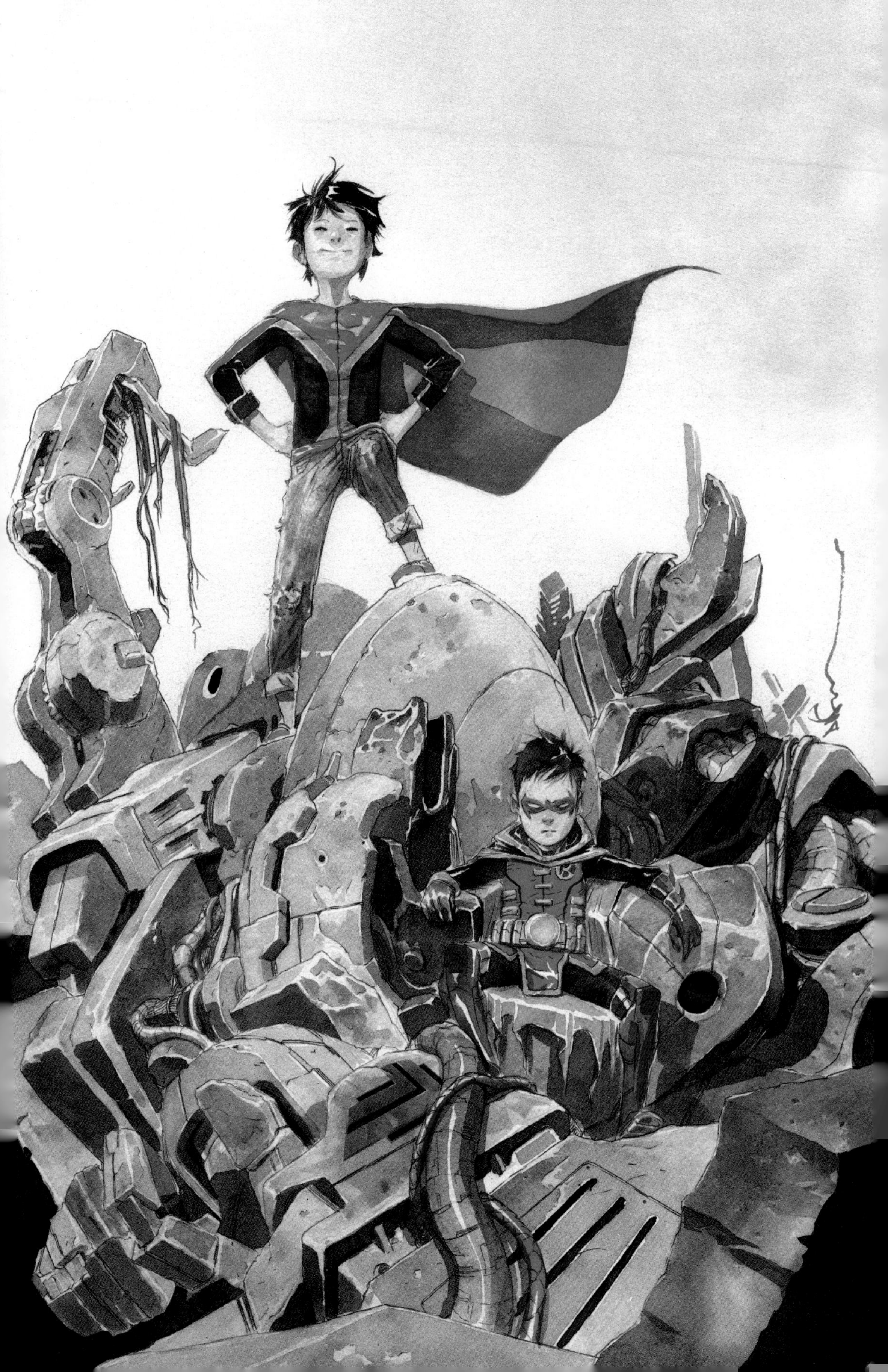

Variant cover art for SUPER SONS #3
by DUSTIN NGUYEN

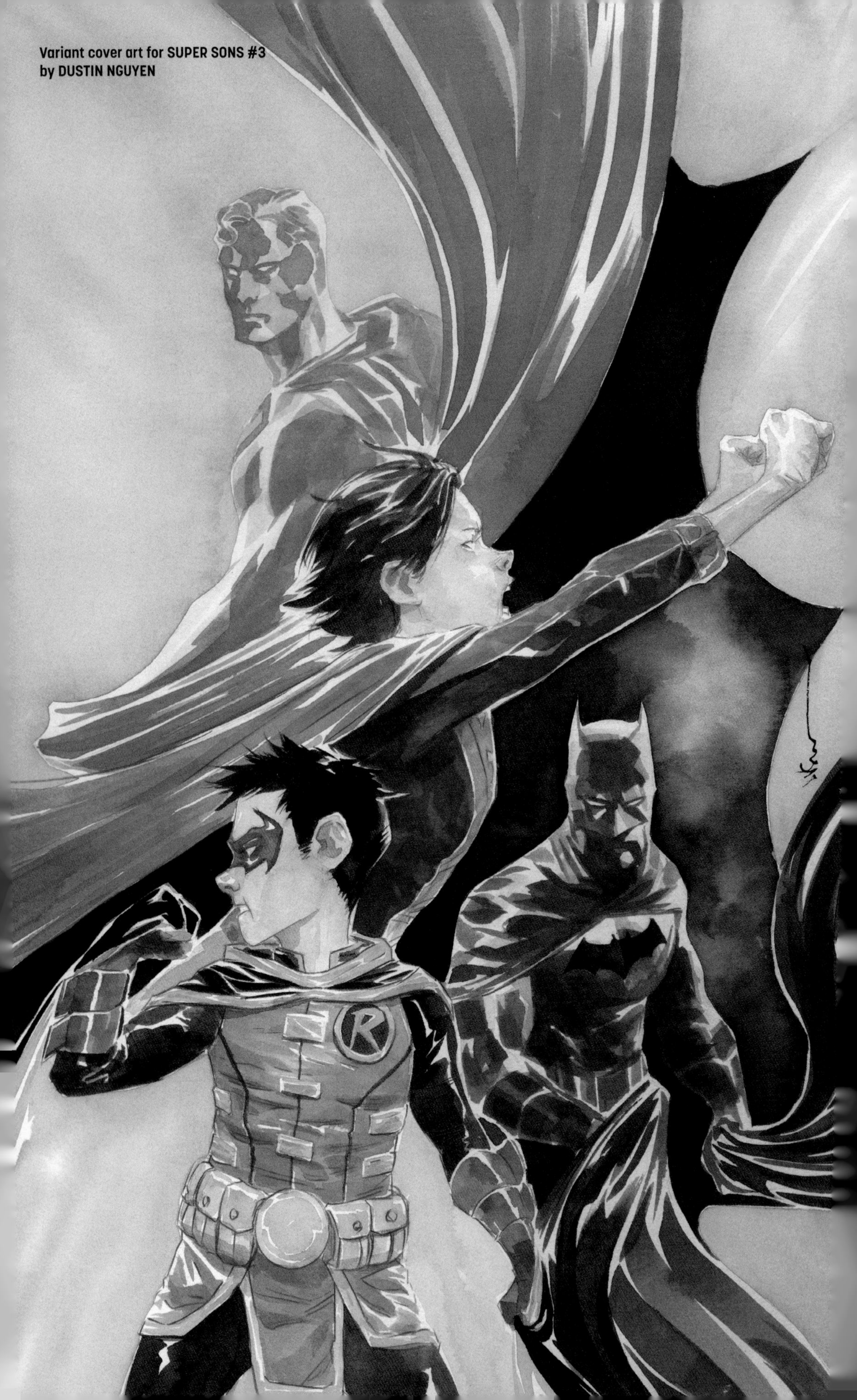

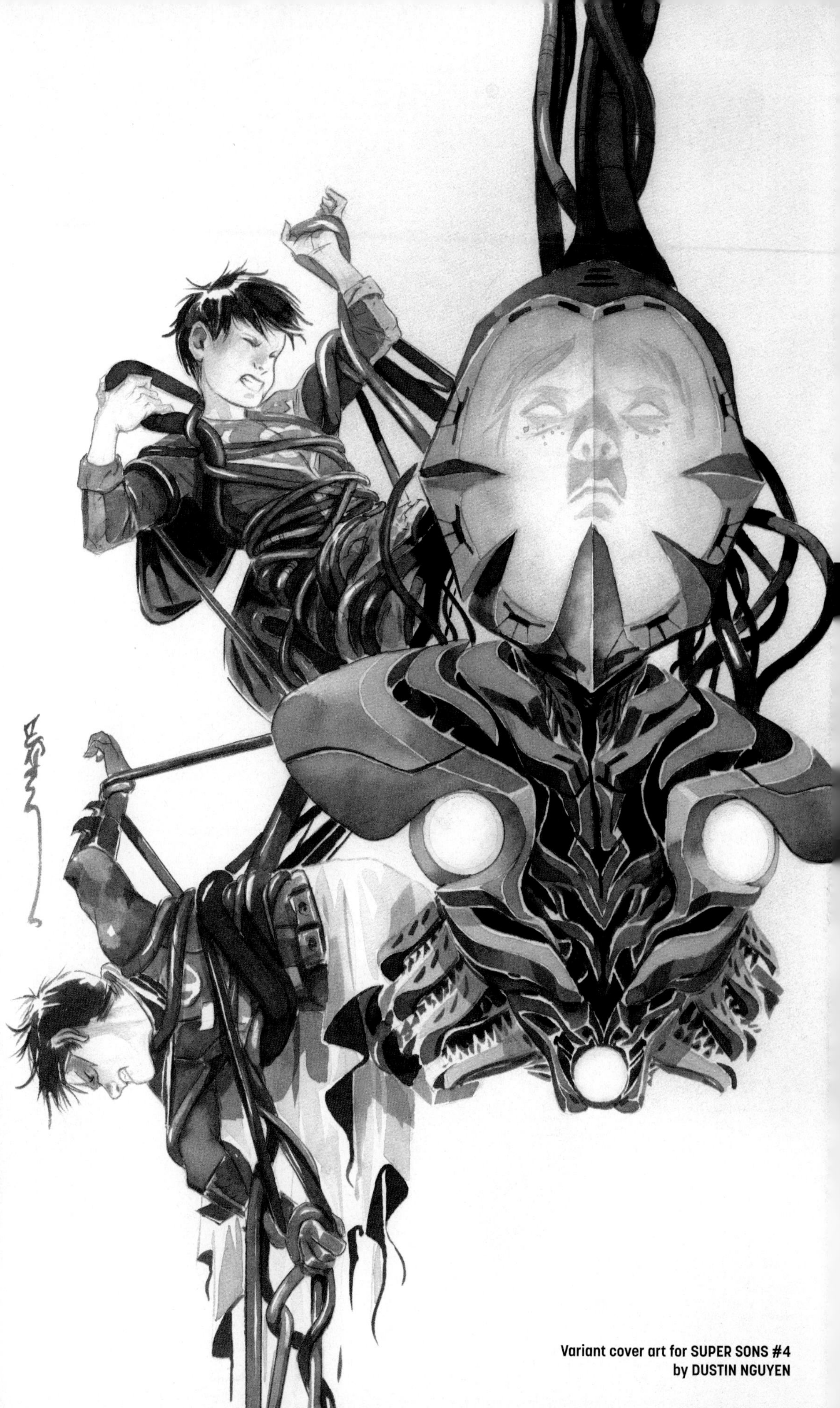

Variant cover art for SUPER SONS #4
by DUSTIN NGUYEN

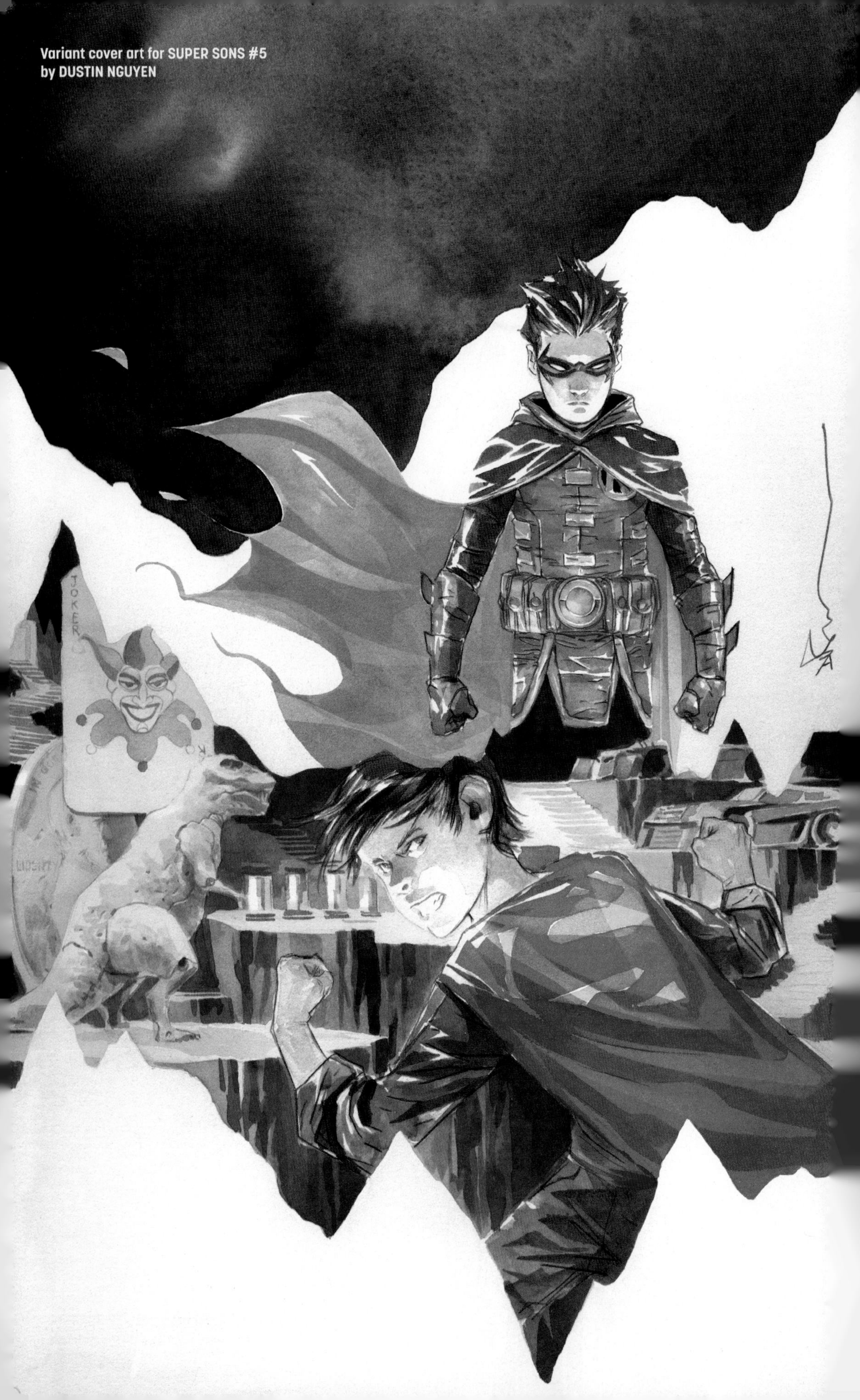

Variant cover art for SUPER SONS #5
by DUSTIN NGUYEN

SUPERBOY DESIGN
BY JORGE JIMENEZ

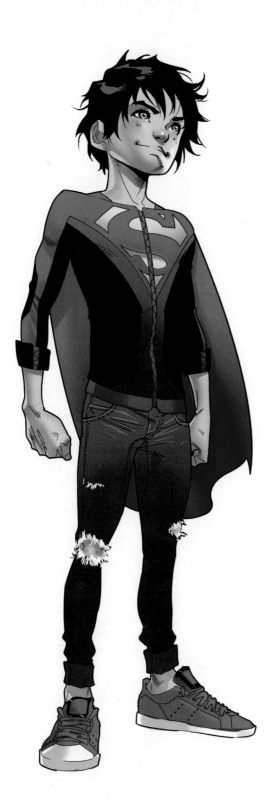

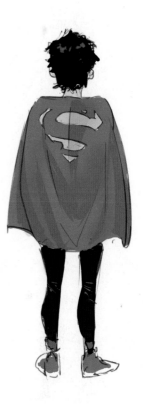

SUPERBOY SKETCHES
BY JORGE JIMENEZ

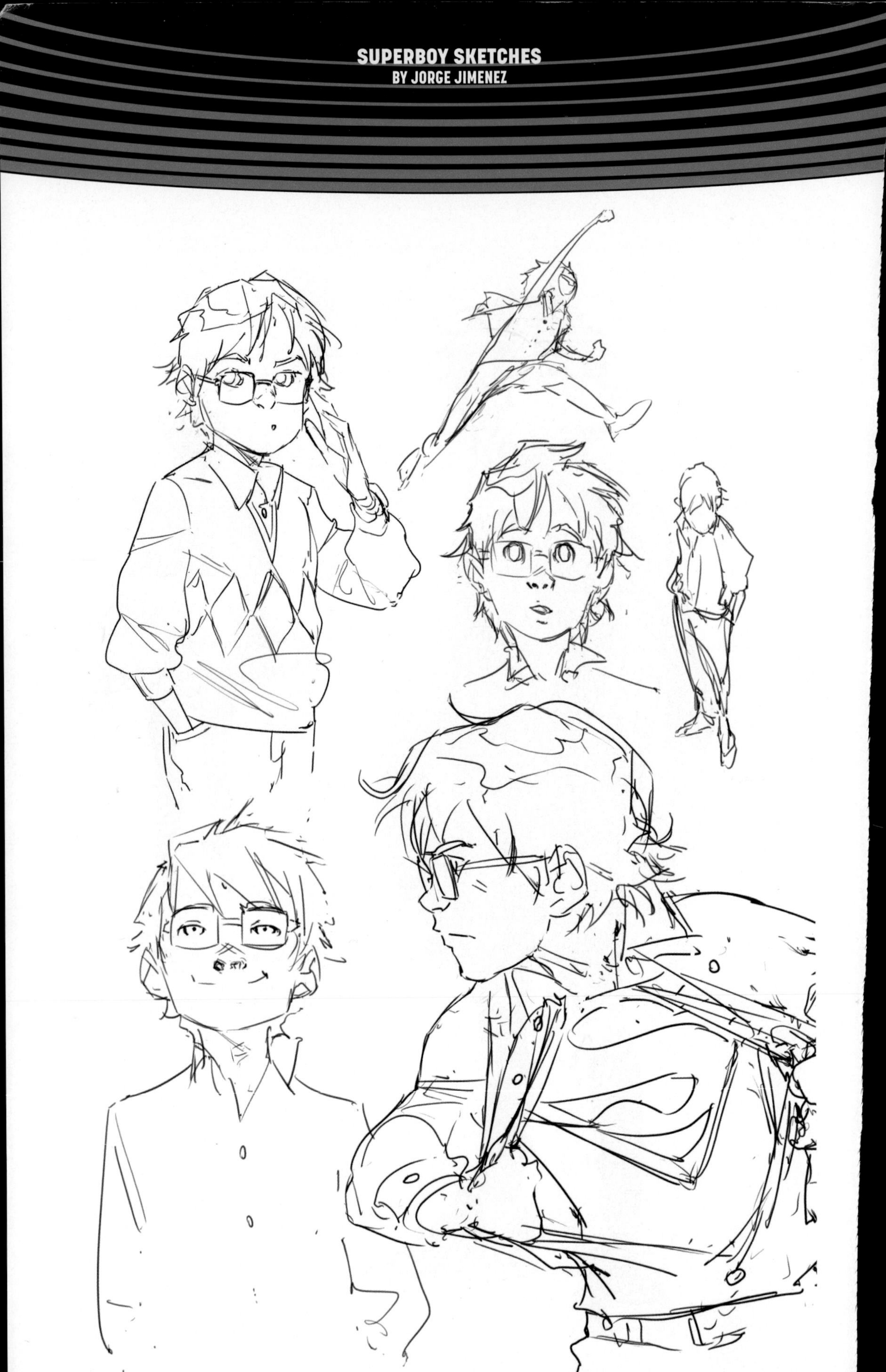

KID AMAZO DESIGN
BY JORGE JIMENEZ

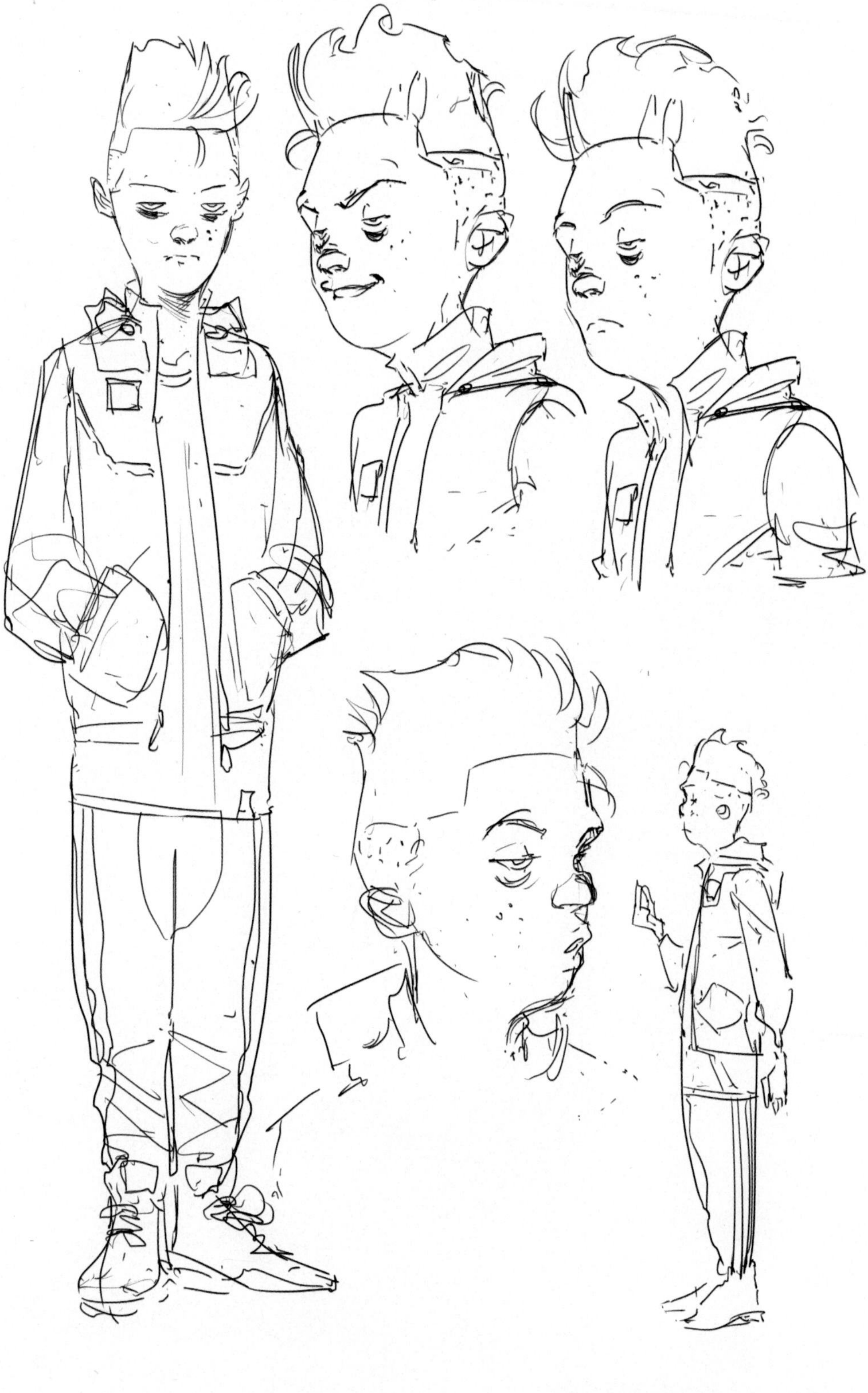

KID AMAZO DESIGN
BY JORGE JIMENEZ

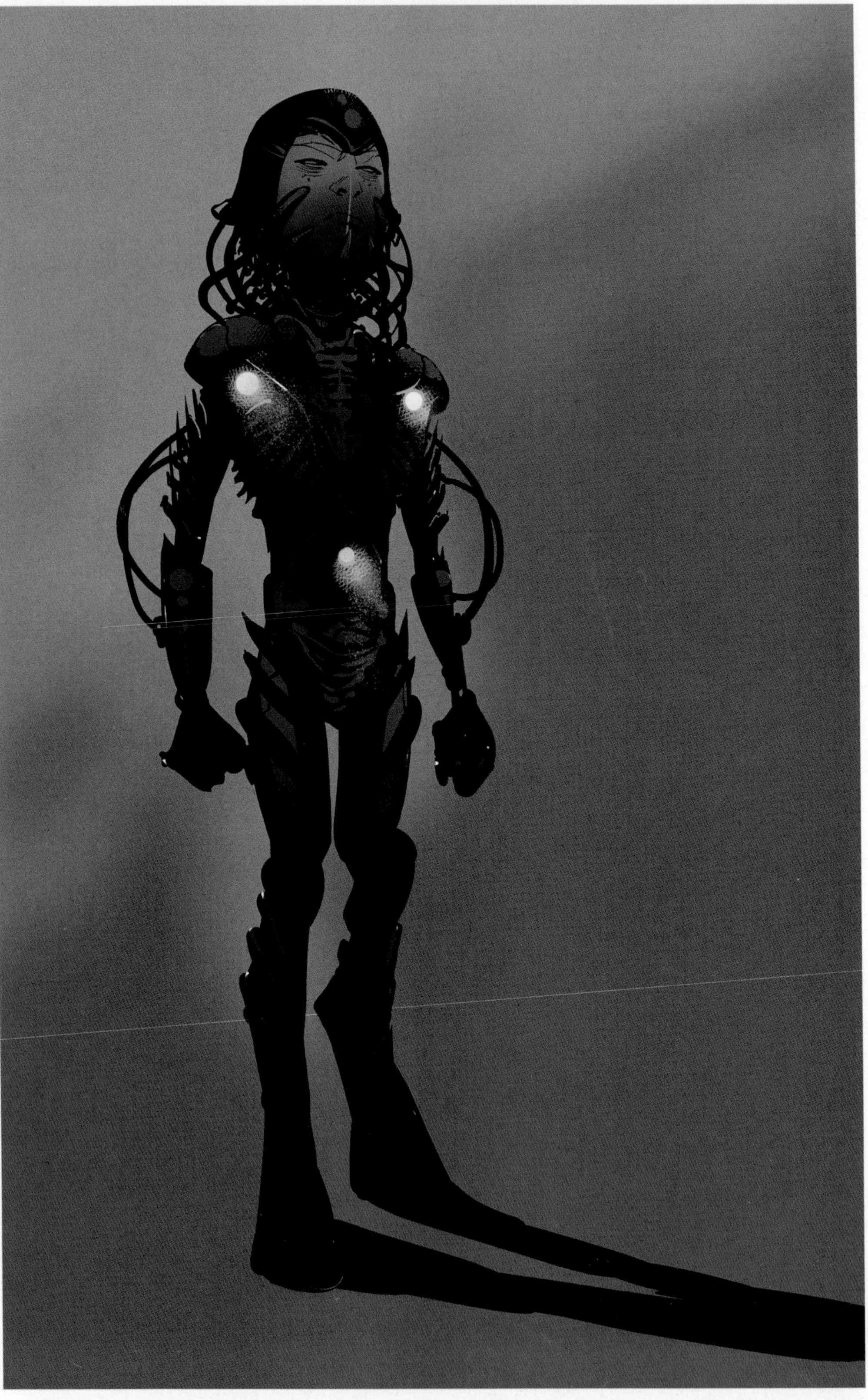

CHARACTER SKETCHES
BY JORGE JIMENEZ

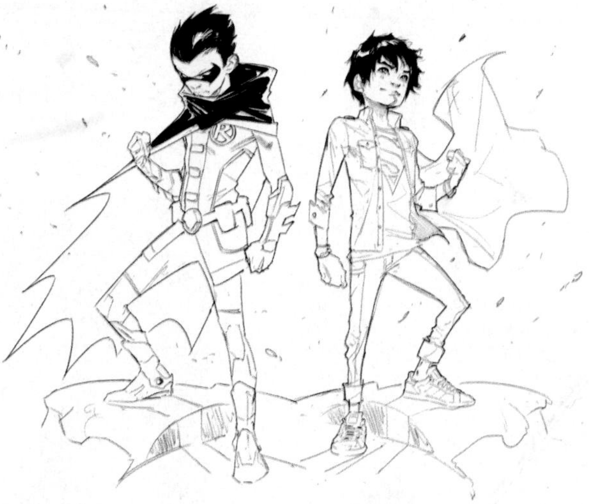

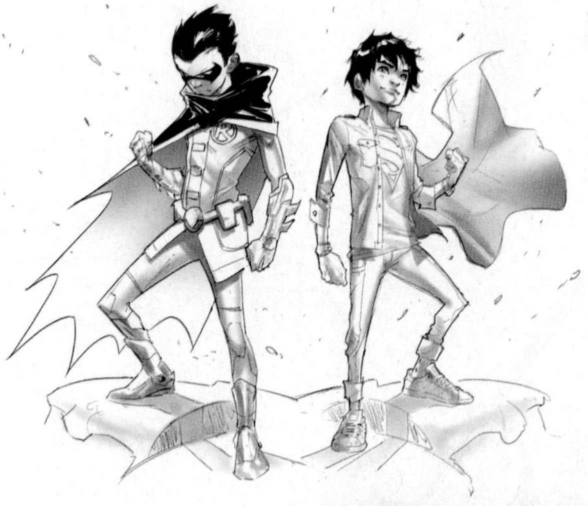

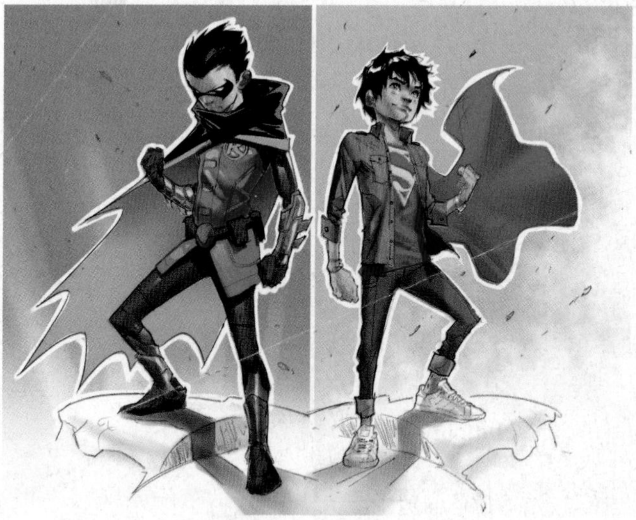

UNUSED SUPER SONS #2 COVER
BY JORGE JIMENEZ

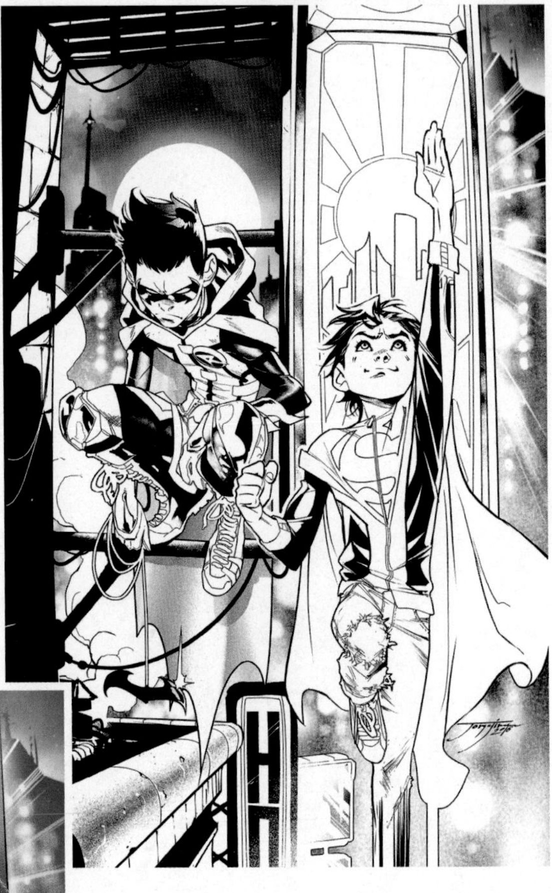

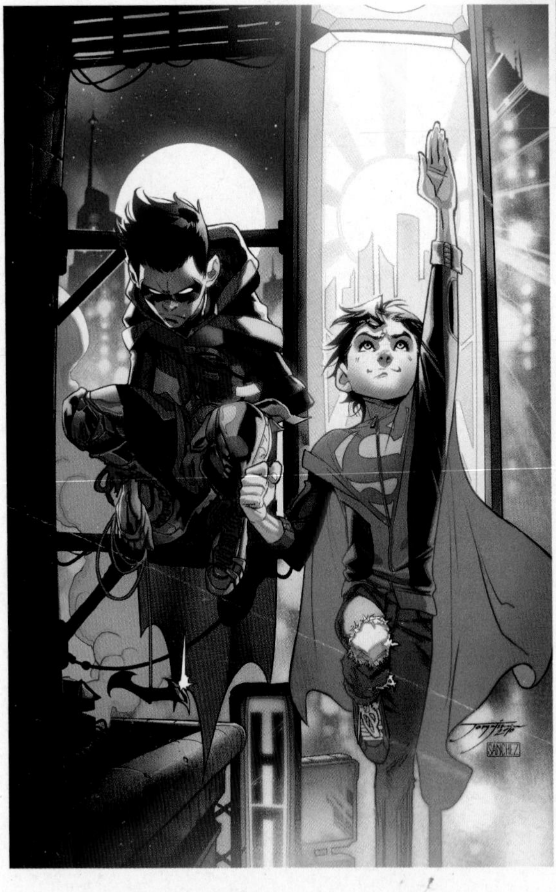
SANCHEZ

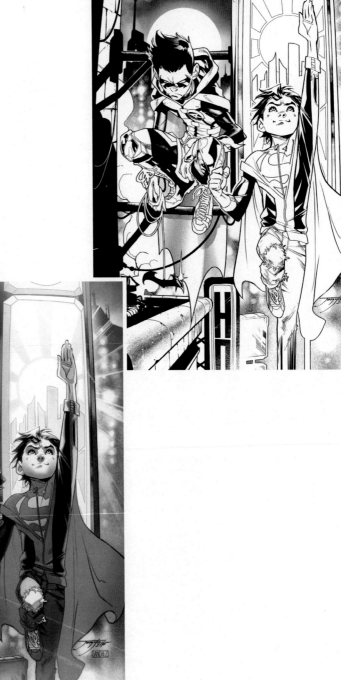